PHILOSOPHY, THEORY, AND METHOD IN CONTEMPORARY POLITICAL THOUGHT

PHILOSOPHY, THEORY, AND METHOD IN CONTEMPORARY POLITICAL THOUGHT

MICHAEL WEINSTEIN

Purdue University

SCOTT, FORESMAN AND COMPANY

Glenview, Illinois   London

ACKNOWLEDGMENTS

From *The Ruling Class* by Gaetano Mosca. Copyright, 1937 by McGraw-Hill, Inc. Used with permission of McGraw-Hill Book Company.

From *From Max Weber,* by H. H. Gerth & C. Wright Mills, New York: Oxford University Press, 1958. Used with permission.

David Easton, *A Framework for Political Analysis,* © 1965. By permission of Prentice-Hall, Inc., Englewood Cliffs, New Jersey.

From *The Political System,* by David Easton, New York: Alfred A. Knopf, Inc., 1953. Used with permission.

From *Man in the Modern Age,* 2nd edition, by Karl Jaspers, 1951, London: Routledge & Kegan Paul Ltd. Used with permission.

From *A Systems Analysis of Political Life,* by David Easton, 1965, New York: John Wiley & Sons, Inc. Used with permission.

From *Political Parties,* by Robert Michels, © Crowell-Collier Publishing Company, 1962. First published by The Free Press of Glencoe, Inc. 1958.

FOREWORD

In his first book, *Identity, Power, and Change,* Michael Weinstein introduced the concept of "the public situation" and used it for a comparative evaluation of the contributions of psychological, systems, and conflict theories to our understanding of that situation. In the present book he shows how an appreciation of the public situation may give rise to appropriate responses to it.

Weinstein's method is entirely straightforward—a critical survey of recent political thinking. His exposition and criticism of schools of philosophy (pragmatism, existentialism, and civilized humanism) and of individual thinkers I find thoroughly admirable. Even more impressive is the way in which he connects philosophical outlooks with political theories and political science. Again, it seems to me, his criticism is both sympathetic and effective, and paves the way for his highly original formulation of what is an essentially existentialist philosophy of life and politics. His analysis of the relations between philosophies, political theories, and methods of inquiry would in itself make this a book of high importance. His analysis of the rise of "formalism" in political thinking is superb, and dramatic is the only word adequate to describe the final confrontation of formalism and existentialism.

My own sense of Michael Weinstein's achievement depends upon two thoughts. The first of these has to do with fundamental types of political thinking, and the other with what may be called, broadly speaking, human dynamics. By the latter term I mean the ways in which our attitudes and our understandings are functionally interdependent.

The type of political thinking that we call liberal recognizes the complexity of human personality and values. This has been the case from Locke onwards, to Rousseau and even Hegel, and manifestly so in the work of the younger Mill, and more recently in the work of thinkers such as Berlin and Plamenatz. Other thinkers, most notably Marx, have sought a single principle according to which all of life's activities could be articulated. They could not abide human ambivalence; instead of psychological equipoise and balance as embodied in the liberal conceptions of individuality and rationality, they find in life a concrete universality, an identity manifesting itself in diverse spheres of activity. So it is with Marx, as it is with his contemporary disciples who would "green" America. Marx thought he saw in the relations of men and women at their best the only natural relations of human beings, and hence he came to advocate that all human relations—social, economic, and political—be placed on a basis of spontaneity, mutuality, and reciprocity. Any other principles of organization, such as specialization and competition, could only serve to alienate man from himself and others.

In this perspective, Michael Weinstein's work stands out as a reformulation of liberalism. Again we hear its authentic notes of diversity blending with balance, integration, and harmony. If the liberal ideal of personality and character can be summed up in the expression *romantic rationalism,* then I think it may be fairly said that Weinstein's book very substantially advances our interpretation of that ideal. Never again will it be possible for anyone who claims to be a political theorist, as distinguished from an ideologist, to attempt to read man as an "identity in difference"—to try to reduce our melody to a single beat.

I incline to think that in the longer perspective of Western political thinking there is displayed a certain rationality. By this I mean that as we better comprehend ourselves and our situation, our moral and political attitudes progressively reflect this improvement in understanding. And this is true despite regressive ideologies and murderously retrogressive behavior, which are the manifestations of stress. The historical record does reveal a rationality in human dynamics which all of our reactive thinking and doing cannot obscure or wash away. In the end, we are moral beings because we are, first of all, intelligent.

In Michael Weinstein's writings I detect an illustration of the principle that ontogeny is a recapitulation of phylogeny. For does he not show us once again how thinking about life and politics in a disciplined, penetrating, and comprehensive manner carries with it an inwardly acceptable morality? Some day, no doubt, we shall understand how this all comes about. In the meantime, it is sufficient that an intelligent morality be displayed. Michael Weinstein regards himself as an existentialist. But I am sure he will forgive us if we choose to think of him as an Aristotelian also.

John W. Chapman

PREFACE

Since World War II there has been a tendency for political scientists to divide political theories into mutually exclusive categories like normative and empirical, prescriptive and descriptive. In this study such hard-and-fast categorization is abandoned in favor of a quest for unity in contemporary political thought. First, the master political philosophies of the twentieth century are presented. These philosophies—pragmatism, existentialism, and civilized humanism—are then related to the respective empirical political theories which are derived from them. These empirical theories—pluralism, organization theory, the theory of political elites, and systems theory—are then related to distinctive methods of political inquiry. After the unity in contemporary political thought has been demonstrated, the outlines of a new and synthetic political theory are presented. Coherent description of twentieth-century political thought and redirection of contemporary political theory to a civilized and socially conscious existentialism are the chief purposes of the book.

As a systematic description of major tendencies in twentieth-century political thought, the book is suitable for a wide range of courses in political science and philosophy departments. It is appropriate for advanced undergraduate courses in twentieth-century political thought, modern political theory, theory and method in political science, political analysis, and social philosophy. It is also suitable for beginning graduate courses in political theory, sociological theory, and social philosophy. Aside from its possible contribution to redirecting contemporary political theory, the book is meant to fill a need in the literature of political thought. No other study has attempted to put contemporary political theories into a historical perspective and to classify them systematically according to relations among philosophies, empirical theories, and methods. The guiding approach to this book is meant to provide students with a comprehensive understanding of political thought in the twentieth century.

Four people have been particularly important in aiding the completion of this book. My wife and colleague, Deena Weinstein, has made essential contributions at each stage of this study. Professor John Chapman of the University of Pittsburgh read the manuscript carefully and made valuable suggestions for improvement.

Susan Schwartz of Scott, Foresman and Company was an excellent editor, who mastered the ideas and made the discussion far more lucid. George Vlach of Scott, Foresman and Company has been a sympathetic and particularly helpful program director and friend throughout this project. I would also like to thank the theory students at Purdue University for their stimulation and criticism.

M. A. W.
Tippecanoe County

CONTENTS

PHILOSOPHY, THEORY, AND METHOD IN CONTEMPORARY POLITICAL THOUGHT

PART ONE

INTRODUCTION

CHAPTER ONE

POLITICAL THEORY IN THE TWENTIETH CENTURY

The study of political activity as an intellectual pursuit is defined by the problems that human beings encounter in public existence. In his book about contemporary political theory, *Scope and Methods of Political Science,* Alan C. Isaak writes that probably "the first question that a present-day student of politics ought to ask is, What is political science?"[1] Isaak's approach to the study of political thought, which is conventional among commentators on American political theory, puts form before content. In his view, the analyst of political thought describes the activity of describing political activity. The present study is guided by a prior question: To what problems in public existence have the significant twentieth-century political theorists attempted to respond? An adequate answer to this question does not depend upon carefully drawn definitions of political science, politics, and theory. As a minimal definition, political activity refers to actions oriented to the maintenance and extension of other actions. This very broad and formal definition is introduced simply as a way of providing some delimitation of politics within the mass of human activity. Any particular study of political activity usually pertains to actions oriented to the maintenance and/or extension of other actions. Around this core, diverse interests are possible. The actual problems to which political theorists will seek to respond will depend in great part on the character of the public situation, or the basic elements that political theorists discover in the projects, relationships, and cultural objects of human beings. Thus, an introduction to political theory in the twentieth century can most profitably begin with a brief discussion of the uncertain and threatening public situation in the contemporary world. While the study of political thought is the description of descriptions of political activity, it gains meaning only after the context in which it appears is understood.

POLITICAL PHILOSOPHY

The Indian political theorist Vishwanath Prasad Varma has written that political philosophy is "the rational synthesis of opinions, information, speculations, maxims, postulates, norms and generalizations relevant to the power-structure, into coherent knowledge."[2] Whether one defines the subject matter of political philosophy as the "power-structure" or actions oriented to the maintenance and/or extension of other actions, Varma's definition of political philosophy is important because it shows the wide range of statements that one can make about political activity. In this study, we will follow Varma's idea that political philosophy is the most inclusive category of thought about political activity. Thus, political theory is a subtype of political philosophy. For Varma, political philosophy, "in a comprehensive sense, includes a rational critique of all types of statements, propositions, generalizations and ethical speculations regarding the political universe which have been or are held in the different civilizations."[3]

Political philosophy has both substantive and methodological dimensions. With reference to substance, one studies political activity and the statements that are made about it. With reference to methodology, one discusses the regularized ways of responding to problems encountered in political activity; that is, the ways in which political activity is studied. In the present study, questions of substance precede questions of method both in order of appearance and order of importance.

Varma identifies four distinct branches of political philosophy. The first is the study of the history of political thought. Here one discusses the statements that past political philosophers have made about political activity. The history of political thought involves the study of political philosophy as an object of civilization, or a cultural object. Varma observes that political philosophy as the history of political thought has to play "a tremendous role in the appreciation and critique of the traditions" present in world culture.[4] In the sense that the present study is an attempt to clarify the major schools of thought that have developed in twentieth-century political philosophy, it is an essay in the history of political thought.

The second major area of political philosophy is the study of political norms, values, and ideals. This branch of political philosophy is grounded in the fact that human beings judge political activity as good or bad, right or wrong. The study of political norms, values, and ideals has several aspects. First, one may investigate the logical relationships among prescriptions and the modes in which prescriptions are justified. Second, one may articulate a standard of evaluation for political activity. Third, one may criticize actual political activities in terms of a standard of evaluation. The present study is concerned with prescriptive theory, or the principles for evaluating political activity, in the sense that it discusses the functions that twentieth-century political philosophers have prescribed for political activity and the moral aspects that they have found in methods of inquiry.

The third major area of political philosophy is the study of the relationships of political ideas, theories, and ideologies with other aspects of human existence. This component of political philosophy, the sociology of political knowledge, includes both the analysis of the contexts in which political knowledge appears and the consequences of political knowledge for other aspects of human existence. The present study is concerned with the foundations and implications of political knowledge in the sense that it is guided by the conception of political philosophy as a response to problems encountered in the public situation, and in the sense that it discusses the sociologies of political knowledge developed by twentieth-century political philosophers and political theorists as integral parts of political thought.

The fourth major branch of political philosophy is the study of empirical theory. This component of political philosophy consists in the development and coordination of general descriptions of political activity. Twentieth-century political philosophy has been characterized by two different kinds of thought structures. First, there have been general political philosophies which have included the analysis and development of principles for evaluating political activity, the discussion of the context of political thought, the creation of visions of human existence, and only secondarily the elaboration of logically coordinated descriptions of political activity. These "master political philosophies," or political world views, are the subject of the following three chapters of this book. The second major thought structure in twentieth-century political philosophy is the empirical theory, which thus far has been primarily an effort to state the most general categories through which political activity can be described. The fifth through eighth chapters of this book discuss the major empirical theories that have appeared in the twentieth century. The master political philosophies and the empirical theories are closely related to one another. The empirical theories tend to be specialized expressions of the fundamental principles articulated in the master political philosophies. The three master political philosophies of the twentieth century—pragmatism, existentialism, and civilized humanism—have their respective empirical theoretic expressions in pluralism, organization theory, and the theory of political elites. The fourth significant empirical theory—systems

theory—is a synthesis of the other three empirical theoretic structures.

Thus, in one of its aspects, the present study can be considered a
philosophical approach to political theory. However, in a more
fundamental sense it can be considered an investigation of the
significant responses to the public situation in the twentieth century.
Varma asserts: "Ours is an age of crisis. Everywhere the human spirit
is subjected to terrible agonies. The tragedy of man is being revealed
in the perpetual threat of human extinction."[5] For Varma, the
worldwide crisis of the twentieth century is fundamental and has
ramifications in every aspect of human existence. He maintains that
the most important role of political philosophy in the modern age is
to provide clarification of the human condition and the public
situation. Political philosophers must construct "models of epochal
crises" which free people from their parochial attachments and
provide them with new possibilities for action in the face of
imposing concentrations of organized power. This same ultimate
goal characterizes the present study.

THE PUBLIC SITUATION IN THE TWENTIETH CENTURY

To what elements in human existence do political philosophers
in the twentieth century respond? For the most sensitive political
philosophers, the contemporary human condition is both uncertain
and threatening. Each master political philosophy and major empirical theory selects a particular set of elements as decisive in constituting the public situation.

Master Political Philosophies

Pragmatism For pragmatists, the uncertainty and threat of the
contemporary public situation arise from the growing importance of
the indirect consequences of human activity and the problems of
communication among human beings in the modern age. All purposive human action involves control over consequences. In the study
of human activity one can distinguish among the direct and indirect
consequences of purposive actions. Direct consequences are intended and affect the parties to a concrete interaction. Indirect
consequences are often unintended and affect people who are not
parties to a concrete interaction.

In the twentieth century, the indirect consequences of
human activity have become increasingly important. When the
United States tested nuclear weapons in the Pacific Ocean after
World War II, political and military decision makers probably

did not intend that Japanese fishermen receive radiation poisoning. However, some Japanese fishermen, who were not parties to the interactions involved in testing nuclear weapons, were poisoned by fallout. These fishermen had no control over the explosion of nuclear devices and no way to protect themselves from the hazards of which they were not aware. The Japanese fishermen were victims of the uncertain and threatening public situation of the twentieth century. Some of those people who learn about the plight of these fishermen are brought to a recognition of the importance of indirect consequences of human activity in determining the quality of contemporary existence.

Of course, the threatening aspects of the indirect consequences of human activity are not confined to occurrences in Asia. People in the United States are becoming increasingly aware that environmental pollution is a significant indirect consequence of industrial activity. Decisions to increase the production of automobiles not only put more people behind the wheel, but also contribute to the emission of carbon monoxide into the atmosphere. Decisions to build industrial complexes on level ground not only decrease construction costs and contribute to the maximization of profits, but may also lessen the amount of crop land available for cultivation. Decisions to nourish livestock in cramped feedlots not only contribute to efficient production of meat, but also result in inefficient waste disposal and the fouling of water supplies. Perhaps the most poignant examples of victimization by the indirect consequences of human activities are the refugees and displaced persons of the twentieth century: Cambodians displaced in a war between North Vietnam and South Vietnam and the United States, Lebanese displaced in a war between Israeli soldiers and Arab guerrillas, Jews displaced in World War II and Arabs displaced after World War II, Indians displaced in Africa and Moslems displaced in India, Japanese displaced in the United States. Very little imagination is needed to describe many more indirect consequences of human activity that have made the public situation in the twentieth century uncertain and threatening.

The second phase of the pragmatic critique of the contemporary public situation concerns problems of communication. In the twentieth century two factors have worked to bring about intensified problems of communication among human beings. First, in Western societies, the rate of specialization of human activity has increased rapidly. This has led to the fragmentation of human knowledge and the proliferation of specialized vocabularies which can be understood only by the initiated few. The problem of coordinating specialized functions, which is partly a problem of communication, has gained great importance in North American and European nations. Second, the peoples of the world have been brought into relations with one another as the result of imperialism, war, trade, and technology. This has created the problem of communication among people who refer their actions to different cultures. Both specialization and cultural encounter breed suspicion and distrust. Human beings tend to distrust that with which they are not familiar. They are uncertain of others who represent arcane specialities or unfamiliar cultures. Their uncertainty is mingled with a feeling of threat. When uncertain and threatened people interact with one another they do not communicate authentically, but experiment upon one another. This does not mean that mutual understanding would automatically result in trust. Part of the reason the public situation in the twentieth century is uncertain and threatening is that people have good reason not to trust one another in many cases. Should the Cambodian refugee trust North Vietnamese, South Vietnamese, or American soldiers? Should the Arab refugee trust Israelis, Jordanians, or Egyptians? While problems of communication are important in the contemporary public situation, they do not exhaust the problems characteristic of twentieth-century political existence. The pragmatic description of the contemporary public situation provides the important elements of indirect consequences of human activity and communicative processes. However, it is not a sufficient description and must be supplemented by elements from the other master political philosophies of the twentieth century.

Existentialism For existentialists, the uncertainty and threat of the contemporary public situation arise from contemporary attacks on human freedom. Varma provides an existentialist interpretation of the human condition in the twentieth century:

> The individual is crushed by the rise of what I would like to call gigantic structuralism. The gigantic structures in the field of political, military and economic technology are appearing as powerful demons which are out to submerge the protestant human conscience.[6]

Existentialists hold that the major element in the public situation is the tendency for human existence to be defined as a function in social organization. They point to the fact that the worst brutalities in the twentieth century have been justified by such arguments as "I was only following orders," "It was necessary to protect national security," "The first responsibility of the manager is to his stockholders," "I did not break the law," and "Everyone else was doing it at the time." To such efforts at rationalization existentialists oppose the concept of authentic existence. They claim that a human being can always choose not to follow orders, hide behind a collectivity, narrowly interpret his responsibilities, obey a law that he deems unjust, and follow the crowd. However, they are painfully aware of the difficulties of assuming the responsibilities of a free human being in the modern age. Most of the person's existence as contributor to civilization and to his fellow human beings is lived in bureaucratic organizations which define his rights and duties as functionary. If he steps out of bounds he is likely to lose his livelihood. If he compulsively stays within bounds he loses his freedom and with it his raison d'être as a human being. Almost everyone in the bureaucratized societies of the West is a proletarian, in that the means to creation are owned and controlled by organizations. The existential sociologist Max Weber went so far as stating that contemporary human beings are "intellectual proletarians" whose thoughts are often owned and controlled by the mass media of communication, or what Hans Magnus Enzensberger calls the "mind machine."

Perhaps the most threatening aspect of the organizational revolution of the modern age is its connection with the increased importance of the indirect consequences of human activity. It is through activities within complex organizations that human beings are made victims of the indirect consequences of human activity. The displaced person is the victim of a bureaucratized army. Thus, the functionary within that army is drawn into responsibility for consequences that he may deem evil. With respect to such consequences as environmental pollution, the functionary may even become the victim of his own activities. He is in a paradoxical position. His bureaucratic role makes him appear as a replaceable part in a vast human machine; he can plead that if he did not perform the role someone else would. Yet the functionary is also responsible for the activities of his organization. Whether or not he could be replaced by someone else, the fact remains that he did perform actions that instrumented organizational plans. As a free human being, at a specific time and place, he chose to follow orders. However, in an organization the consequences of individual actions are not proportionate to the consequences of the organization. If the functionary revolts he will have little effect upon the outcome of the collective activity. Yet he cannot be sure that he is impotent. Why has he failed to join with his colleagues? Would others follow his example of revolt? They might. Such analysis makes up the existential critique of the contemporary public situation.

This analysis supplements the pragmatic description of the indirect consequences of human activity. Through organizations the actions provoking indirect consequences of human activity are mediated, presenting the functionary with some of his most painful moral problems. It is useful to view the existential description of the public situation as the agent's perspective on contemporary political existence and the pragmatic description of the public situation as the patient's perspective on contemporary political existence. Agents performing organizational roles wreak consequences on others. Increasingly the existential and pragmatic viewpoints fuse as functionaries wreak indirect consequences upon themselves.

Civilized Humanism Even together, the pragmatic and existentialist descriptions of the contemporary public situation do not provide a complete account of the fundamental problems in political existence in the twentieth century. Equally essential is the point of view developed in the third master political philosophy of the twentieth century—civilized humanism. For civilized humanists, the uncertainty and threat of the contemporary public situation arise from attacks upon the set of cultural objects that comprise civilization in the modern age. In the twentieth century, along with the increasing importance of the indirect consequences of human activity and the growth of complex organizations in all zones of human existence, has come the experience of barbarism. Through propaganda and advertising, languages have been debased. Ideals of rational thought have been attacked by partisans of romanticism, naturalism, and spontaneity. Fundamental recognition of the values of individuality and personality has become questionable as the brutalities of concentration camp existence and instances of torture, both mental and physical, are progressively revealed. Further, the encounter between different cultures has had a direct and profound effect on Western civilization. During the Middle Ages, much of the West was insulated from knowledge of other civilizations. People could believe that their values and world view were natural to human beings. There were no competing civilizations to provide standards of comparison and criticism. With the age of exploration, Europeans encountered other civilizations. The first response was to proclaim the superiority of the West and to declare other peoples inferior. In this response of missionary's consciousness is found the origin of contemporary barbarism. The second response to the encounter of diverse civilizations was to proclaim that all civilizations are equally good; each one represents an adaptation of human beings to a set of particular circumstances and, therefore, cannot be judged as better or worse than the others. In this response of anthropologist's consciousness is found the second phase of contemporary barbarism—the surrender of the responsibility to judge.

In the twentieth century, new responses to the encounter of civilizations have appeared that represent the zenith of barbarism. In elite consciousness, cultural values are used as myths to mask the pursuit of power and gain by leadership groups. The members of these leadership groups assume that the members of the mass believe in the validity of cultural values. Otherwise the fraudulent use of these values would be self-defeating. The transvaluation of culture into an instrument of power, which has occurred in Nazi Germany, Stalinist Russia, and to some extent in Western regimes, is the barbarism that most disturbs civilized humanists. Frequently, leadership groups characterized by elite consciousness have manipulated populations characterized by mass consciousness. In mass consciousness, people believe that they pattern their lives according to cultural values, while their leaders are corrupt. The people proclaim their own morality and excuse atrocities they commit on the grounds that they are obeying orders. They displace their own responsibility to the shoulders of their leaders. However, the zenith of barbarism is not described by the interplay of elite consciousness and mass consciousness. In experimental consciousness there is neither leader nor led, there are only degrees of power. Each party to the political relationship uses cultural values as myths to mask the pursuit of power and gain. The so-called crisis of democratic leadership in the twentieth century is perhaps due to the ever-increasing importance of experimental consciousness in contemporary political and social relationships.

The negative response to the encounter of civilizations involves a progressive denial of values. First, in missionary's consciousness, one's own parochial values are used as a standard of judgment through which the validity of other values is denied. Second, in anthropologist's consciousness the superiority of any values is denied and standards of judgment drop out of social existence. Third, in experimental consciousness the very existence of values is denied. They are transformed into the components of ideologies and images. They no longer refer to human experiences that are potentially or actually available. For experimental consciousness, the appreciation of many of the objects of civilization has become impossible. This is why experimental consciousness is barbaric.

Over and against the barbarism characteristic of the twentieth century, civilized humanists have set the ideal of a world civilization synthesizing the foremost contributions of the diverse historical civilizations. In accord with this ideal, no particular civilization would be viewed as necessarily superior to others. However, all civilizations would not be considered equal in all respects. Rather than deny values, the synthesizing activity would involve creating a standard of judgment that draws upon the standards present in particular civilizations.

Civilized humanists provide the third and final fundamental component of the description of the public situation in the twentieth century. Both the human decisions and actions that occupy the attention of existentialists, and the social processes that engage the interest of pragmatists, are mediated through cultural objects. Social processes arise when the activities of human beings have consequences for one another. These activities can be defined as usages of cultural objects. For civilized humanists, the uncertain and threatening aspects of the contemporary public situation can be traced to the fear that civilization will be swamped by barbarism. In the modern age, one can never be certain that the other person understands the meanings of the objects of civilization. Similarly, one must always take into account the possibility that the other person may intend to destroy the most precious objects of civilization.

The Public Situation Synthesized From the perspectives of pragmatism, existentialism, and civilized humanism, the contemporary public situation can be defined as one in which the indirect consequences of human activity take on increasing importance, the individual as responsible actor is confronted by complex organizations, and civilization is threatened with dissolution. Within this context some of the most severe aspects of the human condition discussed by the seventeenth-century British political philosopher, Thomas Hobbes, are presented strikingly. As human beings adopt experimental consciousness and attempt to realize their particular private projects at the expense of the plans of others, they enter into a relation of combat. For Hobbes, "without a common power to keep them all in awe," human beings are in a "war of every man against every man."[7] In order to maintain itself, this common power must be both credible and just. In the contemporary public situation, both of these qualities are at a premium.

This uncertain and threatening public situation finds its expression in all aspects of human existence and provides the context in which twentieth-century political philosophy is written. If the study of political activity, as an intellectual pursuit, is defined by the problems that human beings encounter in public existence, the character of the contemporary public situation must be kept clearly in mind as one studies the significant examples of twentieth-century political philosophy. It is likely that if human activity were not mediated through complex organizations in the modern age neither pragmatism, nor existentialism, nor civilized humanism would have appeared as master political philosophies. This does not mean that the content of political philosophy is strictly determined by material or nonconscious conditions. To stress the importance of the public situation as a context for political philosophy is not to hold that thought has no efficacy, but instead, it is to hold that political thought is interrelated with political action.

Until recently, few if any scholars undertook political thought in order to create abstract structures with the elegance of mathematics. Traditionally, political philosophers have been concerned with clarifying significant aspects of the public situation. Sometimes they have concentrated on attempting to define aspects and elements common to all public situations. At other times they have tried to identify the unique factors in particular public situations. In either case, political thought has had the dual functions of catching up to political activity and clarifying its significant elements, and leading political activity in the direction of realizing new possibilities. As responses to the uncertain and threatening public situation of the twentieth century, pragmatism, existentialism, and civilized humanism have performed the traditional functions of political philosophy. In Varma's terms, the master political philosophies of the twentieth century have constructed models of epochal crises which free people from their parochial attachments and provide them with new possibilities for action in the face of imposing concentrations of organized power. Thus, in terms of the present study, the first question that a present-day student of politics ought to ask is not, "What is political science?" but, "What is the public situation?"

Empirical Theories

Pluralism The empirical political theories that follow from the master political philosophies are also, at least in part, responses to the contemporary public situation. Pluralism, organization theory, the theory of political elites, and systems theory each define units of analysis that clarify political relations in the twentieth century. As the expression of pragmatism in empirical political theory, pluralism defines the public situation through the concepts of cross-sectional activity, interest group, and public. Like pragmatists, pluralists fix attention on the consequences of human activity. They derive political activity from the interference in the performance of one or more actions by one or more other actions. When people suffer the indirect consequences of human activity, they form a public. When people organize to maintain or extend the performance of a human activity, they form an interest group. Thus, both publics and interest groups are defined in terms of discriminable cross sections of activity. For pluralists, the public domain is a field upon which interest groups contest to secure the maintenance and extension of diverse human activities at the same time that they wreak consequences on various publics.

The pluralist perspective on political existence is a response to the same elements in the public situation as the pragmatic interpretation of twentieth-century political life. The expansion and specialization of contemporary cultural objects leads to a proliferation of different activities. Each one of these activities can interfere with a multitude of other activities and can suffer interference from a vast number of other activities. In response to interference, interest groups grow up around usages of cultural objects. Thus, interest groups arise from the condition of suffering consequences and, in turn, inflict consequences on other groups. The idea that the basic unit of contemporary political existence is the interest group goes along with concern for the indirect consequences of human activity. Interest groups both provoke and suffer indirect consequences.

Organization Theory As the expression of existentialism in empirical political theory, organization theory defines the public situation through the concept of organization. We have already discussed the importance of complex organizations and functional roles in the existential critique of twentieth-century political life. It remains to point out that interest groups appear in the twentieth century as bureaucratically organized units. While pluralism provides the idea of cross sections of activity that refer to the maintenance and/or extension of other human activities in the face of interference, organization theory contributes the description of the ways in which these representative or political cross sections of activity are organized. Bureaucracy, as the hierarchically directed specialization of human activity, is the dominant way in which powerful interest groups organize to maintain and extend their influence in contemporary political life. While pluralists tend to study the consequences of interest group activities for the attainment of various values or for the fulfillment of different functions, organization theorists tend to study the relationships within interest groups. Thus, they are complementary perspectives on political affairs.

Theories of Political Elites As the expression of civilized humanism in empirical theory, the theory of political elites defines the public situation through the concept of ruling class, elite, or oligarchy. Underlying the idea of a directing minority is the notion of a dominant and organized cross section of activity. For theorists of political elites, ruling classes represent social types, or people whose characters have been organized around particular cross sections of activity. Ruling classes represent the dominance of certain usages of cultural objects and justify their leadership in political formulas that express the public importance of the particular cross sections of activity identified with the regnant social type. Harold Lasswell, the theorist of political elites, has stated that ruling elites are composed of those people who receive the greatest share of socially available values. Thus, they are interest groups which have been conspicuously successful in extending a particular cross section of activity. Among others, religious, military, and economic elites have been socially dominant at various times.

Theorists of political elites note the importance of directing minorities in the contemporary public situation. They attempt to identify the cross sections of activity that mold the dominant social types of the present age. Different theorists of political elites have identified different social types as particularly important. Gaetano Mosca, the Italian theorist of political elites, holds that public administrators are the rising elite group in contemporary societies. Harold Lasswell contends that the world is in the midst of a skill revolution in which experts continually gain more power. For Robert Michels, the ruling class of the modern age is composed of political managers. He finds the contemporary form of domination to be the bureaucratized political party run by an oligarchy. The theory of political elites complements pluralism and organization theory. It provides the notion of a dominant cross section of activity and thereby contributes a linkage between the external activities of interest groups and their internal organization. Interest groups themselves are dominated by elites, and some interest groups are dominant over others. The empirical political theories related to the three master political philosophies of the twentieth century provide the materials for a synthetic political theory when they are taken together.

Theories of the Political System An attempt at bringing together the major empirical theories of the twentieth century has been undertaken by current theorists of the political system in the United States. Around the concept of a system of action, they coordinate the concepts of cross section of activity, interest group, public, organization, elite, social type, and political formula. They also attempt to define a social function for the political system. Least of all are theories of the political system self-conscious responses to the uncertain and threatening public situation of the twentieth century. They build on previous responses to the public situation and take them to a higher level of abstraction. Yet underlying even theories of the political system is the context of the public situation as defined primarily by the master political philosophies of pragmatism, existentialism, and civilized humanism. The primacy of the public situation should be kept in mind even when the discussion of political thought becomes so abstract that it appears to have nothing to do with what is commonly viewed as human existence. Paradoxically, the threat and uncertainty of existence in the twentieth century have been accompanied by the development of formalism in empirical political theory.

Formalism

Formalism in Political Theory Political theory, particularly in its empirical aspect, is more than a response to the public situation that exists when it is written. It is also part of a tradition that is transmitted and altered by each generation of theorists. At certain points in time the tradition is altered decisively by the appearance of a new approach to interpreting the public situation. Almost always this new approach can be retraced to problems encountered in the body of traditional literature as well as contemporary crises in public existence. During the nineteenth century, the tradition of political theory in the West was altered decisively by the appearance of ambitious political sociologies, particularly Karl Marx' interpretation of the public situation. For the political sociologists like Auguste Comte, Marx, and Herbert Spencer, the primacy of law and governmental institutions as variables in the study of political activity could no longer be taken for granted. Underlying both legal rules and governmental institutions were social forces which also specified a plastic human nature.

Early Political Sociology—Comte, Marx, and Spencer The exact nature of the underlying social forces was a matter of dispute among nineteenth-century political sociologists. Comte held that the type of thought characteristic in collective existence is the major determinant of the pattern of that existence. Thus, he divided societies into theological, metaphysical, and positive types, depending upon whether they were characterized by religious, speculative, or scientific thought. Comte believed that the theological, metaphysical, and positive types were also stages in the development of humanity. For Comte, the first theoretical response of human beings to the world and to each other is the attribution of personal causes to events: a tree grows because of the spirit within it; rain falls because a god wants it to fall; one is cured of a disease through God's answering one's prayers. The second theoretical response of human beings to the world and to each other is the interpretation of events as manifestations of a guiding idea or principle: a tree grows because it exemplifies the idea of a tree; rain falls because reality is composed of earth, air, fire, and water; one is cured of disease because the body strives for its natural fulfillment. The third and last theoretical response of human beings to the world and to each other is the explanation of events by observable antecedents: a tree grows because, among other things, it is rooted in fertile soil and receives enough water; rain falls because, among other things, evaporated water is cooled; one is cured of disease because, perhaps, a particular drug has been introduced into one's bloodstream. For Comte, all of the other activities within social existence can be organized around the primary activity of knowing. There is a political activity appropriate to each major kind of society. For example, the scientific society which is emerging in the modern age will be governed by a class of scientific managers who will apply exact knowledge in the interest of humanity. This ideal is still present in the writings of some of the civilized humanists.

The general structure of Marx' theory is quite similar to the structure of Comte's interpretation. However, instead of organizing the elements of social existence around the type of knowledge characteristic in a society, Marx made the mode of economic production and the form of ownership of the means of economic production central to his description. Thus, he divided societies into slave, feudal, capitalist, and socialist types depending upon whether the means of production were owned by slave owners, a landed aristocracy, owners of private industrial property, or the collective representing the workers. Marx also believed that the slave, feudal, capitalist, and socialist types were stages in the development of humanity. He held that all of the other activities within social existence could be organized around the primary activity of transforming nature into objects desired by human beings. Thus, there is a political activity appropriate to each major kind of society. For example, representative democracy appears in capitalist societies as a means through which differences among factions in the ruling class of property holders are reconciled.

Herbert Spencer, too, developed a theory which resembled Comte's interpretation in its structure. He organized the activities of social existence around the differentiation of social function. He saw historical development as a process of increasing specialization of function, through which violent domination by man over man would be replaced by peaceful exchange.

Comte, Marx, and Spencer have their followers in contemporary political theory, just as do St. Thomas Aquinas, Machiavelli, Thomas Hobbes, and John Locke. As long as a cultural tradition is not obliterated, new political theories do not fully supplant the old ones. Thus, the English philosophical sociologists, like Morris Ginsberg, have carried on Comte's tradition in the twentieth century. Outside of the United States and the Anglo-Saxon liberal democracies, Marxism is the dominant contemporary political sociology. In the United States, Herbert Spencer is the usually unrecognized influence behind structural-functional theories of social existence which take as their underlying variable the differentiation of function into many structures. We have already pointed out that interest group theory gains much of its plausibility from the fact that activities have become highly specialized in contemporary Western social existence.

The key to the political sociologies of the nineteenth century is that they organize social existence, including political activity, around a particular kind of activity. Comte takes the activity of knowing as primary, Marx takes the activity of converting nature into culture as primary, and Spencer takes the mode of interaction as primary. This practice of organizing the bulk of social activities around a supposedly primary activity led to the proliferation of conflicting political sociologies. There was no way of synthesizing the insights of one political sociologist with those of another as long as one started from the premise that empirical theory should begin with the assumption that certain activities are primary and others are secondary in determining social existence. The turn of the twentieth century was a decisive moment in the history of empirical political theory, because at that time the doctrine of primary activities was abandoned in favor of a new assumption. The empirical political theories discussed at length in this study—pluralism, organization theory, the theory of political elites, and systems theories of politics—are based on the denial of the doctrine of primary activities and the substitution of the principle of the a priori parity of activities.

Formal Political Sociologies At the turn of the twentieth century, empirical political theory was formalized. While the abandonment of the doctrine of primary activities was not fully self-conscious, it was nonetheless real. Political theorists like the pluralist Arthur F. Bentley in the United States, the organization theorist Max Weber in Germany, and the theorist of political elites Gaetano Mosca in Italy were seeking general descriptions of political activity. They were not willing to accept one of the theories based on the doctrine of primary activities and they did not propose the development of yet another theory based on this doctrine. Instead, they found a way of reinterpreting all of the theories based on the doctrine of primary activities so that they could be compared according to a common standard. The repudiation of the doctrine of primary activities consisted of pushing beyond the contents of social existence to their forms. The formalist revolution in empirical political theory amounted to posing the question, "In what ways are such activities as knowing, producing, controlling, and exchanging alike?" Essentially, the formalist's response to this question was that all of these activities are alike in that they are activities which can be organized and claim resources at the expense of other activities. While this response appears to be quite simple, it has had far-reaching effects on political thought in the twentieth century.

The significance of the formalist revolution can be grasped by comparing formalist empirical theories to Marxist political sociology. The basic unit of analysis in Marxist political sociology is economic class. Marx held that economic classes are the significant groupings in determining major social decisions. For Marx, religious groupings, political groupings, and other noneconomic associative activities reflected the interests of economic classes. The basic unit of analysis in formalist political theory is the group defined as cross-sectional activity. Formalists hold that it is impossible to specify in advance of observation which cross sections of activity will be the most significant groupings in determining major social decisions. Sometimes religious activities will pattern political and economic activities, sometimes military activities will take precedence over all the others, and at other times economic activities will be dominant. Thus, for the purposes of general political theory the formalists suspend judgment on the importance of particular cross sections of activity. In specific instances some cross sections of activity will be more important than others, but specific instances are not the concern of the general political theorist. Thus, the concept of cross-sectional activity makes it possible to compare the nineteenth-century political sociologies according to a single standard. Rather than confronting dogmatic assertions about the primacy of particular cross sections of activity in social existence, the political theorist revalues each claim to primacy as a hypothesis to be tested through observation. For example, Marxism is revalued as a hypothesis predicting that groupings based on economic class will be particularly significant in determining major social decisions. Formalists do not claim that the Marxist hypothesis is false. Instead, they claim that it is a statement to be tested through observation rather than a fundamental analytic category of political theory.

Further comparisons of Marxist political sociology with formalist political theory reveal similar revaluations. For Marx, economic classes organize production into typical economic systems. The form of property ownership, which is closely related to the mode of converting nature into culture, is the basic social institution around which other institutions are organized. Further, the institution of property ownership has a typical organizational expression. The factory and the corporation, for example, are the typical organizational forms of capitalism. In formalist political theory no single kind of organization is singled out as particularly important for the purposes of general theory. Formalists find organization in all human activities and identify a multitude of different kinds of organizations. In the twentieth century, formalists have declared that bureaucratic organization is particularly important in patterning human activity. However, this is an observation rather than a general theoretical postulate. Organization, as the methodic coordination of human activities, includes the patterns of relationships in churches and legislatures, as well as the patterns of relationships in factories and corporations. The kind of organization that is most significant at a given place and time is a matter to be determined by observation.

Similarly, Marx singled out the relationship of economic exploitation as the most important mode of domination in social existence. He placed such means to domination as the organized application of physical force and the manipulation of symbols as subordinate to control of the means to producing livelihood. The state, which organizes the greatest concentrations of physical force, he termed the executive committee of the ruling economic class. Churches, which control activity primarily through the manipulation of symbols, he termed mental opiates which reinforce the domination of the ruling economic class. Marx did not make distinctions among coercion (the use of force or threat of force in controlling human activity), suppression (the use of rewards or punishments in controlling human activity), repression (the bias in a culture for certain kinds of experiences), and oppression (the lack of social opportunity for certain groupings to enjoy particular experiences). He tended to reduce all of the modes of human domination to oppression. They were means of control in an oppressive economic system. In formalist political theory no single type of dominative relationship is set forth as particularly important for the purposes of general theory. The formalist holds that it is possible for any cross section of human activity to become socially dominant and for any of a number of means to domination to be applied. Again, the formalist does not deny that in certain cases economic classes may be ruling classes and oppression may be the most important mode of human domination. However, the formalist holds that whether or not economic classes dominate in an oppressive economic system must be determined through observation. For general political theory, the notion of domination itself, rather than any particular example of domination, is sufficient.

Finally, Marx characterized societies by the adjectives feudal, capitalist, socialist, and communist. This was the summation of his project of organizing all phases of social existence around the economic act. The economic system was the core of the social system. In formalist political theory the notion of system is emptied of all content and is defined as any set of activities chosen for investigation. Whether or not particular systems of interaction appear in human affairs is a question to be resolved by observation. What systems of interaction appear is also a question to be resolved by observation. Some contemporary theorists of the political system attempt to define in advance the content of the interactions that make up the political system by postulating a particular function for political activity in society. This kind of argument represents a return to the political sociologies of the nineteenth century rather than an advance over the formalisms developed at the turn of the twentieth century. However, the notion of a system as a set of cross sections of activity, organized and disbanded, dominant and subordinate, is the capstone of formalism. This concept of system contains within it an exhaustive set of analytic categories for a formal political theory in the twentieth century.

The Formalist Revolution The formalist revolution in empirical political theory can be defined as a suspension of judgment on the question of which particular cross sections of activity are the most important in determining major social decisions. Through the formalist revolution political theorists were able to resolve the problems presented by conflicting political sociologies based on the doctrine of primary activities by overarching them. Questions of importance became matters to be taken care of by observation, and general political theory became an enterprise in refining analytic categories. Political theorists like Bentley, Mosca, and Weber implied that these categories defined the irreducible units of descriptive political analysis. Philosophically, their enterprise can be described as an attempt to identify the categories that make the study of political activity possible. Thus, the efforts of the major twentieth-century empirical theorists imply a minimal definition of political activity. This definition is the one put forward at the beginning of this chapter: political activity pertains to actions oriented to the maintenance and/or extension of other actions. Thus, political activity is representative or reflexive activity. It is activity which refers to other activity. Political activity involves work on other cross sections of activity. It organizes other cross sections of activity and makes some cross sections of activity dominant over others. When the adjective *political* or the noun *politics* is used in this study, the broad and formal definition of political activity is implied.

At this point it is not wise to attempt any justification for defining political activity as a kind of reflexive activity. The discussion of pluralism, organization theory, the theory of political elites, and systems theories of politics as the major twentieth-century empirical theories of political activity should itself provide the justification for this definition. The different branches of twentieth-century formalism each provided a necessary component to empirical political theory. Pluralism, the empirical political theory related to the master political philosophy of pragmatism, contributed the notion of the group as a cross section of activity. Organization theory, the empirical political theory related to the master political philosophy of existentialism, contributed the concept of organization. The theory of political elites, the empirical political theory related to the master political philosophy of civilized humanism, contributed the concepts of dominant cross section of activity, ruling class, social type, and political formula. Systems theories of politics, which attempted syntheses of the other empirical political theories of the twentieth century, contributed the notion of system as a set of cross sections of activity. In each one of these theories the definition of political activity as reflexive activity is implied or stated. It is implied in organization theory and systems theories of politics, and it is stated in pluralism and theories of political elites.

During the first three quarters of the twentieth century, the formalist revolution in empirical political theory has run its course. Already, in systems theories of politics elaborated after World War II there has been a return to an interest in content. However, as previously noted, this interest in content has taken the form of a return to nineteenth-century ideas of ascribing particular functions to political activity, thereby creating anew the problem of determining which particular example, if any, of the doctrine of primary activities is the correct one. In the last chapter of the present study an attempt will be made to go a step beyond formalism and towards a new political theory, rather than take a step backwards into the nineteenth century.

The Key Methods of Political Inquiry

The master political philosophies of the twentieth century have been considered primarily as responses to the uncertain and threatening public situation of the modern age. Pragmatism was viewed as a response to the importance of the indirect consequences of human activity in contemporary social existence, existentialism was viewed as a response to the importance of massive complex organizations in mediating human action in the modern age, and civilized humanism was viewed as a response to the attacks on civilization that characterize the present public situation. Within the three master political philosophies is a model of social action. This tripartite model can be stated essentially in a single sentence: Human beings project purposes into the future which have reference to cultural objects and other people. The projecting activity of human beings is the contribution of existentialism; the analysis of the cultural objects is the contribution of civilized humanism; and the social processes set in motion by the interlacing of human projects is the contribution of pragmatism. This description of human action is the ontological basis for contemporary empirical theories. Whenever the terms *activity* or *action* are used in this study, reference is made to this description of social action.

The major empirical political theories of the twentieth century have been considered primarily as attempts to formalize nineteenth-century political sociologies. This formalization involves the determination of the analytic categories which make the study of political theory possible. Pluralism was viewed as an attempt to formalize the notion of economic class through the notion of group as cross section of activity. Organization theory was viewed as an attempt to formalize the notions of factory and corporation through the concept of organization. Theories of political elites were viewed as attempts to formalize the notions of economic exploitation and ruling economic class through the concepts of dominant cross section of activity, ruling class, social type, and political formula. Systems theories of politics were viewed as attempts to formalize the idea that economic systems are primary determinants of social existence through the notion of system as a set of cross sections of activity chosen for investigation. Within the four major empirical theories of the twentieth century is an interrelated set of analytic categories sufficient for the study of political activity. This interrelated set of analytic categories can be stated essentially in a single sentence: The student of political activity describes systems of cross-sectional activity, organized and disbanded, dominant and subordinate. This definition can be further compacted into the sentence: The student of political activity describes systems of representative activity. This description of analytic categories is the formal basis for political study, which is the study of representative activity. The descriptions of human action and analytic categories, however, do not exhaust the study of political thought in the twentieth century. Each master political philosophy also has a method of inquiry appropriate to it.

Methods and the Public Situation Paradoxically, the discussion of method brings one closer to the public situation at the same time that it appears to take one further away from it. Master political philosophies are primarily descriptions of the public situation. They are responses to vital events taking place in social activity. In one sense, master political philosophies are the perspectives through which human beings mediate their political acts. The great political philosophers reveal and clarify basic elements in the conduct of public affairs that the vast majority of people only dimly grasp. Empirical theories are primarily definitions of the analytic categories appropriate to the description of political activities. Thus, they are one step removed from the public situation. The categories of empirical theory are meant to apply wherever human beings act with reference to one another. Even if they fail, they are attempts to arch over specific public situations. Wherever human beings act, there are cross sections of activity, organized and disbanded, dominant and subordinate. Empirical political theory is an attempt, in Arthur F. Bentley's sense, to fashion tools of analysis. Empirical political theories have a less direct relation to the public situation than do master political philosophies.

Methods of political inquiry, as descriptions of regularized ways to analyze and describe political activity, seem to be the furthest removed of all from the public situation. However, a moment's thought will reveal that any description of the public situation involves a method of data selection and data interpretation. Sheldon Wolin has even observed that the adoption of a method of inquiry in the modern age resembles a conversionary experience. There are three characteristic methods of political inquiry in the twentieth century—the historical method, the functional method, and the method of totalization. Like the master political philosophies and empirical political theories from which they arise, these three methods are complementary.

Historical, Functional, and Totalizing Methods The historical method is the typical approach of civilized humanists. It is primarily a definition of the data that are relevant to the study of political activity. For practitioners of the historical method, the data of political inquiry are contained in the history of mankind. Proponents of the historical method hold that only through the comparison of organized and dominant activities in various civilizations can reliable substantive generalizations about political activity be developed.

The functional method is the typical approach of pragmatists. It is primarily a definition of the kind of generalization sought in political inquiry. Practitioners of the functional method seek to determine the consequences of some human activities for the maintenance and/or extension of other human activities. With special reference to political inquiry, practitioners of the functional method attempt to determine the consequences of certain human activities on the organization and dominance of other human activities. The historical and functional methods of inquiry are compatible because it is only with historical data that one can describe the functional relationships among human activities.

The method of totalization is the typical approach of existentialists. It is primarily a definition of the way in which one attempts to organize functional relationships into a thought structure. Practitioners of the method of totalization seek to relate functional generalizations about political activity at a certain time and place into a whole. They realize that social existence is continually changing its configuration through the projecting activities of human beings, and they claim that the construction of models of epochal crises, like those suggested by Varma, represent the fulfillment of the vocation of a political philosopher and theorist. Practitioners of the method of totalization must continually attempt to catch up with changing social relations and project ahead of them possibilities for new social relations. They try to identify the typical forms of organization at a specific place and time, as well as to determine the dominant cross sections of activity. The method of totalization is compatible with the historical and functional methods. It organizes functional generalizations based on historical data into historically specific wholes, thus providing a compact statement of the essentials of the synthetic method contained in the three key methods of twentieth-century political inquiry.

SUMMARY

The study of political thought includes the study of master political philosophies, empirical political theories, and key methods of political inquiry. Each of these types of thought is related to the others in complex ways, some of which have been defined in the preceding discussion. However, as one investigates these impressive thought structures he should be aware that their final justification and meaning lies in the clarification that they give to actual public situations. Political theory that is completely divorced from any public situation is itself a product of the barbarism deplored by all of the significant twentieth-century political theorists and political philosophers.

NOTES

1. Alan C. Isaak, *Scope and Methods of Political Science* (Homewood, Ill.: Dorsey Press, 1969), p. 3.

2. Vishwanath Prasad Varma, "Political Philosophy in the Modern Age," *Indian Journal of Political Science,* 30 (January–March 1969): 1.

3. Ibid., 2.

4. Ibid., 4.

5. Ibid., 17.

6. Ibid., 19.

7. Thomas Hobbes, *Leviathan Parts I and II* (Indianapolis: The Bobbs-Merrill Co., Inc., 1958), p. 106.

SUGGESTED READINGS

Buehrig, Edward H., ed. *Essays in Political Science.* Bloomington, Ind.: Indiana University Press, 1966.

Isaak, Alan C. *Scope and Methods of Political Science.* Homewood, Ill.: Dorsey Press, 1969.

Kaplan, Abraham. *The Conduct of Inquiry.* San Francisco: Chandler Publishing Co., 1964.

Mackenzie, W. J. M. *Politics and Social Science.* Baltimore: Penguin Books, Inc., 1967.

Martindale, Don. *The Nature and Types of Sociological Theory.* Boston: Houghton Mifflin Company, 1960.

Meehan, Eugene J. *Contemporary Political Thought: A Critical Study.* Homewood, Ill.: Dorsey Press, 1967.

Parsons, Malcolm B., ed. *Perspectives in the Study of Politics.* Chicago: Rand McNally & Co., 1968.

Sorauf, Frank J. *Perspectives on Political Science.* Columbus, Ohio: Charles E. Merrill Publishing Co., 1965.

Varma, Vishwanath Prasad. "Political Philosophy in the Modern Age." *Indian Journal of Political Science.* 30 (January–March 1969): 1–21.

Young, Oran R. *Systems of Political Science.* Englewood Cliffs, N.J.: Prentice-Hall, Inc., 1968.

PART TWO

MASTER
POLITICAL PHILOSOPHIES

CHAPTER TWO

PRAGMATISM

The characteristically American contribution to clarifying the uncertain and threatening public situation of the twentieth century is pragmatism. As an orientation to political science and political philosophy, pragmatism demands that the investigator turn his attention away from the quest for first principles of behavior and the origins of political institutions, and towards the investigation of the consequences of activities and structures. Amelie Rorty has remarked that "there is no set of unambiguous doctrines that define pragmatism."[1] Like most significant movements of philosophic thought, pragmatism "is best thought of as a label for a range of views bearing a general family resemblance."[2] E. A. Burtt has defined the family resemblance among pragmatists as a readiness to recognize "as fact whatever proved to have practical significance in man's ongoing experience."[3] Burtt's definition identifies the core of pragmatism as a theory of truth. Charles S. Peirce, the philosopher who is usually credited with founding pragmatism, developed the pragmatic theory of truth as a tool for clarifying the concepts of reality and of probability. In his influential essay, "How to Make Our Ideas Clear," Peirce enunciated the pragmatic maxim: "Consider what effects, that might conceivably have practical bearings, we conceive the object of our conception to have. Then, our conception of these effects is the whole of our conception of the object."[4]

C. S. PEIRCE

The pragmatic maxim, proposed by Peirce in 1878 as a clarification of the function of concepts in inquiry, was gradually extended and applied by a school of American philosophers to all spheres of speculative investigation. In his later life Peirce repudiated pragmatism "as a system, a universally applicable therapeutic method, or a theory of truth."[5] He coined the word *pragmaticism* to characterize his discussion of rational inquiry. However, even Peirce sometimes succumbed to the temptation of tracing the applications of the pragmatic maxim in the realms of morals and politics. In an 1893 addendum to "How to Make Our Ideas Clear," he remarks that the pragmatic maxim is an application of the Christian principle— Ye may know them by their fruits. He warns against interpreting the maxim in too individualistic a way:

> To say that man accomplishes nothing but that to which his endeavors are directed would be a cruel condemnation of the great bulk of mankind, who never have leisure to labor for anything but the necessities of life for themselves and their families.[6]

The Sociality of Human Existence

Human beings not only effect direct results, but, along with many others, produce a dimly-grasped collective achievement. This collective achievement is a result of social learning. For Peirce, the human being is essentially a possible member of society. Peirce's study of scientific investigation taught him that a single person's experience is nothing if it stands alone. We say that someone who sees what others cannot see is hallucinating. Thus, Peirce claims that the pragmatic maxim points out that it is "not 'my' experience, but 'our' experience that has to be thought of; and this 'us' has indefinite possibilities."[7] Carried to its ultimate conclusion, the sociality of human existence leads Peirce to a romantic conservatism in which the person is subordinated to humanity. Individual action becomes a means, not an end, and "we are all putting our shoulders to the wheel for an end that none of us can catch more than a glimpse at—that which the generations are working out."[8] While we cannot grasp the content of the great end, at least we know that its form consists in "the development of embodied ideas."

Applications of Pragmatism

While romantic conservatism and the subordination of the human being to a collective are not recurrent themes in the literature of American pragmatism, Peirce's discussion of the moral and political applications of the pragmatic maxim reveals several fundamental principles of the pragmatic orientation to the contemporary public situation. First, Peirce distinguishes among the direct effects and the indirect effects of human action. This distinction, vital in the pragmatic orientation to political science and political philosophy, will be used later by John Dewey to clarify the notions of public and private, and by Robert Merton to differentiate the manifest from the hidden effects of social practices.

Second, Peirce bases his description of social existence on the conduct of rational inquiry. The necessity of social relations is disclosed by a study of the processes through which people verify "truth-claims" about the world. The conduct of inquiry as a paradigm for political relations later appears as a dominant theme in the works of John Dewey and Sidney Hook. For Dewey and Hook, democracy becomes continuous with free scientific inquiry.

Third, if the public domain is revealed to Peirce by the study of the processes through which truth claims are verified, society itself is a process of social learning. From one point of view, the collective achievement "takes place by virtue of man's capacity for learning, and by experience continually pouring upon him ideas he has not yet acquired."[9] From another point of view, the ultimate human fulfillment would be the concrete embodiment of the finest human possibilities in activity. For Peirce, as for the pragmatists who followed him, there should be a continuous reciprocity between thought and behavior. Behavior should be informed by knowledge and knowledge should be tested in behavior. Despite his objections, Peirce was a forerunner of the pragmatists who extended the pragmatic maxim into the fields of political theory and political philosophy.

PRAGMATISM AND THE PUBLIC SITUATION

The pragmatic orientation to the public situation has two components. These components follow from the two ways in which the political consequences of human activity can be studied. First, one can study the consequences of activities from the viewpoint of their bearing on the maintenance and enhancement of groups and structures that are present in a given political system. This is the application of pragmatism to descriptive political science. Usually the consequences of political activities are referred to the interests of groups making claims upon the public or to the maintenance of defined patterns of political interaction.

Functionalism

Often, the pragmatic orientation to descriptive political science is called functionalism. One attempts to show how a political practice or activity functions to aid or hinder the fulfillment of a group's objectives, or how that practice or activity functions to maintain or disturb the patterns of interaction in an organization.

Further distinctions can be made in the descriptive study of political consequences. One can differentiate aids (functions) from hindrances (dysfunctions). As was mentioned in the discussion of Peirce, one can also distinguish among manifest functions (consequences that are recognized by political actors and intended by them) and latent functions (consequences that are neither recognized nor intended by political actors).[10] While they are not often made the subject of inquiry, one can, of course, study consequences that are unrecognized though intended, and consequences that are recognized but unintended. The complexities of contemporary policy making have brought into sharp focus these two kinds of consequences. Frequently the goals of government programs are sufficiently vague that it is difficult to determine when and if their intended consequences have been realized. Often, particularly in cases of environmental pollution, contemporary populations come to painful recognition of social consequences that they clearly did not intend. Through functionalism, interest group theory, and systems theory, the pragmatic orientation to the public situation exerts a profound influence on descriptive political science.

Normative Theories

The second component of the pragmatic orientation is normative. The consequences of political practices and activities can be referred to their bearing on the realization of given political values or ideals. Most pragmatists have held that there is a continuity between the descriptive and normative judgments on consequences. Normative theories of pragmatists have been generally characterized by cognitivism and naturalism.

Cognitivism is the position that ethical principles can be known to be either true or false because they affirm or deny that something is the case.[11] A cognitivist would hold that statements such as "X is good" are either true or false, and can be shown to be so through the application of some procedure or standard. Examples of standards that have been used in the past are pleasure, the divine will as revealed in Scripture, and the ability to universalize an act without contradiction.

Opposed to cognitivists are noncognitivists who hold that statements such as "X is good" cannot be known to be either true or false because they do not affirm or deny that something is the case. Existentialists, who will be considered in the next chapter, are noncognitivists.

A kind of cognitivist position is scientific naturalism. Naturalists hold that statements such as "X is good" can be known to be either true or false through applying the procedures of natural and social scientific inquiry. Proponents of scientific naturalism have never been particularly clear about how the scientific method can show ethical principles to be either true or false. Social science can include statements about the values that people hold and the ways in which values can be realized. However, such descriptions seem in no way to imply statements that one value is intrinsically better than another value. Whether or not scientific naturalism is a tenable position, it is clear that the consequences of political practices and actions can be referred to the realization of any number of values and ideals. It is such tracing of consequences, rather than scientific naturalism or even cognitivism, that distinguishes pragmatism from other political philosophies.

The foregoing discussion of the descriptive and normative components of the pragmatic orientation to the public situation should not lead one to believe that the reference of consequences to autochthonous or independent standards is easily accomplished. Political practices and activities always appear in a context of other practices and actions. Since controlled experiments with the consequences of political practices and activities are usually both undesirable and impossible, one must always be tentative about ascribing a consequence to a particular action or practice. Political rhetoric is filled with facile linkages of activities and consequences. For example, the proposition that the consequence of protest demonstrations is "backlash" has at best problematic scientific standing.

WILLIAM JAMES

Pluralism

William James used a political analogy to elucidate his pluralistic and pragmatic theory of reality: "The pluralistic world is thus more like a federal republic than like an empire or a kingdom."[12] In line with his world view, James was one of the first writers to adopt a fully pluralistic view of government and politics. In *The Varieties of Religious Experience* he noted that no major social institution could be defined simply. This was particularly true in the case of government:

> If we should inquire for the essence of 'government,' for example, one man might tell us it was authority, another submission, another police, another an army, another an assembly, another a system of laws; yet all the while it would be true that no concrete government can exist without all these things, one of which is more important at one moment and others at another.[13]

The person who would understand government most completely would be wise not to waste time casting about for a definition purporting to give its essence. Rather, he would enjoy an intimate acquaintance with the particulars of many governments and would "naturally regard an abstract conception in which these were unified as a thing more misleading than enlightening."[14] Government, then, is a name for certain structures and processes which may, at times, attract one's attention and provide the substance for action.

James applied this pluralistic view to the problem of political reform. The successful reformer would not reflect on the nature of the state and the human condition in general. Rather, political reformers have accomplished "their successive tasks in the history of nations by being blind for the time to other causes."[15] In other words, the reformer is a member of a special interest group even when he is working for a good. After all, how could he be otherwise when "government" is merely a name? In his *Pragmatism,* James remarks that "the stock rationalist trick" is to treat "the *name* of a concrete phenomenal reality as an independent prior entity," and place it "behind the reality as its explanation."[16] James did not play rationalist tricks in his political thinking.

Anti-Institutionalism

Along with his nominalist treatment of government, James evinced an extreme anti-institutional bias. In *Human Immortality* he claims that

> when a living want of mankind has got itself officially protected and organized in an institution, one of the things which the institution most surely tends to do is to stand in the way of the natural gratification of the want itself.[17]

Among other offenders, James singled out "laws and courts of justice," anticipating later pragmatists.[18] The fault in the institutions lay with the "place-holders" who frustrate "the spiritual purpose to which they were appointed to minister" because they judge "by the technical light which soon becomes the only light in which they seem to be able to see the purpose, and the narrow way which is the only way in which they can work in its service."[19]

Here James seems to be contradicting himself. While the theme of technical values destroying humane values in complex organizations anticipates some aspects of the uncertain and threatening public situation of the twentieth century, the implication that institutions have definable moral purposes runs counter to the claim that government, for example, has no essence. The apparent contradiction is resolved in James' letters. In a letter to Mrs. Henry Whitman he declared himself against "all big organizations as such, national ones first and foremost," and in favor of "the eternal forces of truth which always work in the individual and immediately unsuccessful way."[20] James opposed the individual as creator and sole source of value to the stultifying institution. This is clearly brought out in a letter to William M. Salter: "*Every* great institution is perforce a means of corruption—whatever good it may also do. Only in the free personal relation is ideality to be found."[21] Institutions are set up to satisfy human wants, but invariably they become congeries of technical processes which work to inhibit the dynamic individual's fulfillment. However, who is this all-important individual? Does he have an integrity and a purpose? James described the ideal human type in *Pragmatism:*

> A radical pragmatist . . . is a happy-go-lucky anarchistic sort of creature. If he had to live in a tub like Diogenes he wouldn't mind at all if the hoops were loose and the staves let in the sun.[22]

Peirce and James

James represents the opposite pole from Peirce in the pragmatic movement. While Peirce finds the greatest value in collective achievements, James holds that values are personal. While Peirce finds the ground of society in the collective verification of truth claims, James derives society from the free personal relation in a multitude of activities. While Peirce was essentially a conservative, James was a reformer and an individualist. Perhaps most striking of all, while James' ideal individual might live in a tub like Diogenes, Peirce's human being put his shoulders to the wheel for an end he could not understand.

It was in the works of John Dewey that the themes of Peirce and James were synthesized and their extremes avoided. While Peirce and James both looked to the consequences of political activity, neither one of them was able to articulate a satisfactory relationship between the public and the private spheres of human existence. For Peirce, the private was absorbed in the public; while for James, the public was absorbed in the private. Dewey attempted to give each domain its proper function.

JOHN DEWEY

John Dewey is probably the American philosopher who has exerted the most profound influence on the development of culture in the United States. While he preferred to call his philosophy instrumentalism or experimentalism he identified himself closely with the pragmatic tradition in American thought. Like James and unlike Peirce, Dewey believed that the philosopher's role should be far broader than that of clarifying the methods and presuppositions of inquiry. While James addressed himself primarily to the significant problems of individual experience, Dewey was most concerned with the dilemmas of social life. Rytina and Loomis maintain that Dewey's overriding goal was to create a situation in which philosophic thought would clarify social action and thought in turn would be clarified by such action.[23] To this end he became involved in educational reform and was a guiding spirit in the progressive education movement in the United States. He was also deeply concerned with political reform and attempted to work out a theory of democracy that would be relevant to the uncertain and threatening public situation of the twentieth century.

Critique of Traditional Theorists

Dewey's major contribution to political thought is contained in *The Public and Its Problems.* Though short and deceptively simple, this work represents a full-scale critique of the Western tradition of political philosophy and the outlines of a pragmatic political philosophy. Dewey's critique of traditional political theorists can be summed up by his statement that they took "causal agency instead of consequences as the heart of the problem."[24] Dewey is not concerned with accounting for the origin of the state. Whatever the origin of the state may have been, it can only be described and justified in terms of its consequences for life in the here and now. Thus, he considers speculation about whether the state was created by divine will or by a contract among individuals, or whether it appeared as some sort of organic growth, as irrelevant to the work of serious political philosophers in the twentieth century. He counters those who investigate the origins of political activity with the statement that "every serious political dispute turns upon the question of whether a given political act is socially beneficial or harmful."[25]

In his criticism, Dewey is probably unfair to the traditional political theorists. They frequently used their descriptions of the supposed origins of the state to illuminate what they thought to be the essence of political activity. More to the point seems to be James' objection that politics, at least in the twentieth century, has no specifiable essence. Of course, Dewey's objection to thought about the origins of the state is an implicit rejection of ascribing essences to politics.

The Individual and Society

In his *Reconstruction in Philosophy* Dewey situates his political theory in the history of social thought. He remarks that no one disagrees that society is composed of individuals. Given acceptance of this basic fact, three alternative social philosophies follow:

> Society must exist for the sake of individuals; or individuals must have their ends and ways of living set for them by society; or else society and individuals are correlative, organic, to one another, society requiring the service and subordination of individuals and at the same time existing to serve them.[26]

Dewey associates the first position with Bentham and rejects it because individuals become isolated and ineffective apart from their participation in social groups. He associates the second position with Plato and rejects it because social bonds depend upon strong and competent individuals. While the third position seems to avoid the errors of the preceding two, it is also defective because it commits one to a "logic of general notions under which specific situations are to be brought" when the significant problem is to determine the worth of social institutions as they operate "under given conditions of definite time and place."[27] The theory that society and individuals are correlative to one another, associated with Hegel, tends to justify established political patterns. The organic relation between society and individuals that is generated in a conceptual dialectic becomes a mold in which are fit a wide variety of social facts. Any general theory of politics that specifies an invariant relation between individual and society promotes a situation in which the "meanings which are found in the general notions are injected into the particulars that come under them."[28] The facts are violated by a preconceived theory.

In order to escape the problem of injecting the meanings of general notions into the description of social particulars, Dewey proposes a radical change in the whole enterprise of political philosophy. In place of a dialectic of concepts he suggests the development of a method of inquiry. There is an answer to the question of how the individual and society are related to one another—while there will always be individual selves and social organization, the relations between them must be determined empirically for each situation. From the normative point of view, the relations that should obtain between individuals and social organization must be determined with regard to the context of each particular situation. For Dewey, there are three dimensions basic to political analysis. First, the individual must be taken as a nodal point of value and experience. Second, social organization, or systems of rights and duties, must be placed in relation to the individual. Third, social relations, or the processes of associating, must be viewed as the crucial factors in the transmission of experience. One would expect Dewey's political theory to reflect an attempt to describe the public situation of his time through all three dimensions. While he did undertake such an enterprise in *Individualism Old and New, The Public and Its Problems* states a more general theory.[29]

Dewey and the Public

Definition of Terms The political theory contained in *The Public and Its Problems* is based on a fundamental distinction between the direct and indirect consequences of social action. Dewey begins his analysis by stating the objective fact that human acts have consequences for other human beings, that some of these consequences are perceived, and that such perception frequently results in attempts to control action. From here, we can observe that there are two kinds of consequences—"those which affect the persons directly engaged in a transaction, and those which affect others beyond those immediately concerned."[30] Given this distinction between the direct and indirect consequences of social action, Dewey defines the fundamental concepts of his political theory. The public is composed of "all those who are affected by the indirect consequences of transactions to such an extent that it is deemed necessary to have those consequences systematically cared for."[31] Officials are those who care for such consequences in the interest of the public. The physical resources used by officials in the performance of their duties compose the commonwealth, and the public so far as organized through officials and a commonwealth is the populace. The organization of officials is the government, and the state is "the organization of the public effected through officials for the protection of the interests shared by its members."[32] Dewey admits that this interconnected set of definitions is purely formal. The indirect consequences that will be recognized and controlled in any given society can only be determined empirically. Also, how the officials perform their function is a matter for empirical determination in each situation. Despite his recognition that the set of definitions is formal, Dewey derives from them a criterion for judging the good state: a state is good to the degree that the public is organized and to the degree that the officials are constituted in such a way that they care for the public's interests.[33]

Weaknesses of the Theory In *The Public and Its Problems* Dewey seems to have produced a theory that would not meet his tests of good political philosophy. First, instead of providing an account of the consequences of political activity, he has put forward another theory of the origin of the state. The state arises from recognition of the consequences of conjoint action and the decision to control these consequences in the interest of those people indirectly affected by them. In a sense, this account is not very different from the descriptions of social contract theorists who derived the state from the inconveniences of human existence without law.

Second, Dewey identifies an essence of political activity. Politics and government serve a distinctive function in human society. They exist to control the consequences of conjoint action in the interest of those indirectly affected by such action. In this connection, we may remark that Dewey's political science and political philosophy stress the public function of the political system over the private interest of the people involved in influencing and making decisions in that system.

Dewey suggests that the function of the political system is caring for indirect consequences of social action. Of course, there are many other functions that the political system might perform. In fact, Dewey himself suggests another function for the state in *Reconstruction in Philosophy.* Here he argues that the state is an "instrumentality for promoting and protecting other and more voluntary forms of association, rather than a supreme end in itself."[34] Dewey contends that in the modern age three developments have occurred with regard to social life: the state has grown more powerful and better organized; the individual has been liberated from traditional attachments; and voluntary associations have multiplied. The last development has been far and away the most important, and "groupings for promoting the diversity of goods that men share have become the real social units."[35] The state is important, but its main function is to regulate and adjust the relations among groups, define the limits of their actions, prevent and settle their conflicts, and foster and coordinate their activities. Again, Dewey stresses public function over private interest in his definition of the essence of the political system. However, the function is different. Dewey would have done well to heed James' warning that those who want to understand government should regard an essential definition of the political system as a "thing more misleading than enlightening."

The third and most important self-imposed test that Dewey's political theory fails follows from attempting to devise an essential definition of the political system. By defining the political system in terms of its public function, Dewey develops the same kind of dialectic of concepts that he finds so offensive in Hegel's work. His set of concepts becomes a mold in which social facts can be made to fit. These concepts also can be used in a justification of the status quo. The government is not a power that stands over and against the individual and weak social groupings. It is a system of roles oriented either to caring for the indirect consequences of conjoint action in the interest of the public, or to harmonizing the relations among all groupings. It is difficult to understand exactly what these definitions mean.

Part of the problem is Dewey's ethical naturalism which commits him to a continuity between statements of fact and statements of value. The vagueness of the boundary between fact and value dulls both descriptive and prescriptive analysis. Descriptively, it is easy to observe that most of what we ordinarily call political systems perform only imperfectly the functions that Dewey assigns them. Dewey himself admits this. In what way, then, are these functions the essence of politics? Prescriptively, Dewey never attempts to justify why these particular functions should be the only ones performed by the political system. This is all the more ironic in view of the fact that in *Individualism Old and New* Dewey predicted that the "problem of social control of industry and the use of governmental agencies for constructive social ends will become the avowed center of political struggle."[36] He argued that the politically lost individual who had no worthy objects for his loyalties should apprehend "the realities of industry and finance as they function in public and political life."[37] He ascribed political apathy to lack of consciousness of "any vital connection between politics and daily affairs," indicted the political parties for maintaining this breach, and concluded that financial and industrial power, organized into corporate interest groups, "can deflect economic consequences away from the advantage of the many to serve the privilege of the few."[38] Here Dewey recognized the role of private interest in the political system and did not attempt to develop essential definitions. Instead of developing a formal standard for the good state in terms of organization, he proposed that the connection of events and the society of contemporaries "as formed of moving and multiple associations, are the only means by which the possibilities of individuality can be realized."[39]

Two Aspects of Dewey's Thought

The side of Dewey's political philosophy presented in *The Public and Its Problems* and *Reconstruction in Philosophy* has exerted much more influence over contemporary political theory and political science than has the analysis of *Individualism Old and New.* The description of politics as group activity and the functional interpretation of the political system have become increasingly popular. Pluralism and contextualism in descriptive analysis are regnant. Much less popular is the activity of continuously making new linkages between the personal plight of the individual, the organizations that he confronts, and the associations in which he lives. In brief, the side of Dewey that is closer to Peirce has been stressed more than the side of Dewey that is closer to James. This has been particularly the case with regard to democratic theory. For Dewey, democracy was an application of the method of experimentation to decision making. Rytina and Loomis summarize the general experimental method in six steps—confused situations, development of alternative solutions, formulation of a clarified problem, transformation of solutions into hypotheses, application of hypothesis to particular situation, and active test of hypotheses and unification of situation.[40] Dewey believed that a democracy with guaranteed civil liberties at its best functioned according to this method. Freedom of inquiry allowed problems to be articulated, alternative solutions to be reviewed, and plans to be proposed. Majority rule guaranteed that hypotheses would be tested. Dewey held that the democratic method should be applied in all social institutions. Thus, he favored a thoroughgoing socialist democracy.[41] He believed that the political system was accessory to the economic system.[42] However, his followers, like Sidney Hook, have tended to treat democracy as "purely and only a form of government," mechanizing its method.[43]

Even at its freest, however, Dewey's method has a serious weakness. It leads to the conclusion that all social problems are problems of communication and inquiry. Dewey concludes *The Public and Its Problems* with the observation that the basic problem of the public is the "improvement of the methods and conditions of debate, discussion and persuasion."[44] While this statement might be true in an ideal social democracy, it is certainly not the case in a society characterized by organized and concentrated blocs of power. Dewey seems often to have taken his essential definitions of the functions of the political system for fact. Unfortunately, this mistake has been made by many writers in the pragmatic tradition.

SIDNEY HOOK

Sidney Hook is widely recognized as the foremost expositor of pragmatic political theory in the period following World War II. While Dewey developed his political theory between the two world wars, particularly in the 1920's, Sidney Hook transmitted Dewey's legacy under the shadow of totalitarian barbarism. This difference between the times in which the two men wrote may partially help account for the defensive tone of Hook's writings as opposed to the more optimistic and expansionist mood of Dewey's work. This defensive thrust in Hook's work can best be appreciated by considering his political philosophy, which is primarily a justification of political democracy in the West. Hook remarks that in its "primary *historical* significance, democracy refers to a form of government and only to government."[45] He follows this statement by defining a government as democratic to the extent that "those who are affected by its decisions—leaving aside children—have a share, direct or more often indirect, through election of its agents or representatives, in determining the nature of the decisions."[46] Like Dewey, Hook holds that it would be desirable for democratic methods to be applied in complex organizations outside of the political system, particularly in industry. However, unlike Dewey, he does not contend that the political system is primarily accessory to the economic system. Rather, he reverses the order of priority. He asserts that while political democracy without economic democracy is incomplete, "economic democracy without political democracy is impossible."[47]

This reversal indicates an important shift in thought about politics that was brought about by the generation of theorists who confronted the brutality of totalitarian regimes. The center of debate about the good society shifted from the controversy between advocates of capitalism and socialism to the discussion of the best way to defend democratic political institutions from totalitarianism. The young pragmatists of the 1930's and the 1940's witnessed the rise of single-party, repressive, and technically advanced regimes that ruled in the name of ideologies of both left and right. They concluded that while capitalist democracies might be imperfect, at least they maintained a high level of civility and held open the possibility of humane social change. The dominant attitude can be summed up by the novelist E. M. Forster's apothegm—"two cheers for democracy."[48] While Dewey considered democracy as a method for attaining public control over the indirect consequences of conjoint action, or as a method for facilitating the healthy growth of voluntary associations, Hook considered democracy primarily as "a *common method* of negotiating differences."[49] For Hook, the method itself is more important than any specific result, and he contends that it is a continuous recognition of this principle that gives meaning to the philosophical heritage of Atlantic democracies. In *The Public and Its Problems,* Dewey had written that no intrinsically best form of political system could be identified: "In concrete fact, in actual and concrete organization and structure, there is no form of state which can be said to be the best: not at least till history is ended, and one can survey all its varied forms."[50] Sidney Hook would find it difficult to agree with that statement.

Justification of Democracy

Sidney Hook represented pragmatism in the post-World War II philosophical debate over how Western democracy could best be justified. In his essay, "The Justifications of Democracy," Hook identifies five generic forms of justification.

Religious Principles The first position states that democracy rests upon belief in religious principles, in the sense that if these principles are denied democracy must be denied. Hook rejects this position on the grounds that only the moral attributes of God can serve as premises to justify democracy, and this is the case because the "attribution of moral qualities to God is an expression of what we think his qualities ought to be."[51] Thus, the attribution itself must be justified. It is unlikely that Hook's assertion that men create God's attributes would satisfy many religious people. Certainly, Hook does not show that the religious position is self-contradictory.

Nature of Reality The second position states that democracy rests upon a theory of the nature of reality. Hook provides a telling rebuttal to this position. He argues that whatever the ultimate nature of the universe may be, the moral interpretation to be given that universe still must be decided by human beings.

Natural Law He advances a similar argument with regard to the third position, which rests democracy on natural law. There are three possible interpretations of natural law: physical law, juridical law, and moral law. Physical law, which describes relations among facts, cannot by itself provide reasons why one political system is better than another. Juridical law simply refers to the rules that are and have been in effect in actual states. This kind of law cannot be used to justify democracy because we want to give reasons why a particular kind of constitution is moral. Moral law, which declares what is good in the nature of things, merely duplicates the defects of the theological and metaphysical positions. Moral laws can be broken. In what sense are they invariably part of the nature of things?

Existential Preference The fourth position justifies democracy simply on the basis that it is the speaker's preference. Hook states that this is not a justification at all, because it raises no moral or intellectual issue. This is not a fair characterization of the position that Hook has called *existentialist.* While existentialists hold that the final justification of anything human can only reside in personal choice, they do not believe that one must always stick to the particular set of preferences that he has at a given time. One can choose to open himself to new experiences just as well as he can choose to hold on stubbornly to a single set of preferences and experiences. However, the choice that he makes is ultimately his responsibility. Existentialism does not eliminate reason from human affairs. Instead, it shows that reason enters human affairs only when people choose to allow it to do so.

Security, Freedom, and Cooperative Diversity The fifth position, and the one that Hook favors, states that if "democracy is taken strictly as a form of political government, its superiority over other forms of government can be established to the extent that it achieves more security, freedom, and cooperative diversity than any of its alternatives."[52] Whether or not the foregoing statement is factually correct, it evidences once again the weaknesses of scientific naturalism. Is it scientifically demonstrable that security, freedom, and cooperative diversity are good, or is Hook merely telling us that some of our presumed preferences are better realized in a democratic political system than in others? While he claims that he is showing the former, he actually does the latter. The existentialist is able to ground values in choice. He can use the method of pragmatism to describe the consequences of different courses of action for the realization of preferences. He does not believe that values can be grounded in a method. He also does not believe that values are necessarily chaotic because they cannot be justified scientifically. The existentialist does not deny that there may be a structure to the human condition; he holds that one must describe it as it appears in human experience.

Social Process

Hook's uncritical naturalism and his subordination of the individual to a method of political decision making can be traced to a theme in Dewey's political philosophy. In *Reconstruction in Philosophy* Dewey opts for the primacy of relational processes over individual experience and extended systems of social organization. He contends that society is the process of associating, and that "to this active process, both the individual and the institutionally organized may truly be said to be subordinate."[53] The individual is subordinate because without relational processes he would be merely a brute animal. Organization is subordinate because it becomes a static domination when it is not used as a means of enriching association. While it is true that individuals would be brute animals without relational processes, it is also true that relational processes would not exist at all without human beings as centers of original experience. Further, while it is true that organizations can stultify relational processes, it is also true that the stable expectations of behavior made possible by organizations provide a context in which new relational processes can be created.

The subordination of the human being to the *process* of associating was the greatest error into which pragmatists could fall in their political theories. It allowed them to elevate social psychology above psychology and political sociology. It allowed Sidney Hook to say that "*today it is the mode of political decision rather than the mode of economic production which is of primary significance.*" [54] In this investigation into contemporary political theories we will take another one of Sidney Hook's statements as our keynote: "The separation of content from form is a myth."[55]

JUSTUS BUCHLER

One recent philosopher who has attempted to purge the pragmatic tradition of some of its ambiguities and restate the idea of social process in such a way that it does not require subordination of the individual human being is Justus Buchler. Buchler, like the other pragmatists, defines social life in terms of processes of communication. However, he emphasizes the plight of the individual with reference to these processes. The individual enters the world and immediately "nature and history begin to communicate their burden to him."[56] Communication is defined so broadly that anything communicates to an individual if, "in consequence of its impact, he directly begins to communicate with himself about it."[57]

Community
Communication among human beings, or social communication, involves community. Community comes into being when two or more people share the same "procept," or something that affects them in any way at all. Thus, neither community nor communication involves the subordination of the individual:

> When a community is intense and rigid, when its bonds are grounded in dedication, this is not because individuality is minimized but because the power of something common to individuals can be appropriated by each individual to conquer or alter . . . the course of his present self.[58]

The fundamental distinction in Buchler's political philosophy is between invisible and visible communities. Like other communities, an invisible community is composed of individuals who share something that affects them in some way. Unlike a visible community, however, it is not organized by symbols, rules of association, and property to cope with the consequences of conjoint human activity. Dewey's public is a type of visible community.

For Buchler, the individual is the crossroads of as many

communities as there are things which affect him and at least one other person. Some communities are stronger than others, and every individual has a hierarchy of loyalties to his various communities. The relation of the individual to any particular community is always precarious because the individual is the crossroads of so many communities. Individuality is a function of the number of intersecting communities. When the many communities are rendered standard and homogeneous by some authority, individuality is sacrificed for unity.

All invisible communities are genuine because they carry with them the potential for unanimity in action and feeling. Visible communities may have already realized their potentialities and become barriers to effective action. This leads Buchler to two conclusions. First, invisible communities are more tenacious and permanent in human existence. They reflect "the more enduring phases of human nature as well as its inevitable subdivision into human types."[59] Second, and more important, a community "can never be here and now."[60] Nothing that affects human beings is ever fully visible in its destiny. Each community has a future, and adequate projections of that future must be produced continuously.

In his discussion of community, Buchler purges pragmatic social theory of essential definitions. The state is not defined in terms of its public function, as in Dewey, or in terms of its principle of decision making, as in Hook. Instead, the state is one visible community among many invisible and visible communities. The function that it performs in any particular situation must be determined empirically. This discussion marks a return to James' nominalist political science, with the important addition that the living wants of mankind have become organized into invisible and visible communities. Sidney Gelber has remarked that Buchler's general philosophy can best be called *radical naturalism*.[61] In political terms, even though Buchler does not take an ideological stand, his theory of community can form part of a ground for a radical or progressive political theory. This is particularly the case because of his affirmation that communities can never be "here and now." As Gelber notes, the futurity of the community is paralleled by the futurity of the individual in Buchler's work: "For Buchler the direction of experience would entail a process of continuing production, articulated by the self, rather than, as for Dewey, a series of consummatory acts, indicative of the self."[62]

Methodology

While Buchler's contributions to political theory have not received the attention that they deserve, his reflections on methodology are widely discussed.[63] In the same way that Buchler eliminated essential definitions from his social theory, he rejects rigidity in his discussion of method. Buchler's discussion of method is founded upon his pregnant insight that man is "the animal that tries deliberately to limit his world in some respects and to make it more abundant in others."[64] Method appears in human affairs when people attain recognition of themselves as manipulators of the world. This self-recognition carries with it an appreciation of human powers, the most elementary of which is the power to repeat any action. This is the origin of methodic action which has the four components of a mode of conduct, directed in a given way, to a particular set of circumstances, for the attainment of a result.

Like the other pragmatists, Buchler does not posit a sharp break between the various spheres of human existence. Thus, he relates method to policy. Policy is an inclination toward a specific kind of activity, and method provides a policy with its identity through recurrent instances of application. For Buchler, there is no one method that can be applied to gain favorable results in all spheres of human existence. This is perhaps his most important deviation from the mainstream of pragmatic thought. No method should be viewed independently of its contribution to fulfilling a purpose. When method is enshrined as an end in itself, first discretion is lost and then its purpose is forgotten. Method becomes habit, a form of death. Justus Buchler's work shows that the pragmatic tradition in political theory can overcome essential definitions and the separation of form and content. In his theory, the individual is the center of activity, and the human condition is to judge the world in every possible mode.

PRAGMATISM IN REVIEW

The pragmatic movement in American political philosophy can be viewed as an attempt to achieve three goals. First, the pragmatists desired to create a method of analysis that would separate the actual consequences of political patterns and practices from the ideological justifications given to them. Second, the pragmatists attempted to develop a standard for evaluating public activities. And finally, they tried to devise a descriptive political science to trace the effects of political activities on social groups and structures.

Social Criticism

In the first of its phases, pragmatism is a way of engaging in social criticism to clear the way for social reform. The core of pragmatic social criticism is quite simple. One studies the effects that a political institution or practice has with respect to the welfare of a given group or the maintenance of a particular social structure and then compares the observed effects with the consequences ascribed to the institution or practice by its defenders. Of course, an adequate analysis of this sort may be quite difficult and complex in its execution. Aside from the difficulty mentioned earlier in isolating the specific consequences of a given practice or institution, one must distinguish between the judgments that social actors make about the consequences of practices and institutions, and their actual effects. This is not the same as either the distinction between intended and unintended consequences, or the distinction between recognized and unrecognized consequences. Both of these distinctions refer to consequences that actually occur. One of the major problems in political analysis centers on the fact that people may believe that consequences are occurring which are not taking place at all.

Legal Realism Perhaps the best example of pragmatic criticism of the political system is found in the literature of legal realism. Morris Cohen has observed that legal realism is defined by a rejection of "the classical view that the law consists of fixed principles and that cases are actually decided by purely logical deduction from them."[65] Legal realists turned their attention to what judges actually did, rather than what they said they did in deciding cases. Judicial decisions were often justified on the grounds that the judge applied the correct rule to the facts presented to him. Legal realists questioned the notions of correct rule and an objective set of facts for each case. They showed that in most complex legal cases conflicting rules could be applied reasonably in reaching a decision. They also attempted to demonstrate that the court never received all of the facts relevant to a complex case. They attacked adherence to legal precedent on the grounds that no two disputes brought to court were the same in all relevant respects and that interpretation of the law should change as social structures change.

Legal realists like Jerome Frank and Karl Llewellyn wanted judges to become conscious of the reasons why they made decisions in a certain way and the social consequences of their decisions.[66] To this end they suggested various judicial methodologies. Jerome Frank recommended that judges undergo a form of psychoanalysis so that they could recognize their prejudices. Karl Llewellyn recommended that judges explain why they chose certain precedents rather than others. The guiding ethical insight uniting the diverse forms of legal realism is the claim that the judge is acting in bad faith if he holds that the compulsion of precedents or external norms are responsible for his decision rather than the commitment he has made after study of the law and moral dialogue.[67]

Pragmatism and Ideology Along with the type of pragmatic social criticism that identifies the actual consequences of political institutions goes a functional analysis of the ideological justifications of these institutions, If there is a gap between actual consequences and proclaimed consequences, several explanations can be given to account for the existence of the disparity. First, people may lack knowledge of the actual consequences of institutions. In the face of severe disparities this explanation has limited force. Second, proclaiming certain consequences may be serving a psychological function for the defenders of the institution. Self-deception about the social consequences of an institution in which one is involved may relieve both guilt and dissonance, while deceiving others about the social consequences may protect one's position in the institution. Third, proclaiming certain consequences may be serving a social function for the defenders of the institution. When governments release communications to the effect that their policies are caring for the indirect consequences of social acts in the interest of the public, such communications may function to legitimize their rule. Howard R. Smith has referred to the practice of all social groups claiming that their preferred policies are in the public interest as the "common good distortion."[68]

In *Reconstruction in Philosophy* Dewey applied functional analysis to Hegelian philosophy. He observed that the "effect, if not the intention, of German idealism as applied in social philosophy was to provide a bulwark for the maintenance of the political status quo against the tide of radical ideas coming from revolutionary France."[69] Dewey argued that German idealism functioned to justify established power in two ways. First, in speaking about the state in general and glorifying its functions, the German idealists diverted attention from evils in the concrete political situation. Second, in claiming that the state and the individual are reciprocally necessary and helpful to one another, they tended to minimize the significance of specific conflicts. These two tendencies in German idealism were useful in justifications of the Prussian state and its bureaucratic absolutism. Here Dewey is not claiming that in some mysterious way German idealism arose out of the material conditions of the Prussian state. Rather, he is stating that regardless of its origin and intention, German idealism functioned to justify the power system of the Prussian state. Political theories may not be determined in any strict sense by patterns of power, but their survival value and popularity are probably related in a significant way to the functions that they can serve in promoting and defending the interests of powerful social groups. Dewey believed that the essential feature of ideology was its effect of diverting attention from special situations. Only a method of criticism that described the actual effects of political institutions could clear the ground adequately for social reform.

Standards of Public Function

The second goal of the pragmatic movement in American political philosophy was the creation of a standard for evaluating public activities. We have already discussed Dewey's notion that a state is good to the degree that the public is organized and to the degree that the officials are constituted in such a way that they care for the public's interests. Sidney Hook developed another standard for evaluating political activities. He argued that intelligent political life "consists in resolving conflicts of freedoms in such a way as to strengthen the security of the entire structure of . . . freedoms."[70] This standard is as formal as Dewey's and gives little aid to decision makers in any concrete situation.

An ambitious attempt to define a standard for evaluating public activities was undertaken by the legal philosopher Roscoe Pound, who founded sociological jurisprudence. Like legal realism, sociological jurisprudence was an attempt to apply the principles of pragmatism to the analysis of legal institutions. Pound suggested that political activities be evaluated "in terms of civilization, of raising human powers to their highest possible unfolding—toward which spontaneous free individual action and collective organized effort both contribute."[71] The ideal of civilization is applied by attempting to resolve conflicts of interest by paying attention to the entire structure of interest satisfaction. Among the interests to be taken into account are individual interests, claims pressed on behalf of a politically organized society, and interests in the security and development of social institutions. Pound's standard is very similar to Hook's and suffers from the same defect of formalism and high abstraction. Perhaps the most telling criticism of the political ideals proposed by pragmatists is that they can be attacked on the same grounds that Dewey attacked Hegelian idealism. Pound, for example, frequently confuses "is" and "ought." He writes that "to enable satisfaction of as much of the whole scheme of demands" as possible "has not merely been what lawmakers and tribunals and jurists have been striving for, it has also been put in one way or another by philosophers as what we ought to be doing."[72] This kind of identification of power and right functions to reduce structural conflicts to problems of social engineering. The superficial reconciliation of conflict in a dialectic of concepts tends to appear in pragmatic philosophy as well as in Hegelian idealism.

Political Science

The third goal of the pragmatic movement in American political philosophy was the development of a descriptive political science that would trace the consequences of political activities on social groups and structures. Only with the aid of such a political science could pragmatic social criticism be accomplished. A pragmatic political science would also provide the knowledge necessary to carry through social reforms aimed at realizing the various ideals espoused by pragmatists. In pragmatism, theory and action are interrelated. Thus, pragmatists expected political science itself to become an active agent in social change. In a later chapter we will consider the descriptive political theories that grew out of pragmatism and evaluate their contributions to realizing the unity of theory and action favored by pragmatic philosophers.

NOTES

1. Amelie Rorty, ed., *Pragmatic Philosophy* (Garden City, N.Y.: Doubleday & Company, Inc., 1966), p. v.

2. Ibid.

3. E. A. Burtt, *In Search of Philosophic Understanding* (New York: The New American Library, Inc., 1967), p. 38.

4. Charles S. Peirce, *Essays in the Philosophy of Science* (Indianapolis: The Bobbs-Merrill Co., Inc., 1957), p. 42.

5. Ibid., p. xxi.

6. Ibid., pp. 42–43n.

7. Ibid., p. 43n.

8. Ibid., pp. 43–44n.

9. Ibid., p. 43n.

10. Robert K. Merton, *Social Theory and Social Structure* (New York: The Free Press, 1957).

11. Felix E. Oppenheim, *Moral Principles in Political Philosophy* (New York: Random House, Inc., 1968), p. 24.

12. William James, *A Pluralistic Universe* (New York: Longmans, Green & Co., 1920), pp. 321–322.

13. William James, *The Varieties of Religious Experience* (London: Longmans, Green & Co. Ltd., 1929), p. 26.

14. Ibid., p. 27.

15. Ibid., p. 339.

16. William James, *Pragmatism: A New Name for Some Old Ways of Thinking* (New York: Longmans, Green & Co., 1925), p. 220.

17. William James, *Human Immortality: Two Supposed Objections to the Doctrine* (London: Archibald Constable and Co., 1906), p. 7.

18. Ibid.

19. Ibid.

20. Henry James, ed., *The Letters of William James* (Boston: The Atlantic Monthly Press, 1920), 2: 464.

21. Ibid., p. 101.

22. James, *Pragmatism,* pp. 259–260.

23. Joan Huber Rytina and Charles P. Loomis, "Marxist Dialectic and Pragmatism: Power as Knowledge," *American Sociological Review,* 35 (April 1970): 308–318.

24. John Dewey, *The Public and Its Problems* (New York: Henry Holt & Co., 1927), p. 20.

25. Ibid., p. 15.

26. John Dewey, *Reconstruction in Philosophy* (New York: The New American Library, Inc., 1952), p. 148.

27. Ibid., p. 149.

28. Ibid., p. 150.

29. John Dewey, *Individualism Old and New* (New York: G. P. Putnam's Sons, Capricorn Books, 1962).

30. Dewey, *The Public,* p. 12.

31. Ibid., pp. 15–16.

32. Ibid., p. 33.

33. Ibid.

34. Dewey, *Reconstruction,* p. 158.

35. Ibid., p. 159.

36. Dewey, *Individualism,* p. 113.

37. Ibid., p. 114.

38. Ibid., pp. 114, 115.

39. Ibid., p. 170.

40. Rytina and Loomis, *American Sociological Review,* 315.

41. Dewey, *Individualism.*

42. Ibid., p. 113.

43. Sidney Hook, *Political Power and Personal Freedom* (New York: The Macmillan Company, Collier Books, 1965), p. 63.

44. Dewey, *The Public,* p. 208.

45. Hook, *Political Power,* p. 52.

46. Ibid.

47. Ibid., p. 56.

48. E. M. Forster, *Two Cheers for Democracy* (New York: Harcourt Brace Jovanovich, Inc., 1951).

49. Hook, *Political Power,* p. 36.

50. Dewey, *The Public,* p. 33.

51. Hook, *Political Power,* p. 67.

52. Ibid., p. 74.

53. Dewey, *Reconstruction,* p. 161.

54. Hook, *Political Power,* p. 378.

55. Ibid., p. 37.

56. Justus Buchler, *Toward a General Theory of Human Judgment* (New York and London: Columbia University Press, 1951), p. 29.

57. Ibid., p. 30.

58. Ibid., pp. 40–41.

59. Ibid., p. 44.

60. Ibid.

61. Sidney Gelber, "Toward a Radical Naturalism," *Journal of Philosophy,* 56 (February 26, 1959): 193–199.

62. Ibid., p. 195.

63. See Michael A. Weinstein, "Ontology and Social Science," *International Review of History and Political Science,* 6 (August 1969): 30–41; and Michael A. Weinstein, "The Paradox of Representation: Criticism," *Journal of Value Inquiry,* 4 (Summer 1970): 119-125.

64. Justus Buchler, *The Concept of Method* (New York: Columbia University Press, 1961), p. 91.

65. Morris Raphael Cohen, *American Thought* (New York: The Macmillan Company, Collier Books, 1962), p. 212.

66. Wilfrid E. Rumble, Jr., *American Legal Realism* (Ithaca, N.Y.: Cornell University Press, 1968).

67. Michael A. Weinstein, "Review of Wilfrid E. Rumble, Jr., *American Legal Realism,*" *American Political Science Review,* 62 (December 1968): 1336–1337.

68. Howard R. Smith, *Democracy and the Public Interest* (Athens, Ga.: University of Georgia Press, 1960), p. 89.

69. Dewey, *Reconstruction,* p. 150.

70. Hook, *Political Power,* p. 321.

71. Louis H. Masotti and Michael A. Weinstein, "Theory and Application of Roscoe Pound's Sociological Jurisprudence: Crime Prevention or Control?" *Prospectus,* 2 (April 1969): 431–449. Roscoe Pound, *Criminal Justice in America* (New York: Holt, Rinehart & Winston, Inc., 1930), pp. 10–11.

72. Dagobert Runes, ed., *Twentieth Century Philosophy* (Ames, Iowa: Littlefield, Adams & Company, 1958), p. 69.

SUGGESTED READINGS

Dewey, John. *Democracy and Education.* New York: The Macmillan Company, 1961.

Follett, M. P. *The New State.* New York: Longmans, Green & Co., 1918.

Friedrich, Carl J. *The Philosophy of Law in Historical Perspective.* Chicago: University of Chicago Press, 1958.

Hsiao, Jung-Chuan. *Political Pluralism.* New York: Harcourt Brace Jovanovich Inc., 1920.

James, William. *Essays in Pragmatism.* New York: Hafner Publishing Co., Inc., 1948.

Mead, George Herbert. *Selected Writings.* Indianapolis: The Bobbs-Merrill Co., Inc., 1964.

Mills, C. Wright. *Sociology and Pragmatism.* New York: Oxford University Press, Inc., 1966.

Rorty, Amelie, ed. *Pragmatic Philosophy.* Garden City, N.Y.: Doubleday & Company, Inc., 1966.

Rumble, Wilfrid E. *American Legal Realism.* Ithaca, N.Y.: Cornell University Press, 1968.

Veblen, Thorstein. *The Theory of the Leisure Class.* New York: The New American Library, Inc., 1953.

CHAPTER THREE

EXISTENTIALISM

The existentialist Karl Jaspers wrote that while pragmatism seemed to be laying new foundations for a philosophy adequate to the concerns of men in the modern age, what it "built thereon was nothing more than an aggregate of crude analysis of life and cheap optimism, was a mere expression of a blind confidence in the extant confusion."[1] The last chapter comprised an attempt to show that pragmatism does not fall easily before such criticisms, and that its guiding theme of describing the consequences of actions and practices for human beings and political systems is a necessary part of any serious analysis of the uncertain and threatening public situation of the twentieth century. However, Jaspers' remark may be more revealing about the nature of existentialism than it is about the defects of pragmatism. The hallmarks of existentialism have been the continued attempts to give a serious analysis of human existence and describe the tragic price that one must pay to live authentically in the twentieth century.

As in the case of pragmatism, existentialism is best thought of as a label for a range of views bearing a general family resemblance. Ernst Breisach, a commentator on existentialism, remarks that nobody "has yet or will ever put down 'the' tenets of existentialism in a systematic work of so many volumes, nor will there at any time appear an 'Existentialist Manifesto' which would neatly spell out easy-to-grasp maxims."[2] This is not only because existentialism is more a school of thought than a doctrine, but also because the existentialists are primarily concerned with describing the structures of concrete human existence. This enterprise of description makes existentialists empiricists. Breisach points out that the existentialist Soren Kierkegaard approached the question—What does it mean to live as a Christian?—by using the "total experience of his life to bring forth an answer."[3] While some philosophers would define empiricism narrowly as the doctrine that grounds knowledge in sensuous experience, existentialists like Breisach and William Ernest Hocking speak of a wider empiricism that takes all human experience as a possible source of knowledge.[4] Under this view, philosophy becomes an experiment in which the philosopher is not an observer detached from the data and manipulations, but a person who "stands in the very core of the experiment himself."[5] Like pragmatists, existentialists do not split thought and action, but take them together in a human situation.

THEMES IN EXISTENTIALISM

Ernst Breisach attempts to isolate the major themes that recur in existentialist philosophy. He identifies the description of human life as a unique adventure, the opposition to thought systems that claim to give a final explanation of human existence, the quest for authentic existence, and the alienation of the human being from himself, as the four central concerns of existentialists.[6] E. A. Burtt makes a similar attempt, isolating the ideas that "the realm of objective truth falls within the dynamic totality of subjective truth," that no set of concepts should determine what is real and what is merely appearance, and that philosophy should aim at transforming the reader's experience in the direction of authentic existence, as the major presuppositions underlying existentialist thought.[7] These efforts to identify the core of existentialism are useful for gaining a sense of the spirit of this philosophic endeavor. However, they do not capture the relevance of existentialism for political theory.

As an orientation to political science and political philosophy, existentialism demands that the investigator turn his attention away from the quest for a set of categories that will fully explain human behavior, and towards the investigation of the structure of the human condition. While it is premature to attempt a synthesis, one can note that as orientations to political theory, pragmatism and existentialism are complementary rather than opposed. Pragmatism tells the political theorist to look away from the origins of political institutions and towards the consequences of political activities and political structures. The major problem of this orientation is its lack of a ground to which these consequences can be referred. With its injunction to study the human condition, existentialism provides part of the ground to which the consequences of political activities and political structures can be referred. Through the definition of authentic human existence, existentialists are able to avoid the pragmatic error of frequently subordinating the human being to a social process.

HUMAN NATURE AND HUMAN CONDITION

The term *human condition* does not carry one very far along the way to understanding the relevance of existentialism to the clarification of the public situation in the twentieth century. The notion of human condition can be explicated by discussing the special relationship that existentialism has to other ways of thinking about human beings, and by describing the position of existentialists in the debate about human nature. First, existentialism has always functioned as an opposition movement in ethical and political philosophy. It has taken the part of the concrete human being in its criticisms of all thought systems that claim to provide a final understanding of human activity. However, it has been dependent upon such thought systems to provide it with materials to criticize and structures against which to define the drama of human freedom. For the existentialist, the human being always has the possibility of surpassing a definition that has been given to him by an ideologist, a philosopher, or a social scientist. However, the way in which the human being can exercise his freedom to surpass is dependent upon the definitions that are being thrust upon him in his particular situation. Thus, existentialism appears as a revolt against systems of thought that reduce the activity of individual human beings to a limited set of well-defined categories.

Existential Revolt

Each existentialist defines his revolt in relation to a particular restrictive system or group of systems. For example, in the nineteenth century the Christian existentialist Kierkegaard rebelled against Hegelian idealism and Danish Protestantism. The American existentialist William Ernest Hocking objects to behavioral social science, the French existentialist Jean-Paul Sartre criticizes Stalinism, and the German existentialist Karl Jaspers opposes himself to racism and Marxism. However, while existentialists have pressed the claims of human freedom against those who propose final definitions of human activity, they have used many concepts and methods developed by their opponents. Thus, Kierkegaard, who rejected Hegel's application of dialectical reasoning to world history, used the dialectic in his description of the unfolding of human experience through aesthetic, ethical, and religious stages. Much of Hocking's description of human existence is present in American political science and sociology, and Sartre claims that his work is a leavening agent in Marxism.

Though highly complex, the relationship of existentialism to systematizing thought about human activity can be summed up as a tripartite revolt. The existentialists *revolt against* reducing all human activities to examples of predefined categories; they *revolt within* systematic theories by appropriating concepts and methods to the project of describing the barriers to human freedom and the possibilities for the realization of freedom; and they *surpass* systematic theories by showing that the possibilities of any human situation always outrun a single description of the situation. This discussion of the relationship of existentialism to other ways of thinking about human beings reveals an important element of the human condition. Part of the definition of the human condition is the freedom to surpass any definition that is thrust upon the person. Recognition of this freedom in thought and action constitutes authentic existence.

Inadequacy of Definitions
   In their treatment of the concept *human nature,* existentialists stress their claim that human existence outruns any conceptual definition proposed for it. Ideologists, philosophers, and social scientists who describe human nature are usually involved in advancing conceptual definitions of human existence. Some hold that man is irredeemably selfish, others state that his destiny is to be judged by God, and still others assert that he is merely a bundle of responses to external stimuli. The list of definitions of human nature that have been proposed through the history of thought is quite long. Existentialists accept none of them as binding on human existence in the here and now. Instead, they express human possibilities that have been realized in the past or that might be realized in the future. There are other possibilities yet uncreated. For the existentialist, each human being must define himself continuously through action that realizes one of his possibilities. The person who denies his freedom to surpass any particular definition of human nature is living inauthentically. Authentic existence involves coming to the realization of one's freedom. This is the basis of most existentialist criticism of political ideologies. Such ideologies define once and for all human possibilities and thereby blind the person to his freedom.
   The existential substitute for a definition of human nature is the description of the boundary conditions of human existence. These boundary conditions are facts that every human being must confront as soon as he attains self-consciousness. While the boundary conditions identified by different existentialists show some variation, at least three are present in nearly every description. Hocking's description of the "lostness of contemporary man" illuminates the three primary boundary conditions of death, being-in-the-world, and being-among-others:

   The lostness of contemporary man is not the lostness that
   weighed on Kierkegaard: it is not the terror toward an

undying Hell that besets us. The source of despair today has an opposite theme: not the malign possibilities of another world but the visible danger that what we see of this world may be all there is to see! What we see is the moment-to-moment boundary of our being, the nothingness that completes itself in death, our own and that of the race: in such a world, riddled the while with horrorfilled actualities, how can a being aspiring and infinite be other than condemned to frustration? And in just this world we are nevertheless condemned to engage and act as men: is it possible?[8]

Thus, Hocking holds that in the contemporary world, human existence is bounded by death and nothingness, a world that the individual did not create and which fills him with despair, and other people similarly situated. Further, he places a "being aspiring and infinite" (a free being with possibilities) within these boundaries. The free human being bounded by death, a world he did not make, and others, describes the elemental human condition for most existential philosophers.

The ways in which human beings dispose themselves towards death and orient themselves to the world and others, vary according to the possibilities of concrete situations and the decisions that actors make. It is the standard of an authentic existence, consciously encountering death, the world, and others in freedom, to which the consequences of actions and structures that are so important to pragmatists can be referred. However, this is not the only ground to which consequences can be referred. Civilized humanism, which will be discussed in the next chapter, is the other relevant ground.

POLITICAL ASPECTS OF EXISTENTIALISM

With regard to political theory, that aspect of the human condition involved with being-among-others is the most important. The existentialist Ernst Breisach defines politics as "that field in which the fateful organization of the power of one man over another is established."[9] This definition shows the sensitivity with which most existentialists approach the encounter of one human being with another.

Groups
The existential orientation to society is quite different from the pragmatic approach of Dewey, who wrote that "groupings for

promoting the diversity of goods that men share have become the real social units." [10] For the existentialist, the real social units are human beings encountering death, the world, and others. This means, of course, that the existentialist does not recognize any purely social units. Group activity presupposes individuals who choose to give their loyalty to the collectivity. Existentialists never tire of pointing out that not even soldiers can escape morally from freedom by pleading that they had to follow orders in every case. While it is true that active support of a group can be described within the existential orientation, membership in a group through sharing consequences with others is much more difficult to understand within this framework. Sometimes we are members of groups by virtue of sharing unrecognized consequences with others. Only a theory of community, such as the one offered by Buchler, can deal adequately with this fact.

The Public Situation

As in the case of pragmatism, the existentialist orientation to the public situation has two components. These components follow from the two ways in which the human condition as it bears on political affairs can be studied. First, one can study the human condition as it appears in the lives of concrete historical actors. In this case, one investigates how human beings in particular times and at particular places encounter death, the world, and others, and the way that they interpret their freedom. The existential political scientist becomes what the French anthropologist Claude Levi-Strauss called an ethnographer using the method of representation: "All that the historian or ethnographer can do, and all that we can expect of either of them, is to enlarge a specific experience to the dimensions of a more general one, which thereby becomes accessible *as experience* to men of another country or another epoch." [11] Existential political scientists are essentially ethnographers of their own societies, enlarging their own specific experiences to the dimensions of more general ones, making them accessible as experiences to men in other statuses within contemporary complex societies. Their efforts can be judged only on what the existentialist Gabriel Marcel called the agreement of personal testimonies. The study of the human condition as it appears in specific space and time frames is the application of existentialism to descriptive political science.

The second component of the existentialist orientation to the public situation involves determining the possibilities for authentic existence within the specific space and time frames described. Here, the thought systems that blind the human being to his freedom must be criticized and a range of alternatives for human action developed. Whether or not the normative component of the existentialist approach to the public situation involves ethical cognitivism is open to debate. Oppenheim claims that existentialism embraces ethical noncognitivism because it is "logically compatible with any substantive theory of private or public morality."[12] This follows from the existentialist's claim that human beings create values through continuously actualizing some of their possibilities. However, the concern of almost all existentialists with the realization of authentic existence creates a problem in Oppenheim's interpretation. Even if existentialists do not presume to tell human beings what to do when they come to the realization of their freedom, they seem to say that human beings should realize their freedom and the boundary conditions of their existence. This is why Burtt can remark that the existentialists believe that philosophy should aim at transforming the reader's experience in the direction of authentic existence. Existentialists are not clear about whether the imperative to face the facts is grounded in an intuition or in a choice. Thus, the issue of ethical cognitivism in existentialism demands a careful interpretation of each specific author.

   This brief introduction to existentialism should not lead one to believe that all existentialists are in agreement on important issues. Religious existentialists like Kierkegaard and Tillich affirm the existence of God, while atheistic existentialists like Sartre begin their philosophizing from the death of God. Existentialists like Sartre and Merleau-Ponty emphasize the difficulties involved in communication among human beings, while some like Buber and Jaspers stress the prospects for intimate communication among persons.
   Existentialists agree, however, that human beings evince certain permanent characteristics that are bound up with the very meaning of "human." The existentialist states that all human beings make judgments of good and bad, true and false, and right and wrong. Further, within the definition of the boundary conditions of human existence, the existentialist identifies permanent qualities of being-in-the-world. What the existentialist denies is that at all times and places the behavior of human beings is necessarily motivated by such impulses as selfishness, altruism, the desire for pleasure, or the love of God. No one impulse or set of impulses can define the possibilities of human existence once and for all. Existentialists introduce a notion of the human condition, not a definition of human nature, into political theory. They are united in a concern with the human freedom to surpass any fixed definition of human nature.

KARL JASPERS

Besides Jean-Paul Sartre, whose work we will discuss at length in another chapter, Karl Jaspers is the existentialist who presented the most serious reflections about political theory and political affairs. In *Man in the Modern Age,* published in 1931, Jaspers undertook to present a thoroughgoing critique of contemporary Western societies that has become a guideline for much existentialist writing in social and political philosophy. In a later work, *The Origin and Goal of History,* he expanded and altered some of the views developed in *Man in the Modern Age* to bring his theory more into accord with modern democratic ideas.

Authentic Existence

Jaspers begins his description of politics and society in *Man in the Modern Age* with a statement about the human condition of being-among-others in the twentieth century: "To-day it is taken as a matter of course that human life is the supply of mass-needs by rationalized production with the aid of technical advances."[13] With this statement as the keynote of his inquiry, Jaspers poses the question of how authentic existence is possible in the twentieth century. He identifies several paradoxes in contemporary life. If one looks at human life as the supply of mass needs by rationalized production, he will be thrown back upon a view of the human being as utterly dependent upon vast external forces. He will see that his survival is tied to vast organizations, sophisticated technologies, and mass media of communication. The performance of those functions securing human life run far beyond any one person's grasp. Nobody understands the whole. However, while the provision of the requisites of survival cannot be grasped by any human being in detail in the twentieth century, it is still correct to say that what human beings become will depend upon the choices that people make about their products. This paradox underlies all of the argument in *Man in the Modern Age.* Will human beings submit to man-made forces which appear to determine everything that they do, or can they create ways of surpassing their situation? In the twentieth century the seeming necessity of organization, technology, and impersonal communications coexists with the insight that human existence outruns any fixed definition that can be thrust upon it. Jaspers' object in *Man in the Modern Age* is to describe the obstacles to human freedom present in contemporary society and look for signs pointing to how these obstacles might be surmounted.

Mass Society

For Jaspers, mass society was created in the nineteenth century and has become dominant in the twentieth. The great populations in the world could not exist "but for the titanic interlocking wheelwork of which each worker is one of the cogs."[14] There is no plan guiding the operation of the "life-order," or the means to survival, and the economy is composed of independent personalities. The situation of independent personalities who are dependent upon others for their survival and the condition of planless coordination breed more paradoxes. The life order cannot function without voluntary cooperation; popular approval must be won for all collective decisions; and all work is at least narrowly purposive. Yet the life order appears as an iron dominion; the individual feels powerless and swamped; and there is no purposive economy in which each person's work has meaning.

This discussion of the structure of contemporary Western societies is only preliminary to the definition of the relevant unit of social and political analysis in the modern age. While Dewey held that the typical unit of contemporary political life is the public formed by people who share the indirect consequences of a series of social acts, Jaspers proposed that the decisive unit is the mass. Jaspers distinguished among mob, public, and mass. The mob appears as an aggregation of persons at a particular time and place who are unified through a common and transient emotion. More stable than the mob, the public is a group of people who are unified by their common adherence to an opinion. Underlying both mob and public is the mass. The masses compose aggregates of individuals who are "articulated in some apparatus of the life-order in such a manner that the will and the peculiarities of the majority among them are decisive."[15] Politically, the components of the mass are interest groups which compete with one another for resources.

It is important to differentiate Jaspers' conception of the mass from that of Hannah Arendt. For Arendt, the term *masses*

> applies only where we deal with people who either because of sheer numbers, or indifference, or a combination of both, cannot be integrated into any organization based on common interest, into political parties or municipal governments or professional organizations or trade unions.[16]

Masses have no consciousness of a common interest and, therefore, they lack the cohesion and sense of direction necessary for the development of limited goals. In Arendt's thought, the existence of masses sets the stage for the rise of totalitarian movements. For Jaspers, the masses are not disintegrated. Contrariwise, they are integrated into the life order where they press their claims against other segments of the mass in a blind struggle. In Jaspers' work the masses do not appear merely in times of crisis. The standard operating procedure of the life order from day to day is based on the "unceasingly operative and effective power" of the masses. The masses are not composed of human beings who consciously organize themselves into groups. One becomes part of a mass by finding himself already incorporated into an apparatus of the life order. Jaspers mentions the proletariat, the general body of the medical profession, and the teaching staff of a university as examples of masses "insofar as in actual fact the majority of the corporation decides the nature, the actions, the resolves of all its members."[17]

The masses breed a standard social type that Jaspers calls the "mass-man." The mass man is the expression of what most people do in a particular apparatus. He is known by his budget—what he has appropriated from the life order. The corporations, which express particular masses, decide what shall happen in contemporary societies. They are organized according to the abstract rule that each individual "counts only as a unit among many having like powers."[18] In contemporary Western societies nobody can escape from contact with masses. If one wishes to communicate with the masses he must do so through advertising.

Public Existence Like Dewey, who wrote that a state is good to the degree that the public is organized and to the degree that the officials are constituted in such a way that they care for the public's interests, Jaspers is concerned with the creation of a politics centered around public issues. He states that the "essential problem of the political history of our time" is whether or not people can accept their responsibilities as citizens, conscious of the effects of their actions and their condition, and "ready as a part of . . . daily life to . . . share in deciding fundamental political issues."[19] The creation of a public life depends upon people surpassing the life order through refusals to be absorbed into social functions and recognition of the paradoxes within the life order itself. The person can become a mass man and surrender his freedom, but he can also enter into relations with others through choices about what to create and preserve in the world. In realizing that such choices are part of authentic existence, the human being is driven to the further insight that creation and preservation of human productions depend upon some unity of will among those who create and appreciate.

Politics Human beings organize their condition and the means to their survival through "power in the whole" which "decides the historical concreteness of life in the whole."[20] This power has two modes. As a continuing cultural tradition it is expressed through education. As an expression of collective choice in the here and now, it is incorporated politically in the state.

The foregoing discussion has cleared a path toward a deeper understanding of the essential political problem. In the life order, two aspects of existence are fundamental for politics. First, in the life order human beings find themselves organized around a lifeless apparatus. They do not participate in any collective determination of their conditions or purpose, but enter already articulated masses. With respect to this aspect of the life order, Jaspers proposes a politics in which self-conscious people take responsibility for their situation and create genuine collectivities out of masses. Second, in the life order the quality of existence in the entire society is the result of "a vast number of voluntary tensions" and "reciprocal conflicts."[21] Objectively, one possibility for human existence is being realized for the society rather than many others. However, no one or group is consciously determining or even prevising that possibility which is actualized at any given time and place. With respect to this aspect of the life order, Jaspers proposes a politics in which people self-consciously take charge of their history. Simply because of the emergence of the masses and the penetration of the principle of abstract equality into contemporary life, this politics must be democratic and depend upon the tragic vocation of each individual "tensing" his will to "act upon things despite a sense of impotence as regards their course."[22] The aim is a common life in which each individual will be enabled to make a meaningful contribution to history.

Function of the State

Following Max Weber, Jaspers observes that the hallmark of the modern state is a removal of force from the ordering of everyday life and a concentration of the application of force at the point where it becomes clear that "without force, actual or potential, human life cannot persist."[23] Thus, in one phase politics is a struggle "concerning the kind and the trend of the unavoidable use of force."[24] In a second phase, following Dewey, politics is the way in which the state performs its function of providing human beings with "opportunities for the free fulfillment of [their] occupational ideals in all their multiplicity—ideals which cannot be fulfilled" so long as they remain functionaries in the life order.[25]

The state harmonizes the activities of human beings who have been educated so that they can participate in their historical tradition. In the modern age, the state should safeguard continually the life order upon which survival depends at the same time that it safeguards authentic existence against the tendency of the life order to reduce the person to a functionary. In *Man in the Modern Age* Jaspers provides few suggestions about how the contemporary state might be brought to perform its public function. Under the heading "methods and sphere of influence of political activity" he calls for dynamic, responsible, and trustworthy leadership, but points out that the masses do not like great leaders. This relatively superficial solution does not at all meet the difficulty of constituting self-conscious collectivities out of masses.

Development of Jaspers' Thought

The differences observed between the political thought of Dewey and Hook are paralleled by the differences between the earlier and later political speculations of Jaspers. Ascendent Nazism and World War II intervened between the publication of *Man in the Modern Age* and *The Origin and Goal of History.* In the second book he embraces constitutional democracy as it appears in the West as the best practicable political system. Here the basis of his discussion is a theme from *Man in the Modern Age:* the political whole can never fully absorb human existence.[26] However, Jaspers gives a new emphasis to this theme. He merges politics with the life order and states that political affairs relate "to a lower plane of humanity, to existence; therefore . . . they have no direct contact with the high goods of inner liberty, of faith and of the spirit."[27] Politics is concerned only with what is common to all human beings in their interest in survival and their desire to have room in which to consummate their private projects. The great political question has been transmuted. Now it is necessary to determine what must be kept out of politics: "The question is, at what point does that begin which is not common to all men: world view, historically determined faith, all the particular tendencies that must have room to move."[28] The aim of politics is no longer to harmonize the activities of historical human beings so that they can realize professional ideals, but instead is "confined to the interests of existence, in which they seek to give scope to all human potentialities that are not inimical to that which is indispensably common to all."[29]

The differences between the Jaspers of *Man in the Modern Age* and the Jaspers of *The Origin and Goal of History* can be summarized briefly. In *Man in the Modern Age* the state is accorded the function of continually safeguarding the life order upon which survival depends at the same time that it safeguards authentic existence against the tendency of the life order to reduce the person to a functionary. In *The Origin and Goal of History,* the state still must safeguard the life order. However, authentic existence is left to fend for itself against the onslaught of technical rationalization.

The extent of the shift in Jaspers' thinking can be gauged by his appeal for a pure politics in his later work. A pure politics is confined to "necessities of existence." When political activity comprehends more than the question of survival it becomes impure and unfree. In *Man in the Modern Age* politics was a means out of the life order. It was hopelessly impure. In Jaspers' later work the goal of collective action in a public domain was surrendered. However, in this work he is unable to meet the fundamental challenge posed in *Man in the Modern Age*. Swamped by the life order, nobody in particular has responsibility for the common results of mass action. Yet common results appear and they are indubitably man-made. It is bad faith to believe that a collective product determines human existence. Authentic existence does not deny a public domain. The challenge to the existential actor in the modern age is the challenge to create a meaningful public domain in concert with his fellows.

Jaspers and Dewey

There is a significant complementarity between the ideas presented in *Man in the Modern Age* and *The Public and Its Problems*. While Jaspers describes the agents of contemporary society, Dewey describes the patients. Masses, organized as incorporated functionaries in the life order, create the consequences which lead to the formation of publics. This complementarity is further shown by the functions ascribed to the state. For Jaspers, the goal of the state is self-conscious harmonization of human production in a meaningful history. For Dewey, the goal of the state is intelligent care for the indirect consequences of social action. Both goals require organization of groups that presently find themselves unified by an apparatus or by suffering a consequence. Further, it is in the consequences of mass action that meaning for this action can be found. In its ultimate extension, caring for the indirect consequences of social action may involve harmonization of human production in a meaningful history.

Critique of Jaspers' Thought

The major weakness in Jaspers' political theory is its silence about the importance of organized concentrations of power in the modern age. In this theory public function overshadows private interest. In the antipolitics of the life order decisions are made by articulated and incorporated masses which act on the principle of majority preference. This description ignores the fact that inequalities of power within the apparatus of the life order make it certain that significant majority preferences will not be honored, even if they are ever expressed.

Jaspers speaks of mass formations without elites; in the politics of the public domain decisions are made by citizens in the interest of harmonizing activities in a meaningful history. This description glosses over the inevitable conflicts that would arise in harmonizing diverse human creations. Even if all human beings were oriented to realizing professional ideals and harmonizing their products with the products of others, they still might come into conflict over the allocation of resources to their respective activities. Is this not, perhaps, just why Jaspers holds that force is irreducible to persuasion in social existence?

Still, despite Jaspers' neglect of problems of power, he has made two important contributions to an existential description of contemporary politics. First, he has pointed out that part of the content of being-among-others in the contemporary world is to find oneself an element in an aggregation unified around part of an organizational, technological, and communications apparatus. Second, he has shown that a manifestation of nothingness in the contemporary world is the lack of a public domain in which one's products have some meaning beyond momentary survival of self. These two contributions make up for the lack of a theory of organization and organized power that is presupposed by the rest of the analysis.

WILLIAM ERNEST HOCKING

The most important American existentialist who wrote extensively about political affairs is William Ernest Hocking. Like Jaspers, Hocking emphasizes the role of the state and political activity in liberating the individual from deadening social function. His major contribution to political thought is an existential description of the human condition as it applies to political life in contemporary America.

The starting point of Hocking's existential political science is his description of the human condition. Hocking's human being confronts two frustrations. First, his own life is bounded by a death which means to him the extinction of consciousness and with it value. Second, he believes that human life itself is bounded by destruction because he observes terrifying modern weapons and hears natural scientists say that the earth is doomed to an inglorious extinction.[30] The idea that humanity is doomed prevents the person from keeping the faith of humanism that his contributions during his lifetime will have worth for future generations of men. This double frustration of the human urge to transcend natural existence is coupled with the situation that once thrown in the world, the person is condemned to engage in social relations. Despair is the attitude toward existence that accompanies the human condition in the second half of the twentieth century.

The Masses

Despair is expressed in contemporary political life by the masses and the "mass-mind." Hocking's masses are not the same as those defined by Jaspers. For Hocking, the roots of political activity are much more in the individual predicament than they are for Jaspers. Encountering pessimism and uncertainty about his future as a free human being, Hocking's man "loses confidence that his own consciousness is directed toward reality."[31] Lacking the assurances of the worth and meaning of effort that individuals in other ages derived from religion or an optimistic evolutionary science, the individual in contemporary society "seeks assurance here and there in lateral corroborations of thought and feeling."[32] He feels secure in his own judgments only when they are in accord with those of significant others around him. The process of seeking lateral corroborations for one's judgments and even one's emotions is the typical manifestation of inauthentic existence in the United States—one takes his standards day by day from the group and surrenders his freedom to create, affirm, and reject standards.

Of course, if universalized the process of lateral corroboration breaks down. If everyone looked to others for his standards there would be no standards. The group must gain its content from somewhere. Hocking held that lateral corroboration is possible in America through the existence of large-scale communications media which employ commercial propaganda.[33] The masses in America are composed of those people who cannot gain vertical corroboration from traditional authorities and who cannot take responsibility for the creation of their lives. The masses substitute lateral corroboration for faith or authentic existence.

Mass Society Hocking approaches Jaspers when he describes the economic and political orders in contemporary society. If commercial propaganda guides judgment in contemporary America, the propaganda itself is rooted in "industrial functionalism" which drives individuals to lose sight of the rights and duties that apply to full human beings. The life order is regnant when "freedoms and equalities within the momentum of vast industrial mechanisms begin to appear abstractions such as men are tempted to trade away in exchange for deceptive economic security in dictatorial states."[34]

Interest Groups Mass communications and propaganda, rooted in the industrial functionalism of the life order, find their political basis in the interest group. The interest group serves two functions for the person. The first is to provide lateral corroboration for judgments and the second is to gratify material desires by influencing public bodies to grant special privileges. The group performs these functions by breeding a double morality. For the person, "life with the group becomes part of one's at-homeness in the world, and of one's self-realization."[35] Gaining part of his self-definition from the group, the individual tends to give his loyalty to the group interest, whatever that may involve for outsiders. He believes that he is a good man as long as his actions are performed to bring benefits to his group. When standards of judgment independent of group interest exist, the proliferation of associations is desirable for the extension of human freedom, because people will be able to assess their participation according to a standard of public good. However, lacking independent standards, the most destructive group egoism is rampant:

> In the absence of a moral vigor not now in evidence, the prevalence in the USA of the *pressure-group function* for all interests—as a useful institution of spontaneous growth—could mean the spread of a polite and plausible bribery subtly undermining our democracy.[36]

In American society, interest groups express themselves through the party system. Parties do not articulate authentic options for social policy, but attempt to "assemble the greatest agreement of the greatest number, and at the same time to appeal to the interests of (right-thinking) potential contributors, while careful to offend no (right-speaking) influential minority."[37] This is the politics of the life order in which the public domain has disappeared in favor of collective results produced by a compromise of group interests. Bound to the process of lateral corroboration, and even more fundamentally to the human condition of despair, Americans believe that democracy means "giving the people what they want," "a fatal policy when 'what they want' is defined in terms of the double morality of pressure groups."[38] Like Jaspers, Hocking holds that the essential problem of the political history of our time is fostering self-conscious awareness of freedom and responsibility among the broad masses of people. Their objective is the creation of citizens out of functionaries.

Function of the State
Unlike Jaspers, Hocking attempted to spell out the kind of state that would surmount the obstacles to authentic existence in the contemporary world. In *The Lasting Elements of Individualism* he gave a decisive answer to the kind of pure politics advocated by Jaspers in his later work. He identified pure politics with Kant's theory of law: "The central fallacy of Kant's theory of law lies in the supposition that the state has nothing to do with motives and is concerned only with external behavior."[39]

The Coagent State For Hocking, the state is the human organization most dependent upon individual sincerity and good will.

If trust and support for the state are lacking, laws will not be effective and the state will have no defense against attack. However, Hocking realizes that granting the state an interest in motivation involves serious problems. If all rights have conditions and the state is the judge of those conditions, how can liberty be saved from the imperfect wisdom of politics? Hocking answers this question by defining a new kind of state, the "co-agent state," which has a function relevant to the predicament of man in the modern age: ". . . it is the first business of the co-agent state to develop and equip that very conscience of its members which may reject and call for revision of the state's efforts at an inward justice."[40]

The coagent state cannot be neutral in transmitting tradition, because it is based on the realization that collective existence invariably has collective results. Each generation has the responsibility of indoctrinating the next, but this indoctrination must be an honest "handing on of the best we ourselves can see, not as finality but as our best judgment."[41] Thus, the state has the educational function of creating citizens out of functionaries, as well as supervising the maintenance of the life order.

Hocking views the state as the center of collective experimentation. All those who agree that collective life has collective results will that some collective experiment proceed and that law be viewed experimentally. In the coagent state there is a living arterial bond between the citizen's will *that* an experiment proceed and the particular experiment supplied by the governmental agency. This bond is grounded in the educational function of the state.

Public Function and Private Interest The aim of Hocking's coagent state certainly includes the goal of protecting the individual from the life order at the same time that the life order is protected. However, there is a profound weakness in the description. The coagent state is called upon to help create citizens who may alter the state in significant ways. If the agent of the state is the government, why should the government work for its own alteration? Again, we run up against the problem of public function and private interest. Hocking recognizes a public function for the state, but he does not show how the state will be enabled to perform that function.

Like Jaspers, in one place Hocking asserted that dynamic leadership would improve the public situation: "There is, in fact, a disposition, for the most part subconscious, to choose leaders in the hope that our habits will be corrected."[42] Perhaps there is a disposition on the parts of existentialists, who are concerned with the concrete individual's existence, to see an individual commitment as the most plausible means for securing political change. However, the importance of leadership is not strictly implied by the concern of existentialists with human freedom and the boundary conditions of human existence. If existentialists like Jaspers and Hocking recognize the appearance of a public domain in the human condition, there is every reason why those who follow them should understand the possibilities for public action within that domain.

MAURICE MERLEAU-PONTY

A very different kind of existential description of the public situation has been presented by Maurice Merleau-Ponty, a French existentialist and phenomenologist who has become prominent since World War II. The core of his political thought is contained in the essay "A Note on Machiavelli." He begins his discussion with an analysis of private interest, rather than, like Jaspers and Hocking, describing the proper function of the state. Merleau-Ponty credits Machiavelli with a key insight into the public situation. The clarification of political values is necessary but not sufficient. History has shown that the loftiest principles can be used in the service of the meanest ends. As long as "we have not chosen those whose mission it is to uphold these values in the historical struggle, we have done nothing."[43] Politics is conflict among men, not a struggle of contending principles.

Conflict

Merleau-Ponty's insistence that politics be described in terms of human conflict is consistent with the existentialist principle that human beings create their values through action that realizes one of their possibilities. However, the emphasis upon conflict leads to a view of the human condition as a war of all against all. At bottom, "collective life is hell."[44] Human beings exist in a condition of mutual fear—"I live my fear in the fear I inspire."[45] However, the suffering that I cause through my aggression drives me to sympathize with my victim. The war of all against all is no solution to the problem of collective life. Politics appears as the mediation between the two poles of fear and sympathy. Power is not the force that goes along with fear or the delegation of wills to a representative that goes along with sympathy, but a thwarting of aggression against the present means to collective life. Such thwarting of aggression is more efficiently accomplished by grants of limited freedom than by terrorism. The successful government consults with outside interests before declaring policy and steers a way between two dualisms: the will to please and defiance, and self-satisfied goodness and cruelty.

Like Jaspers, Merleau-Ponty holds that the best practicable politics is one that creates room for human beings to pursue their projects: "Through mastery of his relationships with others, the man in power clears away obstacles between man and man and puts a little daylight in our relationships—as if men could be close to one another only at a sort of distance."[46] However, unlike Jaspers, Merleau-Ponty believes that a condition of providing room is a politics that enables human beings effectively to recognize one another throughout the world. Politics should bring human beings to a recognition of their common situation and prepare them for the creation of a common history. The way to bring about this recognition and creation is the unsolved problem of political thought.

Leadership

Merleau-Ponty credits Marx with attempting to found a human community on a different basis than adherence to principle. Marx believed that a movement of the exploited, oppressed, and powerless would provide a ground for a power capable of ending exploitation and oppression. However, there is a fundamental difficulty in his project: How is a power of the powerless possible? If one follows mass desires in undertaking political action, exploitation will continue. If one attempts to judge the true interests of the mass, he will become a member of a new ruling class.

Merleau-Ponty remarks that the solution to this dilemma can only be found in a new relationship between leaders and constituents. Leaders are necessary who are capable of "explaining the reasons for their politics to those subject to power, and to obtain from themselves, if necessary, the sacrifices power ordinarily imposes on subjects."[47] The Bolsheviks of the Russian Revolution failed in their attempt to solve the problem in this way. This failure leads Merleau-Ponty to conclude that despite the Marxist revolution in political theory, the problems that Machiavelli posed are still with us. He painfully asks: "Does all power tend to 'autonomize' itself, and is this tendency an inevitable destiny in all human society?"[48]

Unfortunately, like Jaspers and Hocking, Merleau-Ponty ends by making the political problem one of leadership. This is, perhaps, a result of his highly individualistic description of the human condition as one characterized by mutual fear among human beings who must somehow constitute a state. Human beings who are fear-ridden will attempt to autonomize power when they gain it. As Hobbes realized long ago, the exercise of power is an excellent means of keeping intruders out of one's "life-space." Merleau-Ponty is an existentialist who has forgotten the insights of pragmatists and civilized humanists. The pragmatists correctly point out that human beings are continuously involved in a process of social communication that includes many other processes besides conflict. They contribute to political theory the principle that no one social process can be taken as fundamental in all situations. The civilized humanists, who will be discussed in the following chapter, contribute the insight that the content of social communication in the modern age is a civilization available for use. The state of nature situation described by Merleau-Ponty takes place within and against this civilization, not prior to it. In his description of the public situation, Merleau-Ponty is in serious danger of attributing an essence to the human being, rather than merely defining the boundary conditions of human existence. His notion that as long as we have not chosen those whose mission it is to uphold principles in the historical struggle, we have done nothing, ignores the possibility that collective and public action has an important place in political affairs.

An authentic leader-constituent relationship is only one of at least three desiderata for opening up a public domain in the twentieth century. The other two are the creation of self-conscious citizens and the elaboration of organizational forms that will preserve and extend contributions to the civilization. Of the three foundational philosophies for twentieth-century political theory, pragmatism has gone the farthest toward clarifying the conditions for a leader-constituent relationship; existentialism has produced the best analyses of the requirements for citizenship; and the civilized humanists have given the best descriptions of civilized organization. The otherwise trenchant descriptions of Jaspers, Hocking, and Merleau-Ponty are spoiled by the assertion that leadership must create citizens and organizational forms. Hocking was closer to the truth when he implied that only in a well-ordered state could leadership function to proclaim collective experiments, or projects.

PAUL RICOEUR

The French existential phenomenologist, Paul Ricoeur, has presented a theory of political activity that sums up many of the themes discussed in this chapter. In *Fallible Man* Ricoeur grounds politics in private interest. Relations of socioeconomic domination continue "only because they are recognized and guaranteed by institutions sanctioned by an authority which is ultimately political."[49] Political structures "put the seal of institution on all the technological, economic and social forms of man's power over man."[50] However, the state is also a community making historical decisions. Ultimately, politics would constitute "an authority which would propose to educate the individual to freedom, which would be a power without violence."[51] In the world, the human being is subject to having any of his actions politicized: "All the social roles that a man may exercise initiate situations which political institution consolidates into an object."[52] Politics objectifies man's power over man in an institution and provides a focus for the diffuse feelings which gather around the themes of commanding and obeying.

Ricoeur's analysis provides a better description of some aspects of the public situation than is found in the works of Jaspers, Hocking, or Merleau-Ponty. Ricoeur recognized a dualism between public function and private interest that pervades political activity. Politics arises to put a stamp of legitimacy on modes of social and economic domination, but carries with it the possibility of educating human beings to freedom. This possibility arises because of a paradox in the political institution. If political structures "put the seal of institution" on modes of human domination, they also organize a historical community, or create an incipient public domain. Thus, the requirements for protecting private interest are also the requirements for creating public function. While Ricoeur does not say how public function can take precedence over private interest in the modern age, at least he recognizes the presence of both aspects in political affairs and attempts to relate them to one another. He does not reduce one aspect to the other, but keeps them in tension. As with Buchler and pragmatism, Ricoeur moves a step beyond traditional existential analysis.

EXISTENTIALISM IN REVIEW

Existentialists, like pragmatists, can be considered political critics, descriptive political scientists, and normative political theorists. In the mode of political criticism, existentialism is expressed through a comparison of authentic existence and the human condition as interpreted by participants in a political situation.

William Barrett, one of the important interpreters of existentialism to the American intellectual community, traces this type of political criticism to the work of Martin Heidegger. While Heidegger is not primarily interested in the problems of political theory, he draws a distinction that is fundamental to all existential analysis of the public situation. Heidegger holds that human existence is always personal. Thus, he "locates existence, immediately and at the first stroke, in the public world and among other people."[53] Instead of searching out a purified perspective from which to study human existence, he attempts to understand the human condition through an analysis of everyday existence. This approach leads him to identify the subject of ordinary life as the One. We refer to the One in phrases like "one does not eat peas with a knife," or "one takes exams if he is a student." "The One" is "the mere point of intersection of all these prescriptions of the public and external behavior of everyday existence."[54] The One expresses itself through chatter and attempts to busy itself in diversions and distractions from its own existence. Opposed to the everyday existence of the One is authentic existence in which the human being recognizes h freedom and his boundaries in death, the world, and the other.

Authentic Existence

Authentic existence does not remove the person physically from everyday life, but "is only a question of a modification, slight but profound, within our everyday existence, which places this exis tence in a new and altogether different perspective."[55] Barret remarks that while Heidegger claimed that no value judgment separates everyday existence from authentic existence, this claim is untenable because it is only as a seeker after value that the human being makes this distinction among the possibilities of his existence. Barrett's observation leads to a judgment about the kind of political criticism produced in the existentialist orientation to the public situation. The discussions of Jaspers, Hocking, Merleau-Ponty, and Ricoeur can be considered as extended and refined descriptions of the One and comparisons of those descriptions to a standard of authentic existence. The descriptions of the One constitute the component of descriptive political science in the existentialist orientation to the public situation, while the presented standards of authentic existence comprise the normative component of this orientation. Of course, as far as authentic existence is realized in the world, description and prescription are unified.

Heidegger's distinction between everyday existence and authentic existence puts the political thought of existentialism into a context. When Jaspers writes of masses whose fates are determined by transient majorities, he is referring to the One mechanically organized around part of a technological-organizational-ideological apparatus. When Hocking writes of the quest for lateral corroboration of judgment, he is referring to the One mechanically organized around propaganda and interest groups. When Merleau-Ponty writes about the human situation of mutual fear, he is referring to individuals who have not yet come to a realization of the depth of their humanity. Finally, even Ricoeur extends the description of the One when he writes of the abstract existence of performing well-defined social roles. For Ricoeur, in the life order "man finds himself in a situation equivalent to that of vital functions with a finite ending."[56]

Summary

By no means does existentialism provide a complete framework for political theory. The human condition is but one point in a three-sided relationship that defines political theory in the twentieth century. From the human condition proceed actions whose consequences are transmitted through social processes that are described by pragmatists. These consequences affect the structure of civilization, and through these effects rebound back upon the human condition. In turn the structure of civilization provides new and substantive boundaries to the human condition. It is most of all these concrete limitations that existentialists have ignored in the past. However, the limitations of existentialism should not blind one to its contributions. The existentialist point of view assures that the free individual is not, in thought, subordinated to either social process or civilization. The ultimate value of this concrete human being will be a standard marking the rest of this discussion.

NOTES

1. Karl Jaspers, *Man in the Modern Age* (Garden City, N.Y.: Doubleday & Company, Inc., Anchor Books, 1957), p. 176.

2. Ernst Breisach, *Introduction to Modern Existentialism* (New York: Grove Press, Inc., 1962), p. 4.

3. Ibid., p. 20.

4. William Ernest Hocking, *Strength of Men and Nations* (New York: Harper & Bros., 1959), p. 68.

5. Breisach, *Introduction*, p. 21.

6. Ibid., p. 6.

7. E. A. Burtt, *In Search of Philosophic Understanding* (New York: The New American Library, Inc., 1967), pp. 85–87.

8. William Ernest Hocking, "Marcel and the Ground Issues of Metaphysics," *Philosophy and Phenomenological Research*, 14 (June 1954): 467.

9. Breisach, *Introduction*, p. 235.

10. John Dewey, *Reconstruction in Philosophy* (New York: The New American Library, Inc., 1952), p. 159.

11. Claude Levi-Strauss, *Structural Anthropology* (Garden City, N.Y.: Doubleday & Company, Inc., 1967), p. 17.

12. Felix E. Oppenheim, *Moral Principles in Political Philosophy* (New York: Random House, Inc., 1968), p. 166.

13. Jaspers, *Man in the Modern Age,* p. 33.

14. Ibid., p. 35.

15. Ibid., p. 37.

16. Hannah Arendt, *The Origins of Totalitarianism* (New York: World Publishing Company, Meridian Books, 1958), p. 311.

17. Jaspers, *Man in the Modern Age,* p. 38.

18. Ibid., p. 39.

19. Ibid., pp. 106–107.

20. Ibid., p. 89.

21. Ibid., p. 36.

22. Ibid., pp. 89–90.

23. Ibid., p. 92.

24. Ibid., p. 99.

25. Ibid., p. 91.

26. Ibid., p. 90.

27. Karl Jaspers, "The Goal: Liberty," In *The Development of the Democratic Idea,* ed. Charles M. Sherover (New York: Washington Square Press, 1968), p. 579.

28. Ibid., p. 578.

29. Ibid., p. 579.

30. Michael A. Weinstein, "Hocking's Existential Sociology," *Sociology and Social Research,* 52 (July 1968): 406–415.

31. Hocking, *Philosophy and Phenomenological Research,* 465.

32. Ibid.

33. Ibid.

34. Ibid., 463.

35. Hocking, *Strength of Men and Nations,* p. 68.

36. Ibid., p. 90.

37. Ibid.

38. Ibid.

39. William Ernest Hocking, *Lasting Elements of Individualism* (New Haven: Yale University Press, 1937), p. 170.

40. Ibid., p. 177.

41. Ibid., p. 178.

42. William Ernest Hocking, "Leaders and Led," *Yale Review,* 13 (July 1924): 630.

43. Maurice Merleau-Ponty, *Signs* (Evanston, Ill.: Northwestern University Press, 1964), p. 221.

44. Ibid.

45. Ibid., p. 212.

46. Ibid., p. 217.

47. Ibid., p. 222.

48. Ibid., p. 223.

49. Paul Ricoeur, *Fallible Man* (Chicago: Henry Regnery Co., 1967), p. 179.

50. Ibid.

51. Ibid., p. 182.

52. Ibid., p. 180.

53. William Barrett, *What Is Existentialism?* (New York: Grove Press, Inc., 1964), p. 54.

54. Ibid., p. 56.

55. Ibid., pp. 59–60.

56. Ricoeur, *Fallible Man,* p. 152.

SUGGESTED READINGS

Barrett, William. *Irrational Man: A Study in Existential Philosophy.* Garden City, N.Y.: Doubleday & Company, Inc., 1958.

Camus, Albert. *Resistance, Rebellion, and Death.* New York: Alfred A. Knopf, Inc., 1961.

Desan, Wilfrid. *The Marxism of Jean-Paul Sartre.* Garden City, N.Y.: Doubleday & Company, Inc., 1965.

Hubben, William. *Dostoevsky, Kierkegaard, Nietzsche, and Kafka.* New York: The Macmillan Company, Collier Books, 1962.

Marcel, Gabriel. *Man Against Mass Society.* Chicago: Henry Regnery Co., 1952.

Maritain, Jacques. *The Social and Political Philosophy of Jacques Maritain,* edited by J. W. Evans and L. R. Ward. Garden City, N.Y.: Doubleday & Company, Inc., 1965.

Polanyi, Michael. *The Tacit Dimension.* Garden City, N.Y.: Doubleday & Company, Inc., 1967.

Sartre, Jean-Paul. *Search for a Method.* New York: Alfred A. Knopf, Inc., 1963.

Tiryakian, Edward A. *Sociologism and Existentialism.* Englewood Cliffs, N.J.: Prentice-Hall, Inc., 1962.

Weinstein, Michael A. "Politics and Moral Consciousness." *Midwest Journal of Political Science* 14, (May 1970): 183–215

CHAPTER FOUR

CIVILIZED HUMANISM

Both pragmatism and existentialism are schools of thought concerned with the condition of human life—pragmatists are preoccupied with the consequences of human activities, while existentialists discuss the human condition in its particularity. A third group of twentieth-century philosophers also has been concerned with the quality of modern life; these philosophers form no relatively coherent school of thought such as pragmatism or existentialism, but their number includes such men as George Santayana, Alfred North Whitehead, and Bertrand Russell.

Human beings transform the world through their activities, and they act in relation to others through social processes. Within personal and social action objects of some permanence are created. Following Richard La Pierre, these objects may be classified as technological, ideological, and organizational.[1] The objects created in human activity are means to standardized experiences. Such objects constitute the culture of people to whom they are available. Concern about culture can be held somewhat distinct from concern about the consequences of human activities mediated through social processes and the particular character of the human condition. If culture constitutes the achievement of standardized means to human experiences, the experiences that are available to human beings through cultural objects are liable to evaluation according to standards that are themselves cultural. As experiences are judged according to a norm, clusters of them will be separated out from the rest as particularly good. The system of objects that are means to particularly good experiences can be called civilization.

The central concern of the third group of philosophers whom we shall discuss is with the uses that human beings make of their civilization. Since they never grouped themselves into a movement, we shall use the label *civilized humanism* to describe their thought.

BARBARISM

The civilized humanists discern a distinct threat to civilization in the twentieth century. R. G. Collingwood, an English philosopher of civilization, has described this threat by distinguishing among civilization, savagery, and barbarism. He defines civilization as the displacement of force by persuasion, the increasing use of the intellect in resolving human problems, and the tendency to accord all human beings the same rights that are accorded the people in one's particular group. Savagery defines a human condition devoid of civilization. Barbarism defines an attack upon civilization. While savagery is noncivilization, barbarism is anticivilization. Collingwood's particular definition of civilization, which differs from the one presented earlier, is less important than the general distinction among civilization, savagery, and barbarism.[2] In the twentieth century, civilization is threatened by barbarism, not savagery.

One of the bases of human dignity is the ability of human beings to objectify cherished experiences and thereby make those experiences available to others. Civilized humanists find many agents threatening the objects that constitute the means to the best experiences that human beings have been able to create and communicate. They fear a loss of the experiences themselves under the onslaught of various forms of barbarism. The destruction of honest and precise linguistic communication by propaganda, the subordination of science to national passion, the creation of objects that promote massive destruction, and the subordination of art to advertising are themes that recur in the works of civilized humanists. While civilized humanists differ among themselves about the correct definition of civilization and the precise threats that it faces, they all agree that a major feature of the public situation in the twentieth century is the continuous possibility that barbarism will swamp civilization.

Marvin Farber has distinguished between expanding and contracting views of the human condition.[3] Expansionist political theorists look forward to progress and new creations in the world of human beings. Contractionist theorists envision a future marked by threats to the quality of human existence. They see the major moral task as one of preserving worthwhile cultural objects.

Marxism is an expansionist theory in that it looks forward to an improvement in human existence marked by the production of goods for use. The most expansionist theory analyzed here is pragmatism, which looks forward to increasing control by human beings over the indirect consequences of their activities. Existentialism has elements of both expanding and contracting theories. It is expansionist in its assertion that the human being defines himself through his action. However, it has been contractionist in much of its social criticism, especially among writers who see the life order as a juggernaut.

Civilized humanism is the most contracting view of the public situation discussed here, and it is the one most on the defensive. While almost all civilized humanists take account of the importance of creativity in the preservation and extension of civilization, they emphasize the judgment that creations have no transpersonal meaning apart from a system of civilization. Much of their thought is devoted to defining what human beings have achieved and devising means for protecting these achievements.

HISTORICAL CONSCIOUSNESS

Aside from the threat of barbarism within and without Western civilization, there is an important factor which conditions the civilized humanist's concern with previous achievements. Civilized humanism represents a distinctive and significant moment in the encounter between Western peoples and the other peoples of the world. The penetration by Europeans of the rest of the world, beginning with the Age of Exploration, presented a problem to Western civilization—How would the peoples of Europe respond to the discovery of religious, moral, and value systems different from their own? Generally, there were two responses to the encounter. The missionary's mode of response was to proclaim the supremacy of his religious, moral, and value system, and to attempt to convert others to it. The anthropologist's mode of response was to hold all religious, moral, and value systems relative to historical conditions. One could not state with assurance that any religious, moral, and value system was absolutely superior to another. One could only study and understand each system and how it developed.

World Civilization

In the twentieth century the missionary's and the anthropologist's modes of response to the encounter of civilizations have broken down. The peoples outside of Europe and North America have become independent politically and they are no longer merely subjects for conversion or observation. Civilized humanists have responded to this situation in several ways. Some have attempted to sort out what is valuable in all of the widespread cultures in the world to lay a foundation for a world civilization. Others have attempted to define what is most worth preserving in Western civilization. In both cases they have been led to dissociate civilization from such transient collectivities as ethnic groups, nations, states, and empires. In his book about "prophecies of a world civilization in twentieth-century thought," W. Warren Wagar has argued that the civilized humanists have articulated visions of "the city of man."[4] When they look forward to the defeat of barbarism and a "coming world civilization," even the civilized humanists have an expanding view of the public situation.

Idola

The typical unit of analysis in the works of the civilized humanists is the idolon, or key image around which the culture under study is patterned. The term *idolon* appears in the works of the civilized humanist Lewis Mumford. Among civilized humanists, the interpretations of the idolon differ widely. Pitirim Sorokin and F. S. C. Northrop attempt to describe cultures in terms of the type of knowledge deemed most important in them. Thus, they argue that in some civilizations sensory knowledge is most significant; in others conceptual knowledge is most significant; and in still others mystical intuitions dominate. Both Sorokin and Northrop have devised "super-epistemologies" that they hold might serve as grounds for the synthesis of the cultures of the world.

Elijah Jordan and Lewis Mumford have interpreted the idolon as the view of human nature and its possibilities that dominates the culture under study. Both of them have argued that a redirection of the view of human nature prevalent in the contemporary world is necessary before the good life can be attained.

The Marxists and neo-Marxists have interpreted the idolon as the principle upon which the means of production are organized in a society. For example, in capitalist systems the means of production are organized to provide profit for private owners. Of course, Marxists ground the organization of the means of production in the human activity of transforming the world to satisfy needs. However, Northrop and Sorokin ground their interpretations of the idolon in the activity of knowing, and Jordan and Mumford ground their theories of the idolon in a general description of human activity. None of the civilized humanists believes that there is a "spirit of the age" apart from human activity. Keeping this fact in mind should prevent hypostatization of the idolon, or granting the idolon a personal or substantial existence independent of knowing and acting human beings.

Human beings create, preserve, and destroy idola. This fact should also serve to minimize interest in the debate between philosophical anthropologists and sociologists of knowledge. Supposedly, philosophical anthropologists ground civilization in ideas, while sociologists of knowledge ground civilization in existential conditions (social structure). However, guiding ideas of significant knowledge and principles of social organization are never found apart from one another. Most civilized humanists have seen fit not to make dogmatic judgments about the priority of one or another facet of civilization for patterning human action. However, they have tended to stress the importance of particular realms of civilization in their interpretations of the idolon. It is important to note that one never should assume that any civilization is completely unified around an idolon. Within all civilizations there are conflicts, and several idola may compete with one another even on the most abstract level of culture.

As in the cases of pragmatism and existentialism, civilized humanism has a descriptive and a normative component. With respect to description, civilized humanists seek to understand the technological, ideological, and organizational objects that compose a culture and then synthesize them in an idolon. In descriptive political theory, this endeavor consists of understanding political culture. Theorists of political elites, who are the representatives of civilized humanism in political science, range political culture under idola like political formula and myth of legitimacy. They define the social type, or kind of man who is typical of the political culture.

With respect to normative inquiry, civilized humanists attempt to define a standard of the good life with which they can judge the experience produced by using cultural objects. The formation of this standard does not simply arise from the whim of the investigator. It is based first on an inventory of what human beings have found worthwhile in the past and second on an imaginative synthesis of these worthwhile experience-producing objects. The analyses of civilization provided by the civilized humanists form the second ground to which the consequences of human activities can be referred. The first ground is authentic existence, as described by the existentialists. The indirect consequences of human activities can be judged in their bearing upon the preservation and extension, or the attainment, of civilization.

GEORGE SANTAYANA

George Santayana was one of the first twentieth-century philosophers to embrace civilized humanism. Morris Cohen has written that Santayana is the only American philosopher to have developed a "comprehensive, carefully articulated, philosophy of life and civilization."[5] Cohen observed that Santayana's project was an attempt "to trace the ways in which in the fields of art, society, religion, science and common sense, human effort, conditioned by material structures and natural law, finds expression and fulfillment in ideal forms."[6] Essentially, in his five-volume *Life of Reason,* Santayana undertook the task of categorizing and defining human productions according to a standard of the good life. Like many civilized humanists, Santayana's principle was expressed in the terms of the esthetic realm of human experience. Willard E. Arnett notes that Santayana viewed the good life as a work of art in the sense that it is

> an ordered and harmonious whole, which is contem-
> plated as a perfection achieved, pleasing to man as a man
> because of its affinity to his psyche and its needs, but
> potentially pleasing to any free spirit whose sympathies
> are always with wholeness and harmony.[7]

Over his long life, Santayana's political thought went through several stages while retaining a fundamental unity. In *Reason in Society,* he attempted to describe the nature and ground of a civilized ideal. During World War I Santayana's thinking underwent a change in emphasis. In *Dialogues in Limbo,* he became less concerned with the ideal issue of human activity and more inter-ested in the problems that human beings confront in realizing value. Finally, in *Dominations and Powers,* completed after World War II, Santayana attempted to render a naturalistic and dispassionate analysis of political activity. These shifts, however, were primarily in emphasis and point of view. Over his life, Santayana's philo-sophical vantage point shifted from that of partisan and judge of civilized activity to that of dispassionate observer of human activity. The content of his political analysis did not change fundamentally.

Liberty and Civilization

Throughout Santayana's works, one issue guides his inquiry: "What, then, will liberty bring to the free man? That is the great question in morals and politics."[8] This question, which is also fundamental in the present study, implies that there is a difference between freedom and liberty. For Santayana, freedom means the absence of coercion and liberty refers to what the person does when he is free. Santayana holds that the ultimate aim of liberty is the happiness that accompanies the satisfaction of interests that have been harmonized by the individual. He argues that the ideal fulfill-ments provided by the objects of civilization arise from a biologi-cal ground. He contends that it is important to realize that "man is an imaginative animal, that his ideas are biological products, that his genius and happiness are momentary harmonies reached be-tween his organism and the world."[9] The ultimate aim of civilization is a coherent set of objects that are available to human beings for use in fulfilling a harmonized set of interests.

Orders of Social Existence Santayana's political philosophy is based on a definition of the orders of social existence. Each order is a field for the satisfaction or frustration of a type of human interest. In *Reason in Society* Santayana defines the orders of social existence as natural society, free society, and ideal society. These terms do not refer to different existing collectivities, but are aspects of any concrete social system. Natural society is that set of relationships that "unites beings in time and space."[10] It is rooted in the love for human beings on whom the individual depends for his sustenance, and it finds its issue in relations which are experienced and material. Within natural society are found the institutions of marriage and the family, industry, government, and war. In the relationships characteristic of these institutions the person's attention is fixed upon temporal existences and the fortunes of particular natural and corporate bodies. For Santayana, natural society has no logical or moral primacy. While there is no human existence apart from natural society, human existence finds its fulfillment in cumulative reflection, art, and science rather than the infinite process of biological life and its extensions. Human existence in society has a natural ground and an ideal fulfillment. This principle is the core of Santayana's philosophy of civilization. Civilization is the order of objects making ideal fulfillments possible.

Free society has its basis in natural society and it springs from the accidental association of human beings in particular frames of space and time. Free society is expressed in friendship, which in its fullest development is unanimity among human beings in ideal interests such as beauty and truth. The objects of such ideal interests are symbols, and ideal society is the society of symbols.

Ideal society makes civilized existence possible:

> It is an inspiring thought, and a true one, that in proportion as a man's interests become humane and his efforts rational, he appropriates and expands a common life, which reappears in all individuals who reach the same impersonal level of ideas—a level which his own influence may help them to maintain.[11]

While natural society bounds human beings to particular loyalties in restricted space and time frames, ideal society points to a community encompassing all people.

Politics and Government Politics and government appear in the natural order of society as instruments of military conquest or economic domination. Thus, Santayana grounds government and the political life in private interest rather than public function. However, unlike some conflict theorists he does not fail to recognize the possibility that a public domain can be developed. While the origin of government may be in private interest, politics may become legitimate through representative operation. Governments can represent the most abiding interests of human beings by securing their status in natural society and providing them with the protection necessary to cultivate development in free and ideal societies. Thus, the public function, or aim, of government can be stated as the provision of conditions for the protection and extension of civilization.

Government

Timocracy In his writings, Santayana attempts to define the form of government that would best perform the public function of protecting and extending civilization. He is consistently both a descriptive and a normative theorist of political elites. Thus, the ideal regimes that he describes are aristocracies of merit. In *Reason in Society,* Santayana argues that a timocracy is the form of government that unites the advantage of all other forms and avoids their abuses. For Santayana, the timocracy is an open aristocracy which would promote freedom scientifically, have a great diversity of social classes and institutions, display a wide variety of life styles, and encourage art, science, and noble idiosyncracies. In the timocracy, the individual would find his happiness "in seeing his daily task grow under his hands; and when, in speculative moments, he lifts his eyes from his labor, he must find an ideal satisfaction in patriotism, in love for that complex society to which he is contributing an infinitesimal service."[12] Santayana admits that such a spirit of patriotism would have to be maintained by strict training, discipline, and organization.

An industrial timocracy of the twentieth century would be based on guilds and unions that would eliminate a great deal of personal freedom. The timocracy, which would create glory and perfection in civilization, would appeal only to people who were in some degree philosophers and poets. Timocracy furthers a society which the individual finds beautiful. Society, thus, becomes like a work of art or a system of logic. When the individual thinks about his society he becomes happy. Meanwhile, like any work of art, the society must be disciplined and determinate. Hence, it must suppress liberty, or the satisfaction of harmonies of individual interests. Timocracy represents the form of government which follows from a deep concern with civilization, unbalanced by attention to authentic existence and the indirect consequences of human activities. In a timocracy, government itself becomes a part of the ideal society of symbols. It loses its function of preserving and extending access to civilization and becomes an esthetic object. In a sense, the timocracy is an even more impossible ideal than Plato's perfect state governed by philosopher kings. Plato argued that only when philosophers became kings or kings became philosophers could the good society be realized. Santayana goes one step further. The timocracy can be realized only when all human beings become poets or philosophers.

Rational Government In *Dominations and Powers,* written late in his life, Santayana follows Plato by attempting to describe a best practicable form of government. Here Santayana outlines a form of government that he thought might perform the function of preserving and extending civilization. A rational government would be founded on the authority of things in the natural or generative order of society where human action is materially rewarded or punished. The authority of a rational government would be autocratic but not totalitarian, "for it would speak for the material conditions imposed by nature on the realization of any ideal without dictating to any person or society what its ideal should be."[13] The aim of the rational government would be to prevent conflicts of interest among individuals and groups from becoming material conflicts.

In the time between the publication of *Reason in Society* and *Dominations and Powers,* Santayana came to believe that the worst barbarism comes about when conflicts in ideal society intrude into natural society. The attempt to realize one ideal on earth breeds ugly and brutal fanaticisms. Thus, whereas timocracy represents an attempt to idealize society, rational government is a plan for a world order with "a political organ of reason, an enlightened and disinterested government."[14] However, like the timocracy, the rational government would be ruled scientifically by an aristocracy of experts—an Oxford University become political. Ideal society and natural society would be separated strictly. By leaving them alone, government would foster cultural and civilized activities:

> The hot bloods and the ambitious talents would turn to the separate irrational rival forms of culture, and preach and work for some reform in some one of them; but they would be prevented by the police in the service of that uninteresting government from smashing one another's heads.[15]

A comparison of the timocracy and the rational government shows how politics is a mediation between natural society and ideal society in Santayana's work. In the timocracy, natural society is politically subordinated to ideal society, while in the rational government natural society is politically secured by leaving ideal society free. Thus, Santayana's work shows clearly the two ways in which politics can be oriented to the goal of extending and preserving civilization. As in the timocracy, the political system can play a key role in shaping culture by the self-conscious encouragement and discouragement of the creation and preservation of objects that make up ideal society. As in the rational government, the political system can allow for the development of civilization by leaving ideal society alone and protecting it from physical threat.

Development of Santayana's Thought

Orders of Social Existence The depth of Santayana's shift in orientation from *Reason in Society* to *Dominations and Powers* can be grasped by considering the orders of social existence that he describes in the latter work. As in *Reason in Society,* Santayana delimits three orders of society. However, the generative, militant, and rational orders of society do not exactly correspond to the natural, free, and ideal societies. The distinctions in *Dominations and Powers* refer to moral rather than ontological differences. The generative order characterizes social structures which attempt to satisfy basic needs like those for food, companionship, and work. Rooted in the temporal existence of human beings, it corresponds very closely to natural society as described in *Reason in Society.*

The militant order defines an attempt to impose a narrow set of interests on a society. It is the working out of the urge to pattern the world of human relations after a particular ideal: "So when I distinguish a Militant Order of Society I mean to separate, in the sphere of politics and morals, the love of reforming the world from the total mutation that the world is always undergoing."[16] Santayana describes militancy in the strongest terms. It is the incarnation of barbarism in the contemporary world. The militant person is blind to the accidental basis of his passion, fanatical in his pursuit of a single goal, and thirsty to destroy all enemies and to see nothing in the world but his own likeness. When Santayana describes the free society he is looking to the fulfillments possible in human relations. When he describes the militant order he turns his attention to the threats against the very basis of human relations. While free society is defined by shared interests in ideal objects, militancy is defined by exclusivity of interest. Like Jaspers, Santayana went on the defensive after a half century of war and totalitarianism.

The rational order defines an attempt to harmonize the most basic interests present in individuals within a society and provide a means of satisfying this harmony of interests. The rational order excludes militancy, even when some people have a basic interest in being militant. The rational order does not correspond to ideal society. It makes ideal society possible through the conscious harmonization of the interests present in the generative order. For Santayana, reason is the ability to see "identity, affinity, contrast, or irrelevance between essences present in direct intuition."[17] Reason is inclusive and harmonizing rather than exclusive and dissonant. However, Santayana pessimistically avers that reason will only triumph in human affairs through the efforts of a band of militant fanatics obsessed by the idea of a rational government.

Politics and Civilization

Santayana's thought on the relationship of politics to civilization undergoes a shift from according a positive role for government in creating civilization to giving government the more modest function of protecting civilization from the militant order. Both of Santayana's positions present serious problems. The idea of subordinating the natural order to ideal society through political power hardly need be criticized at length in the light of the results of the various totalitarian regimes of the twentieth century. However, the laissez-faire approach to the defense of civilization also has grave weaknesses. In the *Life of Reason* Santayana realizes that it is impossible to draw sharp lines between the various orders of social existence. Collective projects in the natural order have consequences for the ideal society. In *Reason in Society,* Santayana criticizes capitalism for putting "into rich men's hands facilities and luxuries which they trifle with without achieving any dignity or true magnificence in living, while the poor, if physically more comfortable than formerly, are not meantime notably wiser or merrier."[18] Civilization, which ought to provide wealth, safety, and variety reverts to barbarism.

In *Dominations and Powers* the contributions of the economic system to barbarism recede, and the politics of fanaticism becomes the major threat to civilization. However, neither fanaticism nor culture exists without linkages to the economic system, and if politics must regulate economics it must also be involved with civilization. Santayana poses the problem of the relationship between politics and civilization more clearly than any other twentieth-century philosopher. However, he does not solve the problem.

Elitism

An important similarity between the description of the political ideal presented in *Reason in Society* and that presented in *Dominations and Powers* is the presence of a governing elite composed of technocrats. This theme of functional representation and rule by a technical elite is a political formula of great importance for many civilized humanists. Civilized humanists are apt to fix attention on those people who are most prominent in creating and maintaining civilization. In the contemporary world such people are predominantly professionalized or unionized specialists. Like existentialists, whose preoccupation with the concrete individual's existence led them to overemphasize the importance of leadership in politics, civilized humanists, interested in the creation and preservation of meaningful objects, tend to overemphasize the importance of specialists in politics. Even the pragmatists frequently show a bias in overemphasizing the importance of client groups who suffer consequences. With regard to technocracy, it is enough to say at this point that any doctrine which ignores client groups and leadership in the design for a good life is at best incomplete. Santayana's work shows the strengths of civilized humanism as well as most of its limitations.[19]

ALFRED NORTH WHITEHEAD

Alfred North Whitehead is another prominent twentieth-century philosopher who embraced civilized humanism rather than existentialism or pragmatism. Out of the triad of works defining his philosophy—*Process and Reality, Science in the Modern World,* and *Adventures of Ideas*—the last "is in fact a study of the concept of civilization and an endeavour to understand how it is that civilized beings arise."[20] In the sociological section of *Adventures of Ideas,* Whitehead defines the idolon around which he organizes reports of human activities in civilization. For Whitehead, one fundamental idea that affects "every detail of activity" in a human society is the "general conception of the status of the individual members of that group, considered apart from any special preeminence."[21] Within a civilization, for each historical period there is also a "general form of the forms of thought." This paradigm of awareness, or collective epistemology, is so pervasive that the people living within the historical period are not likely to understand it consciously. Like the conception of the status of the individual members of the group, the general form of the forms of thought tinges every aspect of understanding. Thus, Whitehead is intermediary between those civilized humanists who find the idolon in a conception of human nature and activity, and those who locate the idolon in a form of understanding or collective epistemology. He brings together both the idolon of human activity and the idolon of understanding in the conception of a "coordinating philosophy of life." He observes that when such a philosophy of life is not widespread in the community and consciously articulated, the society is exposed to decadence, boredom, and the slackening of effort.

Dualism

Like Santayana, Whitehead is a dualist in many important aspects of his philosophy of civilization. While he grants importance to the ways in which human activity is generally viewed in a society, the types of knowledge that are most significant in a society, and the coordinating philosophy of life in a society, he also stresses that these idola are grounded in what Santayana called the generative order. Thus, Whitehead observes that every age has its "character determined by the way its populations react to the material events which they encounter."[22] He remarks that with respect to clarifying the general conception of the status of the individual members of the social group, the investigator must study what sort of people performed what sort of functions in the society. At best the sociologist would come to understand the factors that aided the progress of civilization and those that frustrated improvement. Since this ideal for a social science is impracticable, Whitehead states that the sociologists and political scientists can "note some indications of relevant tones of mind apparently widely spread in various districts at different epochs."[23]

Social Change Whitehead's dualism is best illustrated by his conception of social change. Two agents operate in the mutation of social arrangements. First, material conditions and unconscious wants and judgments push social groups to new modes of organization. Second, consciously articulated ideals pull human collectivities toward new states of affairs. Both "senseless agencies and formulated aspirations" drive human beings out of the dreary round of habit.

Ideals Whitehead's dualism differs slightly from the dialectic developed by Santayana. For Santayana, all ideal fulfillments had a natural ground. Thus, the free society of kindred spirits had its ground in the accidental association of interdependent human beings. Out of interests and relations bound to narrow frames of space and time arose esthetic and scientific objects that transcended restricted space and time frames. For Whitehead, the relationship between natural ground and ideal is more complex. The development of general ideas out of particular conditions is the hallmark of civilization. Originally, these ideas express judgments about the factual conditions of human existence and the aspirations that people have for the future. However, once they have been articulated, these ideas perform a new function. When they express with precision the aspirations of human beings, they can be used as standards for judging the adequacy of existing conditions and are called *ideals.* Thus, the ideals that arise in civilized life are subversive of social stability. One never knows how they will be applied in given conditions and how people will respond to the strain between the structures of existing and ideal social life.

Whitehead fails to note the possibility that the ideals developed in civilized life can also be used by ruling groups to rationalize existing conditions. It has always been a tactic of ruling groups to declare that the ideals of the social group are in the process of realization at the given moment. In some circumstances, espousing ideals can become a convenient way of ignoring lack of actual fulfillment and frustrated desires. However, this reservation is not a denial of the fact that general ideas can become standards of criticism and thereby function as goads to progress towards ideals. It is to Whitehead's credit that he makes the practice of criticism central in his definition of civilization.

Politics and Civilization

The political phase of Whitehead's philosophy of civilization is also dualistic. Whitehead observes that one of the most general philosophic notions that investigators use in the analysis of civilized activity is "to consider the effect on social life due to the variations of emphasis between Individual Absoluteness and Individual Relativity."[24] Individual absoluteness refers to "the notion of release from essential dependence on other members of the community in respect to modes of activity," and individual relativity refers to "the converse fact of essential relatedness."[25] Thus, Whitehead identifies a polarity in that aspect of the human condition concerned with the encounter of selves in the world. Social life can be defined most basically in terms of aloneness and relatedness. Both independence and interdependence occur in every society. The balance between them and the spheres of existence in which each one is stressed are described in the idolon and are highly variable.

Dominant Groups If the form of the idolon is an attempted reconciliation of individual absoluteness and individual relativity, the content of the idolon describes the mentalities of the dominant classes in the community at a given time. Applying this idea to the sphere of political activity, Whitehead develops a relatively pragmatic view of government: "Governments are best classified by considering who are the 'somebodies' they are in fact endeavouring to satisfy."[26] Thus, Whitehead grounds his discussion of politics in private interest rather than public function. He notes that most political change merely substitutes one ruling class for another, and that most political history is merely a "barren change of names."

Whitehead does make a place, however, for public function. He argues that in the modern world a decisive development has taken place in political culture. The new politics is based on the conscious and deliberate formation of organizations that embody the purposes of special groups within society and are not concerned with the general purposes of the state or the maintenance of a tribal unity. While even the Greeks were enclosed by the unified polis, modern man lives in a multi-group society in which he is ensured that no one power will dominate every sphere of his existence. Plato and Socrates attempted to secure space and time for contemplative freedom. Modern man demands freedom for corporate action.

Professions Whitehead finds the key to public function in the contemporary world in the growth of incorporated professions. For Whitehead, a profession is an "avocation whose activities are subjected to theoretical analysis, and are modified by theoretical conclusions derived from that analysis."[27] The theoretical analysis is adapted to the realization of the social function of the profession. The opposite of a profession is an avocation based upon custom and modified by trial and error.

In the contemporary world, professions become incorporated into associations and, on the basis of their expertise, claim self-government in their spheres of competence. This poses the question of liberty in a new way. The incorporated profession demands both freedom for its members in performing their function and control over its members in the performance of their function. Since they are functionally oriented, professions also tend to transcend national boundaries and myths, and to promote a worldwide solidarity of fellow professionals. For Whitehead, the organized profession is the center of civilized activity in the contemporary world. The more freedom that is granted to responsible professions, the more civilization will be secured.

Public Function Whitehead does not completely eliminate the modern state from his analysis of public function in politics. The "sovereign state of modern legal theory" has its legitimate sphere of action grounded in its function of representing the general wisdom of the community "derived from an experience broader than the topics of the various sciences."[28] Specifically, in the contemporary world, the state plays the role of providing a general judgment on the activity of the various professional organizations. While its moral authority is severely limited by its lack of competence to decide upon questions relating to the performance of functions by scientists and professionals, it can still judge whether or not professional organizations welcome ability and stand high among like professional organizations elsewhere in the world. Thus, there is a minimum public function for government in the contemporary world. The organized professions are the prime movers of civilized activity, and the governmental institutions merely function as review boards overseeing some of their actions.

As is the case with most civilized humanists, Whitehead overvalues the importance of experts in the modern world. Santayana's timocracy in which individual freedom is limited by guilds and unions is paralleled by Whitehead's civilized society in which the organized professions are dominant. One may ask whether the professions necessarily have the interests of their clients at heart and whether they will always be sure to harmonize their activities with respect to one another. More than a watchman state is needed to create a public domain out of a battlefield of contending professional groups.

ELIJAH JORDAN

Elijah Jordan was an American philosopher who carried certain themes in civilized humanism to radical conclusions. Jordan defines the basic political problem in the contemporary world as follows:

> How to fit yourself and your work and its product into the institutions with which they connect most immediately, and through these institutions to fit yourself and them into the total structure of the good life, is precisely the question of politics as it faces the individual.[29]

For Jordan, an institution is the embodiment of a characteristic act, or a set of facts ordered to fulfill a purpose. If ideas are to become significant or meaningful they must become part of a civilization and become realized in some nonmental object. All "characteristic human acts" become objectified in institutions which are "simply the embodiments of these acts or of a culture's leading ideas."[30] The objects realized in institutions are the things in their environment that impel human beings to act. They are objects which produce characteristic experiences when people use them in certain specified ways.

The Public Domain

Jordan held that the objects which make up institutions are public because they are, in principle, available to any human being who has been taught how to use them and who is permitted access to them. The fact that civilization is by its very nature potentially available to human beings led Jordan to a radical critique of contemporary societies. He founded his political economy on the premise that contemporary economic organizations are principled to maximize mere control of resources. The characteristic interaction of business institutions is the sale rather than the trade. In the trade people exchange goods on the basis of need, want, interest, and curiosity. In the sale, the object is control over resources and, therefore, domination over persons. When the basis of economic organization is the sale, control over markets and production is the principle of social activity, and work does not necessarily issue into objects productive of civilized experience.

Jordan held that the institutions of contemporary society are principled to end in subjective advantage rather than objective creation of enjoyable goods. Thus, he retained the dualism characteristic of the philosophies of civilization proposed by Whitehead and Santayana. However, he split the two poles by making them represent two different kinds of social order. The contemporary industrialized society throughout the world was based on subjectivity and private interest. Human activities were organized around group and personal gain, and the public domain of objects realized in institutions was veiled. In the future a social order principled on objectivity and public function might arise. In the objective social order decisions would be made according to the standard of maximizing the access of human beings to a harmonized set of objects composing a civilization. The creator would recognize his work as a contribution to the good life and would appreciate in turn the contributions of other creators.

Function of the State

For Jordan, the subjective social order of industrialized societies is politically represented by the interest group. Clamoring for advantage and gain, interest groups attempt to control the means to coercion centralized in the state to back up their projects. In the objective social order, however, the function of the political state will be "to organize the ends of life into a system of permanent but dynamic objects which shall be maintained as both instruments to action and objectives of action for all persons who are capable of making use of them."[31] The state will be enabled to perform this function because it will be composed of an efficient administrative organization staffed by professionals and a legislature composed of people capable of taking account of the relations among the objects that make up the public domain.[32] Like Santayana and Whitehead,

Jordan overvalued the professional. However, he made the distinct contribution of showing how civilized humanism could be made a devastating weapon of social criticism.

F. S. C. NORTHROP AND PITIRIM SOROKIN

F. S. C. Northrop and Pitirim Sorokin have attempted to base philosophies of civilization on encompassing epistemologies that would categorize and relate all of the kinds of knowledge that have been important to human beings.

Northrop

In *The Meeting of East and West,* Northrop undertook investigations into culture with the purpose of finding a basis for world understanding. To this end, he suggested that the solution of international conflicts would be speeded by an appreciation of the various modes of human experience around the world. His super-epistemology was founded on a distinction between the primary modes of experience in the Occident and the Orient. In the West, he found that theoretical knowledge was the most important. The characteristic kind of knowledge in Western civilization was scientific, where science is a mode of experience in which bits of sensory experience are ranged under concepts placed in a continuum of divisible space and time. The characteristic kind of knowledge in Eastern civilization was esthetic. Here sensory experience appears in an original whole, or a continuum that cannot be broken into pieces. Northrop believed that international conflict in the future would be rooted in the inability of Western peoples to understand the wholeness of esthetic experience and the difficulty of Eastern peoples in understanding theoretic experience. Northrop applied his insights in formulating a program of cultural reform: " . . . the ideal society must return to the primitive intuition of the past with respect to its esthetically grounded portion and advance to the sophisticated science of the present with respect to its theoretically based part."[33]

Specifically with regard to the nature of the good state, Northrop remarks that a satisfactory political life in the future will have to rest upon the conception of man and nature "as determined by immediate apprehension with respect to the esthetic component and by the methods of natural science with respect to the theoretic component."[34] Unfortunately, Northrop is not very specific about the content of the immediate apprehensions or intuitions that should guide conduct in human relations. He attacks political philosophers who commit what he calls the culturalistic fallacy of making the *is* of any particular culture into an *ought* for that or all cultures. He observes that the great moral leaders of the past have held that human activity should be guided by one's real nature. However, the great moral leaders of the past have differed in specifics about the content of human nature. Northrop expects his super epistemology to help adjudicate such differences. However, this epistemology must be viewed more as a speculative experiment than as a final synthesis of knowledge unless it is to become another domination.

Sorokin

Pitirim Sorokin has presented a philosophy of civilization very similar to Northrop's effort. For Sorokin, there have been three main consistent answers given by human beings to the fundamental question of human existence: "What is the nature of the true, ultimate reality-value?"[35] Some cultures have been based on sensory knowledge and have formed sensate supersystems. Other cultures have been organized around supersensory or mystical truth. These ideational cultures have expressed the ultimate reality-value in such terms as God, Tao, Brahma, Divine Nothing. Still other cultures have found the ultimate reality-value in a Manifold Infinity which is qualitatively and quantitatively infinite. While the human mind cannot fully grasp the manifold, human beings can identify its three components of sensory truth, supersensory truth, and rational, logical, or theoretical truth. All three aspects, harmoniously united in the manifold, are real. Sorokin calls this "typically three-dimensional conception of the ultimate and the supersystem built upon it" the "idealistic" or "integral" supersystem.[36]

Sorokin notes the close comparison between his work and Northrop's efforts. As Santosh Nandy observes, Sorokin is not an organicist who subordinates everything within a culture to a single truth system, but an integralist who attempts to show how different truth systems are coordinated. Like Northrop, Sorokin held that the good society would "assign an effective role to each of the three factors."[37]

Their Contributions

The same reservations that were made about Northrop's work can be entered against Sorokin's effort. However, both philosophers should be given credit for attempting imaginative syntheses of world civilization. They present expanding views of human experience in outlining projects for world understanding. They have attempted to resolve the problems in the encounter between Western civilization and the rest of the world by clearing a common ground for all human beings. They have attacked the culturalistic fallacy that leads either to the militancy of the missionary or the relativism of the anthropologist. Unfortunately, in their own system-building they introduced a contracting element through their preoccupation with defining once and for all the primary modes of human experience.

LEWIS MUMFORD

Lewis Mumford has presented an approach to civilized humanism through the philosophy of emergence. For Mumford, new systems of organization can appear in nature that have dynamics different from those of the ground from which they arose. The human being and human society are emergents out of biological life and constitute a special realm for study. Like Santayana and Whitehead, Mumford holds that human existence has a natural ground and an ideal fulfillment. Like Northrop and Sorokin, he states that the absence of an independent standard for human achievement leads to the culturalistic fallacy, or "giving to the present an ideal significance it does not possess."[38] Like Jordan, he locates the core of the human condition in the culture-creating act: "Man's nature is a self-surpassing and self-transcending one: his utmost achievements are always beginnings and his fullest growth must still leave him unsatisfied."[39] However, Mumford's most significant contribution to civilized humanism is his analysis of the relation between freedom and culture.

Freedom and Culture

Mumford argues that the ultimate goal of human beings is to give a new destiny to humanity through contributing to a cumulative culture. Human freedom never exists apart from cultural patterns of cooperation, and moral freedom consists in selecting, modifying, and augmenting the objects of civilized life. There is no moral freedom to reject one's cultural heritage. The human condition remains opaque apart from consideration of particular cultural moments in history:

> All our questions as to the condition of man, then, remain bottomless until one places man in the frame of a particular culture and a particular historic moment: for his nature reveals itself only in the acting out of his particular drama; and it cannot be understood by a static external analysis, since time and purpose and development are of its essence.[40]

The idea that there is a double movement in human activity will become important in later chapters when method is discussed.

Humanistic Method

In his work, Mumford has developed the outlines of a humanistic method for political theory. This method is founded on a synthesis of human self-transcendence and human historicity. Through prevising possibilities and acting on them, human beings objectify their aspirations in culture. In turn, culture creates an environment for human beings that limits their activity. However, culture is always undergoing mutation in the sense that objects are continuously being selected, modified, and augmented. Thus, it is impossible to characterize human activity once and for all at any time. Human action will outrun any total and fixed description of it. The humanistic political scientist will attempt to grasp the pattern of possibilities and actualities of the political culture of his time without making the mistake of absolutizing them for all times and places. In this view, political theory is a continuous activity of catching up and projecting forward. Mumford's version of civilized humanism offers the beginnings of a way out of the technocracy favored by other civilized humanists.

CIVILIZED HUMANISM IN REVIEW

While there has never been a self-conscious movement in philosophy built around civilized humanism, a group of important twentieth-century philosophers became concerned about the problem of civilization and accorded culture a centrality in their theories. In doing this, they sketched out the third aspect of the three-sided relationship that provides the background for political thought in the contemporary world. Out of the nineteenth-century penchant for systematizing social existence came three movements of protest. The pragmatists realized that in complex industrialized societies the consequences of human activities could not be determined easily. They recommended that students of political activity pay greater attention to the social processes through which human actions are mediated and the various kinds of consequences that resulted from political, economic, and social activity. The pragmatic revolt was particularly important in weaning political and sociological theory away from single-factor deterministic schemes. The existentialists seized upon the insight that individual human existence could not be reduced to any systematic explanatory system of human behavior devised by finite men. Thus, they reinstated the concrete human being into political theory and thereby provided one ground to which the consequences of human activity can be referred.

The civilized humanists realized that the characteristic product of human activity is culture, and that culture is continually being organized into systems. Through developing standards of the good life they provided the second ground to which the consequences of human activity can be referred—civilization. Each master philosophy of political science achieved a characteristic representation through a working political theory. The next section will be devoted to the discussion of the three theories that applied the master philosophies to specific problems in political existence.

NOTES

1. Richard T. La Piere, *Social Change* (New York: McGraw-Hill Book Company, 1965), p. 253.

2. R. G. Collingwood, *The New Leviathan* (London: Oxford University Press, 1942).

3. Marvin Farber, *Basic Issues of Philosophy* (New York: Harper & Row, Publishers, 1968), p. 216.

4. W. Warren Wagar, *The City of Man* (Baltimore: Penguin Books, Inc., 1967).

5. Morris Raphael Cohen, *American Thought* (New York: The Macmillan Company, Collier Books, 1962), p. 390.

6. Ibid., pp. 391–392.

7. Willard E. Arnett, *Santayana and the Sense of Beauty* (Bloomington, Ind.: Indiana University Press, 1955), p. 10.

8. George Santayana, *Dominations and Powers* (New York: Charles Scribner's Sons, 1951), pp. 58–59.

9. Cory, Daniel, *Santayana: The Later Years* (New York: George Braziller, Inc., 1963), p. 181.

10. George Santayana, *Reason in Society* (New York: The Macmillan Company, Collier Books, 1962), p. 108.

11. Ibid., p. 149.

12. Ibid., pp. 131–132.

13. Santayana, *Dominations and Powers*, p. 435.

14. Ibid.

15. Ibid., pp. 435–436.

16. Ibid., p. 177.

17. Ibid., p. 297.

18. Santayana, *Reason in Society*, p. 56.

19.   Michael A. Weinstein, "Santayana: Conservative or Philosopher of Reason?" *Modern Age,* 13 (Winter 1968-69); 51-61.

20. Alfred North Whitehead, *Adventures of Ideas* (New York: The Macmillan Company, 1933), p. vii.

21. Ibid., p. 11.

22. Ibid., p. 125.

23. Ibid., p. 99.

24. Ibid., p. 54.

25. Ibid.

26. Ibid., p. 56.

27. Ibid., p. 72.

28. Ibid., p. 78.

29. Elijah Jordan, *The Good Life* (Chicago: University of Chicago Press, 1949), p. 90.

30. Elijah Jordan, *Essays in Criticism* (Chicago: University of Chicago Press, 1952), p. 6.

31. Jordan, *The Good Life,* p. 10.

32. Elijah Jordan, *Theory of Legislation* (Chicago: University of Chicago Press, 1952), pp. 380–390.

33. F. S. C. Northrop, *The Meeting of East and West* (New York: The Macmillan Company, Collier Books, 1966), p. 459.

34. Ibid., p. 470.

35. Pitirim A. Sorokin, *Sociological Theories of Today* (New York: Harper & Row, Publishers, 1966), p. 23.

36. Ibid., p. 24.

37. Santosh Kumar Nandy, "Pitirim Alexandrowicz Sorokin: Integralist or Organicist?" *The Modern Review,* 124, 5 (September 1969): 670.

38. Lewis Mumford, *The Condition of Man* (New York: Harcourt Brace Jovanovich, Inc., 1944), p. 13.

39. Ibid., p. 7.

40. Ibid., p. 13.

SUGGESTED READINGS

Collingwood, R. G. *The New Leviathan.* London: Oxford University Press, 1942.

Hocking, William Ernest. *The Coming World Civilization.* New York: Harper & Bros., 1956.

Jaspers, Karl. *The Origin and Goal of History.* Translated by Michael Bullock. New Haven: Yale University Press, 1953.

Lippmann, Walter. *The Public Philosophy.* New York: The New American Library, Inc., 1956.

Mukerjee, Radhakamal. *The Social Structure of Values.* London: Macmillan and Co., Ltd., no date.

Russell, Bertrand. *Human Society in Ethics and Politics.* New York: Simon & Schuster, Inc., 1955.

Sarkar, Benoy Kumar. *The Science of History and the Hope of Mankind.* London: Longmans, Green & Co., Ltd., 1912.

Schilpp, Paul Arthur, ed. *The Philosophy of Sarvepalli Radhakrishnan.* New York: Tudor Publishing Co., 1952.

Toynbee, Arnold J. *Civilization on Trial.* New York: Oxford University Press, Inc., 1948.

Wagar, W. Warren. *The City of Man.* Baltimore: Penguin Books, Inc., 1967.

Whyte, Lancelot Law. *The Next Development in Man.* New York: The New American Library, Inc., 1950.

PART THREE

EMPIRICAL
POLITICAL THEORIES

CHAPTER FIVE

PLURALISM

The typical expression of pragmatism on the level of descriptive political theory is pluralism. John Chapman has traced the origins of pluralism to Greek and Judaeo-Christian thought. He identifies the core of pluralism in the judgment that articulation of activities through voluntary and private associations "permits a resilient rationality to the politics of a society, offers its members the satisfactions of both cooperative and competitive achievement, and works to stabilize their common conception of justice."[1] He states that the objective of pluralism is the separation of moral and economic progress from political instability. In the twentieth century this general doctrine, which has both descriptive and normative components, was given a new descriptive expression in the United States. Through its history, the background of the general doctrine of pluralism has been philosophical systems ranging from Thomism to utilitarianism. In America, pluralism has been predominantly a pragmatic political science.

EARLY AMERICAN PLURALISM

James Madison

The origins of American pluralism can be traced to the essay "Factions: Their Cause and Control," written by James Madison as one of *The Federalist* papers. In *Federalist* 10 Madison defines a faction as

> a number of citizens, whether amounting to a majority or minority of the whole, who are united and actuated by some common impulse of passion, or of interest, adverse to the rights of other citizens, or to the permanent and aggregate interests of the community.[2]

Through this definition of faction, Madison delimits a universe of discourse in which a long line of American pluralists, culminating in the interest group theorists and systems theorists of contemporary American political science, would advance their analyses.

Four Components of Faction Madison's definition contains four components which are decisive in the understanding of American pluralist theory. First, the definition of faction is political rather than socioeconomic or psychological. For Madison, factions are important because they press claims upon and against other groups within the community, and upon and against the community itself. A faction is defined through its opposition to other interests and would not exist without these other interests. This political definition of faction marks some deviation from the center of pluralist thought identified by Chapman. Madison does not maintain that factions permit a "resilient rationality to the politics of a society." Factions are conflict groups that act in terms of private interest, even if that interest is some communitywide goal such as the realization of a redistribution of property or a new structure of public authority. Factions do not perform any public function. Rather, they are controlled by agencies of the government which perform public functions.

Second, and more important for descriptive theory, Madison defines faction as a cross section of activity rather than as a distinct entity with its own integrity. He defines faction operationally and behaviorally as a group of human beings "united and actuated by some common impulse of passion." With respect to activities in support of a given impulse, a human being is a member of a particular faction. While Madison does not work out the full implications of this position, later pluralists point out that if the human being gains membership in a faction through some of his activities, he is a member of as many factions as his activities define. Thus, the individual can be a member of factions that oppose one another, as well as claiming membership in factions that support one another. Since Madison does not follow this line of argument very far, he proposes the control of factions by governmental and constitutional means. In more recent work, theorists have claimed that there are social controls to factions through the membership of individuals in overlapping and crosscutting factions. Opposed to Madison's definition of group in terms of cross-sectional activity is the type of pluralism that treats groups as entities with spirits, minds, or wills existing apart from the feelings, ideas, or projects of their members. For American pluralists there are no natural or organic groups that grow up apart from the activities of human beings, or that mold and shape the activities of human beings.

Third, Madison's definition of faction places the problem of political groups in the context of private interest. The members of a faction are united and actuated by some common impulse of passion, or of interest, adverse to the rights of other citizens, or to the permanent and aggregate interests of the community. Here Madison identifies the central problem of political science in America and, perhaps, all political science: Does politics have a public function, or is it merely the expression of private interest? Madison contributes one part of an answer to this question that has been particularly significant in American political thought. For Madison, the raw material of politics is private interest, whatever the finished product of political activity may be. Later theorists of political pluralism like Arthur Bentley, David Truman, and David Easton have made Madison's assumption in their work. This has given a turn to their political thought which has produced a debate over whether government is a technique for the expression of the most powerful interests in the society, or a set of interactions through which interests are balanced and regulated. Of course, these are not the only possible descriptions of government. For example, Dewey holds that the function of government is to regulate the indirect consequences of human activity, while Jaspers contends that the function of government is to make cultural contributions possible. However, when private interest becomes the basis of political theory the debate about government tends to be in terms of domination by private interest and adjustment of private interests.

By introducing the "permanent and aggregate interests of the community" into his discussion, Madison opens up a problem subsidiary to that of the relation between private interest and public function. Are these "permanent and aggregate interests of the community" widely held interests that are essentially the same as the interests actuating factions, or do they refer to some public interest, common good, or general will independent of human actors? The American pluralists have tended to discard the notions of public interest and common good in favor of an interpretation of permanent and aggregate community interest as a widely held interest in regulating group conflict and group power by specific means.

Fourth, Madison defines politics in terms of conflict. Factions attempt to gain resources at the expense of other groups, and these other groups mobilize to prevent this disturbance. Madison states that the "most common and durable source of factions has been the various and unequal distribution of property."[3] The propertied and the propertyless always form distinct interests in society, as do creditors and debtors, land owners, manufacturers, merchants, and financiers. The conflict among these interests is the great political problem of modern times: "The regulation of these various and interfering interests forms the principal task of modern legislation, and involves the spirit of party and faction in the necessary and ordinary operations of government."[4]

The four components—a political definition of faction, a definition of the group in terms of cross-sectional activity, a ground for political theory in the concept of private interest, and a conflict theory of politics—are the permanent contributions that Madison made to American pluralism. Thus, American pluralist theory is relatively free of social and psychological definitions of faction, descriptions of the group as an entity independent of human activity, grounds for political theory in the common good, and views of politics stressing harmony and cooperation.

Controlling Faction Like most American pluralists, Madison develops a pragmatic political science. He remarks that one can cure the "mischiefs of faction" in two ways. One may remove the causes of faction or one may control its effects. With respect to removing the causes, two methods can be followed. One may curb the liberty which is required for the expression of faction or one may attempt to give every person the same opinions, the same passions, and the same interests. Madison does not look favorably at either way of controlling the causes of faction. The method of curbing liberty constitutes a remedy that is worse than the problem of faction, and it is impossible to give every person the same opinions, the same passions, and the same interests. From these considerations Madison is led to turn away from the causes of faction, which cannot be controlled, and toward the effects, or consequences, of faction, which can be treated.

There are two ways in which the deleterious effects of faction can be controlled, corresponding to two kinds of factions. If a faction consists of a minority it may "clog the administration and convulse the society," but its "sinister views" can be defeated by the majority in its regular vote. There is a greater problem if a faction consists of a majority. In this case, Madison holds that many of the features of the American Constitution will militate against majority tyranny. The complex method of legislative representation will prevent precipitous action; the separation of powers will work against single-minded domination; checks and balances will create jealousies among the various agencies of government; and the very size of the republic will prevent efficient organization by the majority.

Madison's constitutional methods for controlling faction have been severely criticized by many later American pluralists. They have shown that majorities are so disorganized and ill-informed that minority factions with tight organization, good intelligence apparatus, plentiful resources, and intense interest can often have their way against majority interests. They have also shown that intense majorities can be organized in the context of improved communications media. However, while American pluralists have moved away from Madison's legal formalism, they have not abandoned his interest in controlling the effects of faction rather than the causes of faction. Even Dewey is a Madisonian in his preoccupation with controlling the indirect consequences of human activities. Contemporary pluralists are divided among those who believe that faction is socially controlled through multiple memberships in crosscutting groups, those who hold that faction is controlled through countervailing organizations, and those who judge that faction should be controlled through further legal norms.

John C. Calhoun

Another precursor of contemporary American political pluralism is John C. Calhoun. In his apology for the slave system in the South prior to the American Civil War, Calhoun is led to formulate a political theory based on multiple interests. He observes that if an entire community had the same interests "so that the interests of each and every portion would be so affected by the action of the government that the laws which oppressed or impoverished one portion would necessarily oppress and impoverish all others," direct democracy would be a perfect form of government.[5] However, he points out that the very problem of government is the equalization of public action with respect to the diverse interests within the society. The easiest course of government is to "pervert its powers into instruments to aggrandize and enrich one or more interests by oppressing and impoverishing the others; and this, too, under the operation of laws couched in general terms and which, on their face, appear fair and equal."[6] Thus, Calhoun gives private interest precedence over public function in descriptive political science.

Private Interest vs. Public Function For Calhoun, conflict among interest groups occurs in all societies, whatever the degree of technological, organizational, and ideological sophistication. He does recognize that opportunities for the realization of private interest increase as the society becomes more complex:

> . . . the more extensive and populous the country, the more diversified the condition and pursuits of its population; and the richer, more luxurious, and dissimilar the people, the more difficult is it to equalize the action of the government, and the more easy for one portion of the community to pervert its powers to oppress and plunder the other.[7]

This view that the opportunities for the triumph of private interest over public function increase as the society becomes more complex seems opposed to the principle held by many contemporary pluralists that multiple memberships in crosscutting groups are factors in curbing the pursuit of private interest. The two principles can be reconciled by stating that as society becomes more complex the opportunities for domination by private interest increase with respect to demands relevant to specialized activities and are moderated with respect to general demands. The idea that in contemporary industrialized societies private interests dominate with respect to policies concerning specialized activities will be vital in later discussion and critique of recent pluralist theories.

Calhoun continues his discussion of interests by remarking that each interest enters an arena of conflict in which it strives to obtain access to the means to coercion organized by government with a view to protecting itself against other groups and advancing its particular interests without regard to the interests of other groups. In democracies, interest groups combine in coalitions to attain majorities. Once such organized majorities are formed, struggles are expressed through major and minor parties striving to maintain or capture control of the means to coercion. Calhoun remarks that political conflict is so basic that even in a relatively undifferentiated society, the advantages of possessing "the control of the powers of the government, and thereby of its honors and emoluments, are, of themselves, exclusive of all other considerations, ample to divide even such a community into two great hostile parties."[8]

Concurrent Majorities Like Madison, Calhoun does not propose to eliminate the causes of faction, which he believes lie in human nature, but attempts to devise a way of controlling the effects of faction. He proposes to control factional activity by a system of concurrent majorities in which the claim of each interest that might be adversely affected by an action of government would be determined, and the consent of each affected interest would be required before government acted. Like Madison, Calhoun devises a constitutional mechanism for implementing his idea for controlling factional activity. He favors dividing and distributing governmental powers so that each interest would have, through a political institution, a concurrent power in making and executing laws or a veto on the execution of laws.

While Calhoun's system of concurrent majorities was never formally institutionalized in the American political system, it frequently works informally in political activity. The prime example of concurrent majorities applied to contemporary political affairs is the government regulatory agency that becomes captured by the group that it is supposed to regulate.

Calhoun favored concurrent majorities as a way of preserving the slave economy. Regardless of the particular interest that he represented, Calhoun was a pragmatic political scientist. In the activity of descriptive political science, he was concerned with tracing the consequences of group activity on other groups and on the maintenance of the political system. In the activity of normative political philosophy, he was interested in devising a way in which various interests could be harmonized. In consonance with the pluralist tradition begun by Madison, Calhoun's basic unit of analysis was the cross section of human activity.

Characteristics of Pluralist Theory

American political pluralism is a distinctive political theory. It has three basic characteristics—the unit of political analysis is the cross section of human activity; political activity is viewed as representing demands grounded in social and economic activity; and political actions are judged in terms of their effects on specified groups or on the maintenance of the political system as a whole.

American political pluralists give private interest precedence over public function. Some of them hold that public function is a myth; others assert that government has a public function of regulation; and still others equivocate between these two interpretations. All political pluralists face the problem of explaining how group conflicts are moderated in such a way that organized human existence is possible. Their solutions to this problem, which follow from their grant of precedence to private interest, comprise the history of pluralist theory.

ARTHUR F. BENTLEY

Arthur F. Bentley is the political theorist who best represents pluralist thought in America. His *Process of Government,* published in 1908, has influenced much of the development of descriptive political theory and political science in the United States. In 1926 he published *Relativity in Man and Society,* in which he attempts to systematize political and sociological analysis around a small number of units. In this work he also attempts to apply rigorously the concept of relativity to the study of human activity. After a long period of work in epistemology, Bentley collaborated with John Dewey on a theory of knowledge that was published under the title *Knowing and the Known* in 1949. Thus, late in their lives the foremost American pragmatist and the most important American pluralist worked out a common ground and demonstrated the affinity between pragmatism and pluralism.

Bentley's work has been viewed in a wide variety of perspectives. One might say that a writer's interpretation of Bentley reflects more his own point of view than it illuminates Bentley's meaning. Thus, David Easton has written that Bentley "stands as the water-

shed between the simple realism of Wilson and the more complex realism of the group approach. . . . "[9] A similar approach has been taken by David Truman. In both cases Bentley is identified as a precursor of the behavioral approach, to which both writers adhere. However, Morris Cohen has written that Bentley's *Process of Government* is "the most vigorous expression of legal realism in America."[10] He is most interested in Bentley's attack on the study of legal institutions to the exception of analyzing the activities of legislation and administration. In this section, we will view Bentley's work as an attempt to establish a pragmatic sociology of knowledge. This is not the only interpretation of Bentley's writings that can be supported by his words, but it is one that unifies his various works.

Critique of Metaphysical Theories

In the first section of *The Process of Government,* Bentley undertakes a detailed criticism of theories that make feelings and faculties, and ideas and ideals, the causes of political events. Essentially he argues that when such statements as "men are selfish" and "Americans are a free people" are used to explain specific political activities, the supposed cause merely duplicates the effect. Explanations by feelings and ideas amount to making statements like "people who take LSD have visions because the drug has hallucinogenic powers."

Bentley criticizes the political theorists and legal philosophers of the nineteenth century for inventing *soul stuff* and *spooks* to explain political behavior. He accuses them of taking the view of the human being contained in everyday speech and attempting to make it serve the purposes of science. In ordinary language, we regard human beings as "persons who possess qualities or motives which are phases of their character and who act in accordance with these qualities or this character, under certain conditions of life in which they are placed."[11] We say that someone told the truth because he is an honest man, as though one can have honesty in the same way that one has two eyes. However, honesty, unlike having two eyes, is not a physical trait. To say that someone told the truth because he is an honest man, is simply to say that someone told the truth. There is no entity called *honesty* behind the act of telling the truth. Further, one cannot acquire honesty in the same way that one acquires a consumer good. One can habituate oneself to telling the truth or be habituated to telling the truth. Honesty is an activity. Thus, political theorists who use *soul stuff* and *spooks* to explain political activities are merely concealing their fundamental ignorance with words.

Bentley summarizes his critique of explanations by feelings and ideas by showing how they can be absorbed into activity. If one explains a political act by a specific feeling or idea, such as "love of theater-going" or "some detail of ballot-law reform," the feeling or idea almost becomes the activity itself. If one explains a political act by a general feeling or idea such as benevolence or the "theory of representative government," it is necessary to particularize the explanation by filling in social content, which amounts to describing social activity. In both cases the feelings and ideas are absorbed into the activity. Bentley's criticism of explanations by feelings and ideas constitutes only half of his critique of nineteenth-century political science. In his time, the alternative to the "various forms of so-called psychical interpretation" was "a dead political science." This dead political science was "a formal study of the most external characteristics of governing institutions."[12]

Critique of Legalistic Theories

The political scientist who embraced formalism would describe the details of written constitutions and statutes and would, perhaps, compare various constitutions. He might also suggest modest institutional reforms to make the formal structure more consistent. Bentley holds that legal forms are only a small part of the political process. Laws are not self-subsistent entities, unrelated to the activities of human beings; nor are they molds into which human activities flowed. Bentley urges a study of the processes through which law is made, from efficient demand to actual application.

Thus, Bentley sees the political science of his time as split between the physical interpretation of political activity and the study of legal forms. He proposes to reform political science by placing human activity at the center of investigation. However, by activity he does not mean blind behavior. Harmon Zeigler has remarked that Bentley's writings are "dated by an uncompromising hostility to introspective psychology, which he regarded as an 'immeasurable element.'"[13] However, Bentley did not object to introspective psychology so much as he opposed freezing mental activity and other human experience into things. Throughout the *Process of Government* Bentley repeats that "each man is a feeling, thinking being." Repudiating physical determinism he writes that it is "not the mountains at all, but the 'meanings,' the practical, actual uses that form our material of social study."[14] However, he viewed these meanings as social. A person's ideas and feelings could only be identified through language, a set of symbols built up by myriads of men. In a striking passage, Bentley describes the core of pragmatic social psychology: "I know myself, so far as I have any knowledge that is worth while, by observation of my actions, and indeed largely not by my own observations, but by what other people observe and report to me directly or indirectly about my actions."[15] Like Dewey, Bentley made social process the cornerstone of his theorizing. This did not mean that part of the social process did not take place as mental activity. It meant that mental activity had to be functioned in terms of its contribution to the social process rather than frozen as an entity split off from the rest of human activity.

Sociology of Political Knowledge

Bentley's political theorizing comprises an extended attempt to relate political language to the rest of political activity. Myron Q. Hale has pointed out that Bentley "embraced the sociology of knowledge in *The Process of Government.*"[16] Essentially, one question guides Bentley's work: What is the cash value of political rhetoric in terms of particular demands? Bentley answers this question generally by stating that political theories, platforms, policies, and even laws were primarily reflections of the interests of groups of human beings in continuing or expanding some activity. Like Madison and Calhoun he defines groups as cross sections of activity, gives them a political description, sets them in conflict, and grounds them in private interest rather than public function. However, he adds two more components to American pluralism, one of which has been emphasized by later writers and the other of which has been relatively ignored.

Interlacing of Groups The contribution that has been stressed in behavioral political science is the idea of gathering up the various cross sections of activity into a process. Hale has remarked that for Bentley "the universe was the contemporaneous struggle which was the boiling equilibrium of a closed total social system."[17] However, while the closed system sometimes appears in Bentley, he usually defines a dynamic process in his work: "We have a great moving process to study, and of this great moving process it is impossible to state any part except as valued in terms of the other parts."[18] While Bentley states that the cross sections of activity, or groups, are interlaced in this process, this should not suggest a closed system, because he argues that "the interlacing itself is the activity." This view that the interlacing of human activities is continuously proceeding is the core of the most advanced methodological reflections of Jean-Paul Sartre and C. Wright Mills. Even as they have taken the idea of a political process from Bentley, writers like David Easton and David Truman have not developed the insight that the interlacing itself is the activity.

Socioanalysis Bentley's second contribution to American pluralism is his sociology of knowledge. Anticipated in the *Process of Government,* it was fully developed in *Relativity in Man and Society.* Bentley called his sociology of knowledge "socio-analysis" and compared it to psychoanalysis. Socioanalysis can best be viewed as an attempt to function political rhetoric in terms of the rest of the social process. Bentley states that

> everywhere around us parts of our social activity are casting their demands absolutely against the social sky, ignoring their relativity, stating themselves in language-thought structures which split themselves off from their origin in activity and attempt to justify that from which they arise.[19]

This statement contains the basic idea behind socioanalysis.

Bentley claims that human beings are alienated from themselves because their social activity has been split in two. On one side are the day to day activities performed by groups of human beings. On the other side are opinionative activities in which demands are made in terms of the public interest, the common good, the general will, or some other absolute. These demands originate in human interests in extending and maintaining particular day to day activities. The function of the opinionative activities is to represent the day to day activities by furthering the satisfaction of particular interests. They are weapons in the political process just like bribery and force. Opinionative activities amount to fraud: " 'Is' and 'must' are the great tools of obscurantism. 'Is' and 'must' with sneer and jeer and arrogant assertion are the backbone of propaganda and they hide the weighted value of what is behind the propaganda."[20] For Bentley, the "weighted value of what is behind the propaganda" is group interest. He expected socioanalysis to develop clear statements to replace propaganda. Such clear statements would give "the meanings of words and thoughts, slogans and ideals, policies and doctrines in terms of their groupal origins and groupal bearers."[21]

Socioanalysis as Therapy If Bentley had merely been a descriptive political scientist he would have ended his discussion with the analysis of how human beings tend to state demands in absolute terms while deceiving themselves or lying to others about the origin of these demands in particular interested activities. However, he was interested in changing the world as well as understanding it. Socioanalysis was not only a keen tool of social criticism; it was also a therapy as important as psychoanalysis. Once people have been educated in socioanalysis, the "conflicts which are now obscure and concealed, not unlike the analyst's inhibitions in the unconscious he studies, will come up into full view, ready for resolution into something of peace and harmony of living and effectiveness of action."[22]

Like Dewey and other pragmatists, Bentley ultimately believed that social conflicts could be resolved through effective education in the consequences and functions of human activities, and through the honest communication that would presumably result from such education. In holding this belief, Bentley implied the proposition that the basic cause of political conflicts is the absolutization of particular interests. In view of his own basic principle that opinionative activities function to represent underlying day to day activities, usually economic, socioanalysis seems to be, at best, a measure preparatory to other change.

Bentley and Marx

Like all of the political theorists who speak significantly about the uncertain and threatening public situation of the twentieth century, Bentley owed a great debt to the writings of Karl Marx. While many contemporary political theorists ignore this debt, Bentley says matter-of-factly about his work: "The starting point for practical purposes is, of course, Karl Marx."[23] It is not too much to say that the three great political sociologists of the twentieth century—Bentley, Max Weber, and Gaetano Mosca—were essentially revisionists of Marx. The revisions accomplished by Weber and Mosca will be discussed in later chapters. Bentley's revision of Marx was to revalue economic classes as interest groups, thereby placing them on a par with other groups for the purposes of theory.

Bentley argues that Marx' theory of classes is not a good representation of the political process because the definition of class as relation to the ownership of the means of production is too hard and fast, because Marx does not systematically function political rhetoric to the group process, and because the economic basis of group activity was given too crude a definition. By putting all groups on an equal theoretical footing, Bentley gains great advantages of generality over Marx. However, what he gains in generality he loses in the analysis of actual human activity. Bentley never implies that all groups are equal. Some groups are more intense than others; some are better organized. However, to be operational Bentley's theory needs a set of rules for determining the importance of the various cross sections of activity in the political process. Such rules would inevitably have to specify that at particular times and places some contents of cross-sectional activity are more important than others.

Thus, Bentley substitutes a theoretical formalism for a legal formalism in his work. He makes the wise theoretical move of suspending judgment on the importance of the various contents of cross-sectional activity so that he can generalize from Marx' class to the interest group as the primary unit of political analysis. However, he never makes the next move of recognizing that the political process is always interlacing contents that are available in the culture. In fact, the analysis of culture is completely lacking in his theory. In actuality, some of these contents are more important in the interlacing process than others. From rarified political abstraction, one must move to the identification of significant contents.

Contributions to Political Theory

It is, perhaps, ironic that Bentley is best known for those aspects of his theory that are already present even in Madison's *Federalist* 10. He gives interest groups a political definition, having them represent underlying social activities in governmental activities. He defines the group as cross-sectional activity and sets groups in conflict with one another. He holds that governmental activities represent private interests and do not recognize the possibility of public function. If he frequently states that governments function to balance interests, he equally often explains that they balance interests in accordance with the relative power of those interests. Bentley explains how a political process is possible in the light of group conflict by proposing that the expansion of day-to-day activities is limited by a set of cross sections of activity called a *habit background.* The habit background comprises a widespread set of tendencies to limit conflict in certain ways. The notion of a habit background has played a key role in recent pluralist theories under such titles as "consensus on basic norms" and "agreement on the rules of the game." Bentley's major contribution to political theory is his generalization of class into interest group. It is this contribution that makes him a leading figure in post-Marxist political theory in the West. Political theorists are still working within the age of Bentley, or the age of theoretical formalism. This is why his statement of pragmatic political science is so important.

DAVID TRUMAN

David B. Truman is the contemporary American political theorist most responsible for reviving that aspect of Bentley's theory relevant to the activity of political interest groups. In his *Governmental Process,* published in 1951, Truman begins his discussion of political affairs in the Madisonian tradition with a section entitled "The Alleged Mischiefs of Faction." He observes that factions appear in every political system where freedom of association is present, and that a conception of political affairs "broad enough to account for the development and functioning of political groups is essential to a reliable evaluation of the alleged mischiefs of faction."[24] Truman remarks that the development of just such a conception of the political process is the purpose behind his writing the book.

Truman and Bentley

Truman makes central to his inquiry the basic question of how a political process is possible in the light of group conflict. Guiding his approach is the query: "How can we account for the existence of a going and generally accepted polity in a context of diverse interest groups?"[25] In attempting to answer this question, Truman makes several revisions in Bentley's political theory. Truman departs significantly from the conception of a group as a cross section of activity. He argues that the individual is less affected by the whole society in which he lives than he is influenced by the various groups to which he belongs. He holds that the actions and attitudes of individuals differ from one another according to the array of group memberships. He asserts that from infancy onward, every individual "tries to make himself an accepted participant in a group, or, more properly, a set of groups, that makes up his social environment."[26] Finally, he concludes his discussion of the relation between the individual and his groups with the comment that the group experiences and memberships of the individual are the primary, but not the only means, through which the individual knows and interprets his society.

Groups as Cross Sections of Activity Bentley would have disagreed with each one of these assertions. For Bentley, there is no whole society which contains groups, only cross sections of activity interlacing one another. Thus, he would never pose the question of whether people were influenced more by their whole society than by their particular group memberships. Bentley would certainly not declare that from infancy onward, every individual attempts to become an accepted participant in a set of groups. This contention amounts to arguing that human beings have a disposition to seek approval, just as LSD has a disposition to produce hallucinations. Bentley would call this an explanation by *soul stuff.* Further, Bentley would not argue that while the group experiences and memberships of the individual are primary in determining his character, they are not the only means through which the individual knows and interprets his society. Since Bentley defined groups as cross sections of activity, he viewed language as part of the social and group process. He would have asked Truman how an individual can know and interpret his activity without language.

In all, Truman's revision of Bentley was often to take the group as more than merely a cross section of activity. He argued that the "justification for emphasizing groups as basic social units . . . is the uniformities of behavior produced through them."[27] For Bentley, groups have no further reality after one has stated and valued purposive human activity. Uniformities of behavior are never produced through groups. This discussion should not be interpreted as meaning that Truman never employed the Bentleyan perspective on groups. He approached this perspective when he wrote that the group is merely interactions or relationships among human beings. This is not quite Bentley's position that the group is a cross section of activity, but at least it does not make the group an entity separate from human activity.

Group Equilibrium Truman's first revision of Bentley's theory prepared the way for his second revision. While Bentley never argued that groups tend to seek a specific equilibrium, Truman held that institutionalized groups have a tendency to maintain or revert to an equilibrium. With this idea as his basis, Truman argued that political activity arises when one group disturbs another's equilibrium, or when a group's equilibrium is disturbed by other factors. Disturbances to equilibrium set the stage for the appearance of interest groups, which on the basis of shared attitudes, make "claims upon other groups in the society for the establishment, maintenance, or enhancement of forms of behavior that are implied by the shared attitudes."[28] When an interest group makes claims on other groups in a society through the institutions of government, it is a political interest group.

Associations Truman worked these definitions out to clear the ground for his discussion of the association as the typical interest group in contemporary Western societies. While any group may function as an interest group, the association is a specialized means of coping with disturbances to equilibrium. Associations are grounded in tangent relations, or relations among groups that are similarly affected by an event or activity. Associations arise when people in tangent relations interact with one another on the basis of these relations. Associations function to maintain or restore equilibrium to underlying groups in tangent relation. For example, if a number of textile manufacturers are confronted by competition from foreign firms exporting inexpensive goods, the equilibrium of the textile market will be disturbed and the manufacturers may get together and form an organization to press for a tariff on textile imports. That organization is an association because it arises out of the tangent relations of textile manufacturers which are in turn created by a common situation of disturbed equilibrium through inexpensive imports. For Truman, associations are the typical units of political activity in contemporary industrialized societies. Bentley did not make this claim, because he wanted to allow for the influence of informal elite groups on the course of social activity.

Truman relates his discussion of associations to governmental institutions. The term *government* describes a set of structures through which a measure of order is maintained among groups for various purposes. Governmental activities are representative in Bentley's sense because the order maintained is relative to the groups and purposes that are most influential. Here Truman presents a view of government grounded in private interest. However, he also sometimes appears to give government a public function. He argues that the tendency for a diversity of groups to attach themselves functionally to government reflects the needs of a complex society. Further, he holds that government has a special function of ordering the relations among groups, this role being derived from the specialization of function in contemporary industrialized societies. Increasing specialization increases interdependence which in turn engenders expectations about the performance of specialists. When these expectations are not met, equilibrium is disturbed and associations are created out of relevant tangent relations. These associations press claims on governmental institutions for the restoration of equilibrium. If their demands are met, new disequilibriums may be created elsewhere setting off the formation of new associations. The process is continuous and dialectical, and government seems to have the constant public function of making sure that the fabric of interdependence is not rent. This is similar to Dewey's suggestion that the public function of government is to harmonize the relations among groups.

Political Cohesion

Truman answers his question—"How can we account for the existence of a going and generally accepted polity in a context of diverse interest groups?"—by developing a concept similar to Bentley's notion of a habit background. Truman argues that if interest groups are shared attitude groups, then in stable political systems one can assume widespread agreement on rules for limiting the scope and methods of conflict. This agreement is not usually well organized in formal associations, but exists as a series of potential groups that can be mobilized when there is a flagrant breach of the norms limiting the scope and method of conflict. Thus, a consensus on the rules of the game is one way in which the mischiefs of faction are curtailed.

Truman also adds a refinement to the concept of habit background. Many individuals are likely to be members of potential groups supporting the rules of the game as well as members of formally organized associations pressing claims on other groups and governmental agencies. Many individuals are also likely to be members of groups pursuing conflicting goals. In both cases the individual carries an internal check on the scope and methods of conflict that he will support. Multiple membership in crosscutting groups is, thus, another way in which the mischiefs of faction are limited.

A third way in which faction is moderated is through the provision of many points of access to the government. Most generally, the political strategy of interest groups is to gain access to decision-making centers and convert these centers into instruments of their own policy. Thus, if a law is passed that disturbs a group's equilibrium, it may attempt to gain access to the legislature to change the law, access to the executive to nullify the enforcement of the law, access to the administration to mute enforcement of the law, or access to the judiciary to reinterpret the law. Multiple and relatively open points of access moderate the effects of any one group's policy, as does the presence of countervailing groups formed over successive waves of disequilibrium.

Of course, the conditions for a going and generally accepted polity are not necessarily found everywhere and at all times. Potential groups may lack widespread membership, multiple memberships may be cumulative rather than crosscutting, points of access may be monopolized by established and powerful groups, countervailing groups may lack the resources necessary to check stronger factions, and the rules of the game themselves may be so biased in favor of specific groups that under certain conditions movements may mobilize against potential groups and the other groups supported by them. Each of these considerations has been raised to show that Truman's description of the political process in the United States is inadequate. However, they are definitely not objections against Truman's general theory of the political process, because that theory allows for the appearance of such conditions.

Equilibrium

Like Bentley's theory, Truman's pluralism is a pragmatic political science. The central unit, the association, resembles Dewey's public. The association is grounded in sharing a consequence of human activity—the consequence of having an equilibrium similarly disrupted by outside intervention. Group equilibrium serves Truman as a standard to which the consequences of human activity can be referred. However, group equilibrium, defined as the persistence of patterns of interaction, seems to be an arbitrary standard for the reference of consequences, particularly in light of Truman's statement that the most "significant feature of group politics is that it is a dynamic process, a constantly changing pattern of relationships involving through the years continual shifts in relative influence."[29] In the present work, the standards to which consequences are referred are philosophically derived from existentialism and civilized humanism, rather than arbitrarily derived from the fiction of a group equilibrium.

Bentley's view of complete group relativity prevented him from referring consequences to equilibrium. For Bentley, judgment of consequences was fully relative to group interest, which might or might not imply an interest in equilibrium. Thus, Truman's second revision of Bentley's theory, like his first, amounts to separating the group out of human activity and freezing analysis. Of course, this does not mean that Truman made a radical departure from the pluralist framework. He is ambiguous on the matter of whether groups are cross sections of activity or something more, but he never adopts the position that groups are organic growths or that they have minds. He resolves the crucial question of multiple membership in favor of the cross-sectional approach. His definition of interest groups is clearly political, as evidenced by the importance of tangency in the formation of interest groups and the centrality of access as the aim of interest group activity.

Truman sets groups in conflict with one another and he derives political activity from private interest. However, he is vague about the possibility of government serving a public function. Truman develops those themes in political pluralism most prominent in *Federalist* 10. He is concerned with determining how the mischiefs of faction are controlled, and he takes the standard American position of studying the effects of faction rather than faction's cause. His contribution to American pluralist thought was to mark out clearly the position that the abuses of faction are moderated by social controls like multiple memberships in crosscutting groups (including potential groups) and countervailing powers. These ideas were implicit in Bentley's writings but were never fully worked out by him because he was more interested in developing his socioanalysis and his view of the political process as an interlacing activity. Unfortunately Truman does not follow up these two concerns. For socioanalysis he substitutes stable expectations about specialized activities, and for the political process as an interlacing activity he substitutes equilibrium analysis. This does not vitiate the significance of his ideas about how faction is controlled.

ROBERT DAHL

Another way in which faction is moderated has been described by the American pluralist Robert Dahl. In his *Who Governs?*, a study of decision making in New Haven, Connecticut, Dahl traces historically a progression from cumulative inequalities in political resources among groups in New Haven to dispersed inequalities in these resources among groups. By dispersed inequalities, Dahl means that while a group may have the ability to gain satisfaction of its interests in its particular and specialized sphere of activity, it will not be able to have its way with respect to activities outside of its sphere of competence. By cumulative inequalities, Dahl means that an advantage in one sphere of activity tends to create advantages in other spheres. Earlier, in the discussion of Calhoun, we called upon dispersed inequalities to explain how in complex societies both opportunities for exploitation of the public domain and multiple memberships in overlapping groups increase. Dispersed inequalities are a variant of the countervailing powers argument. Factional abuse is limited by countermobilization.[30] Dahl adds the observation that a system of dispersed inequalities will function stably if "only citizens who expect the decision to have important and immediate consequences for themselves, or for those with whom they feel strongly identified, try to influence the outcome."[31]

Dahl's position amounts to the complete triumph of private interest over public function. Dewey's public, formed by those who suffer the indirect consequences of a human activity, is left disorganized and impotent. Political activity functions in a private preserve rather than a public domain. Yet Dahl's pluralist construct is a pragmatic political science. He recognizes that human activities have indirect consequences, but he would have these consequences taken care of by the elected official or political entrepreneur who adjusts them to the claims of other interests. In the contemporary world, where the indirect consequences of human activities are particularly severe and threatening, Dahl's idea that in liberal societies, "politics is a sideshow in the great circus of life," appears to be a retreat into an Epicurean garden.

THEODORE J. LOWI

In the United States, the theory of political pluralism has gone through several stages of development, the most important of which are illustrated by the ideas of key writers like Madison, Calhoun, Arthur Bentley, David Truman, and Robert Dahl. From its origins to the present, American pluralist thought has been concerned with factional activity and its control. James Madison, the first American pluralist, recommended that the consequences of factional activity be controlled by legal and constitutional means. A constitution, which through separation of powers and checks and balances prevented any one faction from gaining control of the political system, would create the conditions for a public domain. Calhoun, too, took a legal approach to the regulation of faction's abuses, as evidenced by his doctrine of the concurrent majority. However, after Calhoun the legal approach to controlling the consequences of factional activity gave way to doctrines of social control. Arthur Bentley recommended that faction be regulated through widespread education in socioanalysis, so that people would not be deceived by the propaganda of interest groups. David Truman argued that built-in social controls like multiple membership in crosscutting interest groups and countervailing interest groups automatically regulated the consequences of faction. Robert Dahl held that in a system of dispersed power centers, the abuses of faction tend to be moderated. The latest development in American political pluralism represents a swing back to the Madisonian idea that law is the most effective means to curb excesses of factional activity.

Law and Faction

In *The End of Liberalism* Theodore J. Lowi describes the results of the practical experiment of basing public policy on the idea that factions are socially controlled and that law is merely a register of which groups have gained effective access to the political system. He points out that in the New Deal era a public philosophy of interest group liberalism became ascendant in the United States. The triumph of interest group liberalism marked a profound revision in American attitudes toward faction. While Madison defined a faction as a group whose interest was "adverse to the right of other citizens, or to the permanent and aggregate interests of the community," and held that the consequences of faction should be purposefully regulated, the interest group liberals regarded factions as good. Since they existed in a system of built-in social checks to their activity, groups did not need purposeful regulation. Rather, it was the function of government to provide access points for groups and to attempt to meet their most intense demands. Lowi remarks that "pluralist thinkers today sentimentalize the group, the group member, and the interests."[32] Of course, the norm that interest groups should have access to decision-making centers and should have their most intense interests satisfied, is not logically implied by Truman's and Dahl's descriptive pluralism. The current descriptive theory of interest groups merely provides a congenial background for this norm which, Lowi holds, has become the central standard of American policy making for almost half a century.

Decline of Law

For Lowi, American jurisprudence since the Roosevelt era has substituted bargaining for law and participation for adjudication. Lowi claims that *"modern law has become a series of instructions to administrators rather than a series of commands to citizens."*[33] He traces the development of public controls over economic activities in the United States through eight stages since the formation of the Interstate Commerce Commission in 1887. The Interstate Commerce Commission, which regulated railroads, was guided by a concrete, specific, traditional, rule-bound, and proscriptive delegation of authority. Since that time, the delegations of authority to regulatory agencies have become increasingly general, abstract, novel, discretionary, and prescriptive. Along with the surrender of the law-making function by legislatures has gone increasing participation of the groups that are supposed to be subject to regulation in the regulatory process itself. The policies of regulatory agencies are, therefore, decided on a case by case basis through a process of bargaining. There is no adjudication of cases on the basis of clear rules, and the public domain is parcelled into private preserves in a corporate state characterized by dispersed centers of power. This situation has resulted in an acute crisis of public authority.

According to Lowi, the present social conflict in the United States has a political root. The contemporary revolution is a revolution to instate a just political order rather than a movement to gain a redistribution of economic values. The profound alienation of our time is the alienation of public authority to private interest groups. Lowi disagrees with the view that the rise of delegation and the decline of law are the result of increased technical complexity in contemporary industrialized societies. He argues that "the real problem is one of abstraction rather than one of complexity."[34] Abstraction in the law permits uncontrolled discretion and the system in which interest groups participate in the regulatory process. Lowi holds that the tendency towards abstraction in delegations of authority can be reversed only if leadership chooses to reverse it. He argues that a change of public values in the United States is essential for the realization of law and a measure of justice.

Critique of Pluralism

In *The End of Liberalism,* Lowi presents one of the most radical critiques of American pluralist theory possible. While other critics have shown that the conditions for self-limiting pluralism, such as multiple membership in crosscutting groups and countervailing powers, do not always apply in the United States, Lowi has argued that current pluralist theory lacks a conception of the independence of law. For Lowi, when laws are more than abstract delegations of authority they become an independent variable in patterning human activity. Lowi recommends that a public philosophy of juridical democracy replace the present public philosophy of interest group liberalism. A juridical democracy would reverse the drainage of

public authority from the government to interest groups by formulating clear rules for the centralization of responsibility. With responsible government in being, the crisis of public authority would end,
since the dynamic underlying the crisis is progressive loss of the
idea of law itself.

One can agree with Lowi's idea that laws can be independent
variables in patterning human activity without assenting to his
diagnosis of the contemporary public situation. Lowi's critique of
interest group liberalism is essentially a cogent description of the
juridical expression of the deeper crisis in the contemporary public
situation. There are significant factors, other than increased technical complexity in industrialized societies and increased use of
abstraction in delegations of authority, working in the alienation of
public authority to private interest groups. Lowi remarks that
interest group liberalism was "the New Deal rationalized." It consisted in "making the best of one of our worst periods of history by
buying time and support with sovereignty."[35] He is surprised that
interest group liberalism remained the American public philosophy
through the 1960's, even in periods of national strength. There is no
reason to be surprised about the persistence of interest group
liberalism if one realizes, like Bentley, that multiple access points
and participation of the regulated in the process of regulation
represent the importance of certain cross sections of activity in the
political process.

Juridical democracy will not emerge out of a change in the
values of leadership groups, nor will abstract delegations become
concrete when people realize that the idea of law itself is in
jeopardy. Interest group liberalism does not rest on a mistaken set of
values or a mistaken set of ideas about law. It rests on the fact that
certain cross sections of activity control enough space, time, and
resources to influence governmental activity in their favor. It is
certainly not legitimate to state, like some apologists for the present
American regime, that the participation of the regulated in the
regulatory process is true pluralistic democracy. In fact, interest
group liberalism as a normative theory is utterly opposed to John
Chapman's definition of the pluralist goal as the separation of moral
and economic progress from political instability. However, in aban-
doning interest group liberalism, one should not abandon the
advances in political sociology secured by Marx, Bentley, and
others. The sociology of law arose because investigators saw that
much of the legal system in modern nations was systematically
biased in favor of some groups. Law may have an independent effect
in human affairs, but it is ultimately supported by underlying
activity. It expresses the projects of people acting in social groups. A

return to legal formalism in political theory would merely provide another screen behind which interest groups would continue to act. The Western nations have gone that route before.

PLURALISM IN REVIEW

The great contribution of American pluralism to political theory was made by Arthur Bentley in his definition of the cross section of activity as one of the essential forms in political analysis. Marx' revolt against legal formalism and Bentley's generalization of class into group are permanent contributions to political theory as a cumulative undertaking. These contributions, as well as the advances of the other significant empirical political theorists of the twentieth century, were made under the influence of positivism. Positivism, whose most famous exponent was Auguste Comte, is the doctrine that the most advanced and reliable knowledge is scientific knowledge. Empirical political theorists at the turn of the twentieth century were positivists in the sense that they aimed at discovering the most general categories through which political existence could be described. The notion of cross-sectional activity is, in part, a result of the positivist doctrine applied to constructing empirical political theory.

Aside from providing the definition of the interest group as cross-sectional activity, American pluralists have developed the sociology of political knowledge, described the contemporary association, discussed the problem of faction, and contributed to the functional analysis of social structures. They have paid close attention to the relations among law and social activities. Some of them, like Madison, Calhoun, and Lowi, have emphasized the importance of law as an independent causal factor in social existence, while other pluralists, like Bentley, Truman, and Dahl, have emphasized how law serves the functions of maintaining and extending other human activities. American pluralism as classically expressed by Arthur F. Bentley is one of the most significant examples of post-Marxist political thought.

Pluralism, however, is not a self-sufficient empirical theory of political activity. It must be supplemented by organization theory, which describes the basic structures within cross sections of activity; the theory of political elites, which describes the fundamental relations of domination; and theories of the political system, which describe the relations among cross-sectional activity, organization, and domination. In the following three chapters we shall consider these other theories in preparation for taking a new step in political thought.

NOTES

1. J. Roland Pennock and John Chapman, eds., *Voluntary Associations* (New York: Atherton Press, Inc., 1969), p. 91.

2. Alexander Hamilton, John Jay, and James Madison, *The Federalist Papers* (New York: Washington Square Press, 1964), p. 12.

3. Ibid., p. 18.

4. Ibid.

5. John C. Calhoun, *A Disquisition on Government* (Indianapolis: The Bobbs-Merrill Co., Inc., 1953), p. 13.

6. Ibid., pp. 13–14.

7. Ibid., p. 13.

8. Ibid., pp. 14–15.

9. David Easton, *The Political System* (New York: Alfred A. Knopf, Inc., 1953), p. 177.

10. Morris Raphael Cohen, *American Thought: A Critical Sketch* (New York: The Macmillan Company, Collier Books, 1962), p. 213.

11. Arthur F. Bentley, *The Process of Government* (Cambridge, Mass.: The Belknap Press of Harvard University Press, 1967), p. 465.

12. Ibid., p. 162.

13. Harmon Zeigler, *Interest Groups in American Society* (Englewood Cliffs, N.J.: Prentice-Hall, Inc., 1964), p. 9.

14. Bentley, *The Process,* p. 194.

15. Ibid., p. 187.

16. Myron Q. Hale, "The Cosmology of Arthur F. Bentley," in *The Bias of Pluralism,* ed. William E. Connally (New York: Atherton Press, Inc., 1969), p. 40.

17. Ibid.

18. Bentley, *The Process,* p. 178.

19. Arthur F. Bentley, *Relativity in Man and Society* (New York: G. P. Putnam's Sons, 1926), pp. 196–197.

20. Ibid., p. 196.

21. Ibid., p. 197.

22. Ibid.

23. Bentley, *The Process,* p. 465.

24. David B. Truman, *The Governmental Process* (New York: Alfred A. Knopf, Inc., 1951), p. 13.

25. Ibid., p. xi.

26. Ibid., p. 18.

27. Ibid., p. 23.

28. Ibid., p. 33.

29. Ibid., p. 65.

30. Robert A. Dahl, *Who Governs?* (New Haven: Yale University Press, 1961), p. 305.

31. Ibid., p. 297.

32. Theodore J. Lowi, *The End of Liberalism* (New York: W. W. Norton & Company, Inc., 1969), p. 296.

33. Ibid., p. 144.

34. Ibid., p. 154.

35. Ibid., p. 311.

SUGGESTED READINGS

Almond, Gabriel A., and Sidney Verba. *The Civic Culture.* Boston: Little, Brown and Company, 1965.

Connolly, William E., ed. *The Bias of Pluralism.* New York: Atherton Press, Inc., 1969.

Dahl, Robert. *A Preface to Democratic Theory.* Chicago: University of Chicago Press, 1956.

Galbraith, John Kenneth. *American Capitalism.* Boston: Houghton Mifflin Company, 1952.

Key, V. O. *Politics, Parties, and Pressure Groups.* New York: Thomas Y. Crowell Company, 1964.

Kornhauser, William. *The Politics of Mass Society.* New York: The Free Press, 1959.

Lipset, Seymour M. *Political Man.* Garden City, N.Y.: Doubleday & Company, Inc., 1960.

MacIver, R. M. *The Web of Government.* New York: The Macmillan Company, 1947.

McCoy, Charles A., and John Playford, eds. *Apolitical Politics.* New York: Thomas Y. Crowell Company, 1967.

Pennock, J. Roland, and John W. Chapman, eds. *Voluntary Associations.* New York: Atherton Press, Inc., 1969.

CHAPTER SIX

AUTHORITY, POWER, AND ORGANIZATION

Pluralism is a pragmatic political science both in its historical development and in the content of its fundamental concepts. Arthur Bentley, the foremost pluralist, and John Dewey, the most important political philosopher in the pragmatic school of thought, even coauthored *Knowing and the Known,* a contribution to epistemology. Bentley and Dewey frequently corresponded with one another, and towards the end of their lives both their intellectual interests and their conclusions about the theory of knowledge converged. No single political theory has been associated with existentialism in the same way that the histories of pragmatism and pluralism have been intertwined. Jean-Paul Sartre claims that existentialism is a movement aimed at humanizing Marxist thought. Edward A. Tiryakian has observed that because "the existential perspective views society as the seat of objectivity and therefore antagonistic to the subjective existence of the individual," and since "all existential thinkers deny that society has any authentic, true, reality," existentialists have not developed complete sociologies.[1] However, there is no lack of political theorists and political scientists who have discussed the basic problems raised by the existentialist movement.

Existentialists are primarily interested in the structure of the human condition, including the boundary conditions of the human situation. One of these boundary conditions is the necessity of being-among-others, and the modes of human relationship vary through time. For existentialists, there is a double relationship of the individual to the other person. The individual is dependent upon the other person for his very being-in-the-world, and at the same time the other person poses a drastic threat to the individual's existence.

In the twentieth century, existentialists have concretized this all-pervasive dialectical relationship by opposing creative freedom to the life order, community to organized exploitation, and authentic existence to lateral corroboration. Each of these dualities has been a source of significant work in political and sociological theory in the twentieth century. Some political theorists have studied the life order, or the bureaucratic apparatus through which collective tasks are performed in contemporary industrialized societies. Other political theorists have investigated the power relationship as the typical political activity. Still other political theorists have explored the dynamics of lateral corroboration in contemporary political systems, and have discussed the multiple tensions between leaders and masses. These concerns are complementary in that bureaucracy, in one of its aspects, is a system of power, and because the bureaucratic situation is the center of lateral corroboration, or other-directedness. Perhaps the most important contribution made by the political theorists who explored the problems raised by existentialists was the development of the general theory of organizations. Organization theory, which describes the general principles of coordination in human activity, accomplishes a generalization of Marxism equal in importance to Bentley's idea of the group as a cross section of activity.

ORGANIZATION THEORY

Herbert Kaufman has observed that the problems of organization theory duplicate the traditional questions asked by political theorists.[2] Throughout the history of political thought, philosophers have discussed the structure and goals of the ideal state and have compared the structure and goals of actual political systems to the description of the ideal. Plato's description of a polity governed by philosopher kings, in which each person performs the social function for which he is best suited, is the first and most famous essay in organization theory in the West. However, the history of the contemporary theory of organizations begins with the work of Max Weber.

Consistency with Existentialism
Karl Jaspers remarks that Max Weber is the first sociologist to present a theory consistent with existentialism. Jaspers observes that the movement in political theory which

> first establishes knowledge as knowledge and therefore liberates man, is taken when the significance of an objective cognition of the manifestation of will is not merely sharply distinguished in theory from the contemporary historical situation, but also remains the goal of radical activity in life itself.[3]

For Jaspers, Max Weber secured such a political science.

Weber did not view political science as a self-sufficient philosophy of human existence. Instead, he defined political sociology as a special science of human behavior and its consequences. Weber regarded every observable human relationship as relative and held that any image of the entire social existence of the human being "can be nothing more than one aspect contemplated as an object, and cannot be a knowledge of the real whole."[4] Weber's definition of empirical political science as the study of probability distributions ensured that authentic existence would not be violated by a dogmatic and deterministic positivism or materialism. Weber's sociology, based on the creation of imaginative structures that illuminate significant aspects of social experience, provides the human being with insights into the possibilities and limitations of his existence. However, such ideal types do not absorb the self into an object that can be known.

Authentic Choosing

For Jaspers, Weber's sociology becomes an essential component of authentic existence in the modern age. The insights of sociology, while they are relative, should be grasped by the person and should be immediately present to him when he is choosing. One cannot make responsible decisions without apprehending the significant structures of social existence in his time. However, the person should reject the idea that his responsibility in deciding should be "shuffled off upon a dogmatic knowledge considered to be endowed with objective accuracy, and it demands that the dangers and the hazards of genuine activity in the world should be accepted."[5]

Weber separated the observation of successive human actions from authentic human existence. A two-fold political science followed from this separation. First, political scientists would develop imaginative constructions of social relationships that illuminated significant possibilities and limitations in social existence. Second, political scientists would investigate the probabilities of the occurrence of such relationships. In *Man in the Modern Age,* Jaspers used such imaginative constructions, or ideal types. The description of the life order is, perhaps, the most striking ideal type in his work.

MAX WEBER

Max Weber combined in his work all of the important themes that characterize the existentialist description of social existence in the twentieth century. He developed the definition of power that is most widely used in contemporary political sociology and political science, presented a description of the types of authority that has not been surpassed, founded organization theory with his description of bureaucracy as a technology of coordination, generalized the theory of stratification from its roots in economic class, defined the state in terms of technique rather than function, and presented a definitive discussion of the nature of political responsibility. Along with Arthur Bentley and the Italian theorists of political elites, Weber stands as one of the seminal thinkers for contemporary political theory.

Fundamental Concepts

The fundamental concepts of Weber's political sociology are abstract and correspond to the notion of cross section of activity found in Bentley. Like the pluralists, Weber attempted to grasp the forms without which the study of social existence would be impossible. He defined sociology as the science which aims at "the interpretative understanding of social conduct and thus at the explanation of its causes, its course, and its effects."[6] In order to understand this definition, one must grasp the meaning of social conduct. For Weber, the most general category relating to human beings is behavior, or the sheer movement of the human organism. A subset of the set of human behaviors is conduct, or movement combined with some subjective meaning. Finally, a subset of the set of conducts is social conduct, or those actions in which the intention is related by the actor to the conduct of others. A further refinement of social conduct is defined by the social relationship, in which two or more people engage in conduct the meaning of which is directed from one person to the others. Weber remarks that a social relationship "simply consists in the probability that human beings will act in some (sensibly) determinable way; it is completely irrelevant why such a probability exists."[7]

These definitions are essential rather than merely stipulative. They define the ideas that make discussion about social existence possible. Thus, they are formal and do not contain any judgments about the relative importance of the various kinds of social conduct and social relationships. Given Weber's definitions of social conduct and social relationships, one cannot determine whether a complex set of human actions is organized around economic activity, political activity, religious activity, some other cross section of activity, or several cross sections of activity.

Weber's view of social conduct and social relationships is a generalization of the Marxist proposition that sociology is concerned with the way in which human activity is organized around "the prevailing mode of economic production and exchange" which is expressed in conflict relationships between "exploiting and exploited, ruling and oppressed classes."[8] Weber's generalization arises from an exploration of what is involved essentially in the relationships between exploiting and exploited, and ruling and oppressed. In the most general sense, only the notion of two or more people engaged in conduct—the meaning of which is directed from one person to the others—is involved in essentially describing such relationships. In other words, the essential structures of human existence are constituted by neither domination nor reciprocity, but by mutual orientation. Marx' fundamental mistake was in grounding social existence in the relationship of economic domination. Weber argues that the ground of social existence is in mutual orientation itself. However, this does not mean that Weber recommends according every social relationship equal importance in describing concrete political situations. Contrariwise, he agrees that economic relationships are often the nuclei around which other relationships are organized. The determination of importance is a problem for empirical investigation rather than for social ontology. The relative importance of the various cross sections can not be determined a priori.

Types of Conduct and Authority

Given his definitions of the forms of social existence, Weber defines the ways in which social conduct can be determined. *Purpose-rational conduct* is action oriented towards a goal and governed by the efficient use of means to attain that goal. Purpose-rational conduct is essentially the activity of economic man, who aims at maximum satisfaction of his goals. *Value-rational conduct* is aimed at the realization of an action which is considered intrinsically good apart from any ulterior goal. Telling the truth for its own sake would be an example of value-rational conduct. *Affectual conduct* expresses an emotion. Its aim is simply the release of that emotion, rather than any ulterior goal or pattern of conduct that is considered intrinsically good. Finally, *traditional conduct* is aimed at doing what is customary. In traditional conduct, the individual neither attempts to realize a goal of his own, exemplify a pattern of right action, nor express an emotion. He acts in a certain way because a particular set of actions is performed in the collectivity with which he is associated.

Political Legitimacy Weber uses his types of conduct as the basis for his discussion of the types of political authority. He observes that acquiescence in the imposed order of a political system normally has grounds other than fear or gratification of personal goals. A going political system usually presupposes "the belief that the power of domination of him or those by whom the order is imposed is in some sense legitimate."[9] Weber defines four ways in which actors can ascribe legitimacy to an order. These four grounds for legitimacy correspond to the four most important philosophies of law and theories of obligation in the tradition of Western political philosophy.

First, the order can be defined as legitimate because it is consonant with traditional practice. Here the order is obeyed because the actor perceives it as part of "inveterate usage." While usage is normally strengthened by the interests that create it or gain satisfaction through it, orders grounded in usage are legitimated by the sacredness of tradition. Legitimation through tradition finds its philosophical correspondent in Western legal thought in theories of customary law. Conservative writers like Edmund Burke have argued that the prescriptions of a legal tradition exemplify a wisdom greater than the reasonings of any single human being.

Second, the order can be defined as legitimate because it issues from a prophet who reveals a holy will. Here the basis of legitimacy is in affectual conduct. The actor has faith in the revelation and the gift, or charisma, of the prophet to reveal it correctly. Legitimation through affect finds its philosophical correspondent in Western legal thought in theories of revealed law. The entire Judaeo-Christian philosophy of law and political obligation rests on the revelation of God's law.

Third, the order can be defined as legitimate because it is deduced from the postulates of a rational ethics. Here legitimacy is based on value-rational conduct. The actor obeys the order because he believes that it prescribes an application of intrinsically good conduct. Legitimation through ethical reason finds its philosophical correspondent in Western legal thought in theories of natural law and rational will. The notion that law is or should be an expression of reason is found in Plato, Aristotle, the Roman lawyers, Catholic legal philosophers in the Thomist tradition, and contemporary idealists.

Fourth, the order can be defined as legitimate because it has been issued in a formally correct way. This type of legitimation is not grounded in purpose-rational conduct, but in legal validity. One obeys the order simply because it is a procedurally valid regulation. Legitimation through legal validity may seem unsatisfactory on its surface. One may wish to push beyond the particular order and to the legitimation of the procedures themselves. Procedures may be legitimated in any of the three preceding ways or through agreement of those bound to the procedures. However, while one may wish to push beyond legal validity for philosophical purposes, political sociologists need only note that many people in the contemporary world ascribe legitimacy to orders simply because they are legally valid. Legitimation through legal-rationality finds its philosophical correspondent in Western legal thought in theories of legal positivism. Legal positivists hold that law is valid when it is made through accustomed procedures. They do not attempt to set up ethical standards by which laws can be judged as good or bad.

In considering the legitimacy of the procedures themselves, recourse is often made to the agreement of those living under the laws, or to contract. Legitimation of procedures through contract finds its philosophical correspondent in Western legal thought in theories of social contract. Thomas Hobbes, John Locke, and Jean-Jacques Rousseau, among many others, presented contract theories of law and political obligation.

Authority Weber's discussion of the types of legitimation parallels his more famous description of the types of authority. Traditional authority is obeyed because it is rooted in usage. Charismatic authority is obeyed because of personal devotion to the prophet and his gifts of grace. And legal-rational authority is obeyed because it is constituted through recognized procedures. While Weber did not develop a type of authority based on legitimation through value-rationality, David E. Willer has suggested that "ideological authority" resting on "faith in the absolute value of a rationalized set of norms" can serve as the correspondent type.[10] The pure type of ideological authority is the party organized around a system of absolute value.

The Existential View From the existentialist point of view the types of legitimations categorized by Weber are myths obscuring authentic existence. However, from the viewpoint of the existential sociologist or political scientist they comprise basic ways in which individuals relate themselves to political objects. If the aim of existential political science is to help free people for authentic existence, a significant aspect of its analysis must be the exploration of the various ways in which people rationalize their obedience to commands.

Weber believed that the most common form of legitimacy in the contemporary world "is the belief in legality, i.e., the acquiescence in enactments which are formally correct and which have been made in the accustomed manner." [11] For existentialists this observation is particularly important in view of the widespread tendency for contemporary individuals to excuse their actions with the claim that they were "only following orders."

Bureaucracy

For Weber, the most fully developed expression of legal-rational authority is the bureaucracy, and with his discussion of bureaucracy he rounded contemporary organization theory and gave a generation of existentialists the concept of the life order. Weber considered bureaucracy to be the most efficient organizational technology invented by human beings. Essentially, bureaucracy is a way of coordinating human actions in such a way that the purposes of those who control the organization are efficiently realized.

Organization of Bureaucracy As an ideal type, bureaucracy combines many principles of coordination into a complex pattern. The most important feature of bureaucracy is the allocation of fixed jurisdictional areas, ordered by regulations, to the organization and its component agencies. The activities required for achieving the goals of the organization are distributed as official duties, the authority to give commands in the organization is distributed in a stable manner and is limited by rules prescribing legitimate sanctions, provisions are made to insure the continuous functioning of the organization, and only people who have certain formal qualifications are employed by the organization. The bureaucracy is a system of graded authority in which the higher levels systematically supervise the activities of the lower levels. The management of each bureau within the organization is based on written documents, or files. In the bureaucracy, the means of labor and the fruits of labor are separated from the private control of the individual official. Officials are paid a salary and they do not purchase their offices to exploit them for profit. Organizational tasks usually demand expert training and take up the full working capacity of the functionary.

The loyalty of the official is devoted to "impersonal and functional purposes," behind which certain collectivities like state, church, party, or enterprise stand. Weber remarks that these collectivities are "*ersatz* for the earthly or supra-mundane personal master," create a false sense of community, and "provide an ideological halo for the master."[12] Thus, unlike the civilized humanists who believed that functional excellence would be a sufficient principle on which to base a regime, Weber argues that there will always be a political master ruling in the name of the destiny of a collectivity. Weber emphasizes the importance of technical specialization in bureaucratic development, but like the existentialists he gives primacy to leadership and political power.

Power and Limitations Weber remarks that once a bureaucracy is fully established it is almost impossible to destroy it. Bureaucracy is "*the* means of carrying 'community action' over into rationally ordered 'societal action.' "[13] Bureaucracy regularizes and rationalizes power relationships and, therefore, has been and is an instrument of power for the individual in control of the "bureaucratic apparatus."[14] Methodically organized societal action is nearly always more effective than relatively disorganized mass or communal resistances. Weber observes that where the bureaucratization of administration has been completely accomplished "a form of power relation is established that is practically unshatterable."[15] The bases of bureaucratic power are in the technical advantages gained by dividing a collective task into specialized components, the organizational advantages gained by allocating authority into strictly delimited portions in a hierarchy, and the dependency of individuals on the rewards offered by the organization and the functions performed by it.

In passages reminiscent of Jaspers' description of the life order, Weber explores the situations of the functionaries and the administered population when they confront a bureaucracy. The official "cannot squirm out of the apparatus in which he is harnessed."[16] He is dependent for both his material and his spiritual existences upon the wealth, status, and power held by the bureaucracy. For the most part, he is merely a "single cog in an ever-moving mechanism which prescribes to him an essentially fixed route of march."[17] The single official has no authority to stop or start the functioning of the organization. He can only perform his own specific tasks within the boundaries set for him by the administrative regulations. In Jaspers' terms he is part of a mass, integrated into and around a mechanism. He is a member of a "community" of all the functionaries in the organization. However, the interest of this community is in the sheer continuation of the functioning of the organization. The official in a bureaucracy has subordinated his freedom to technique. The bureaucracy itself is the most efficient technique for performing collective tasks.

The individual administered by the bureaucracy is in no better condition than the functionary. The ruled cannot replace the bureaucratic structure of authority once it has been created and has begun functioning. Since the bureaucracy is based on "expert training, a functional specialization of work, and an attitude set for habitual and virtuoso-like mastery of single yet methodically integrated functions," if an official stops working or is disturbed in his work, social chaos results. The ruled population is not organized so that it can perform a vital community function if a key bureaucracy is disrupted. In the contemporary world, the material fate of entire populations is bound up with the successful functioning of massive bureaucracies. For Weber, the bureaucracies have become the life order, and the life order progressively monopolizes more and more space and time.

Perhaps the single most important political implication of the extension of bureaucratic authority is that once an apparatus is functioning it can be made to work for anyone who gains control over it. Since bureaucratic authority is impersonal, in that officials do not owe personal allegiance to a particular leader, it can operate in the name of any collectivity and for the benefit of any interest group. The results of this characteristic of bureaucracy are plainly evident in the twentieth-century experience of totalitarian and authoritarian regimes which have turned preexisting bureaucracies to their service.

While bureaucracy is the most efficient technique for accomplishing collective projects, it is not monolithic. If Weber provided a generation of existentialists with a description of the life order, he also discovered dilemmas within the structure of bureaucratic organization that are central in contemporary American theories of complex organization. The efficiency of bureaucracies is limited by built-in contradictions. For example, bureaucracies provide security of employment for officials. Such provision of tenure for life makes for increased efficiency by encouraging undisturbed performance of function. The official can concentrate on his work without being distracted by fear that he will be removed at the whim of a superior. However, a strong development of security of employment militates against efficiency by making it more difficult to staff offices with regard to technical efficiency. Provision of tenure for life and seniority systems decrease the "career-opportunities of ambitious candidates for office."[18] Each bureaucracy attempts to resolve this dilemma, but no bureaucracy fails to confront it.

Bureaucracy and Democracy An even more fundamental dilemma concerns the relationship between democracy and bureaucracy. Weber holds that there is a profound ambivalence in the relationship between the two. Historically, democracy has played a major role in the spread of bureaucratic authority through its encouragement of equal and impersonal justice. The democratic revolutions in the West have been aimed at abolishing the special privileges and status relationships involved in feudal societies, and bureaucracy has been one of the primary instruments in prosecuting these revolutions. Functional competence (achievement) has been substituted for personal characteristics (ascription), and adherence to legally specified rights and duties (universalism) has replaced personal and family loyalties (particularism). If a goal of the democratic revolutions has been equality under the law, bureaucracy has been an important means to this end. Further, democracy requires that the projects of the majority's representatives be realized as efficiently as possible. Bureaucracy, as the most efficient technique for realizing collective aims, became an instrument of democratic regimes.

However, Weber points out that "'democracy' as such is opposed to the 'rule' of bureaucracy, in spite and perhaps because of its
unavoidable yet unintended promotion of bureaucratization."[19] This
opposition is revealed most clearly in the phenomena of specialized
examinations and educational requirements in bureaucratic person-
nel practices. While specialized examinations and educational requirements are means of assuring that officials will be competent in
carrying out their functions and will not be chosen on the basis of
personal characteristics, they also tend to create a privileged caste.
Only the wealthy can afford the education necessary for taking high
positions in bureaucracies and only certain classes provide the
environment in which children can develop the characters necessary for bureaucratic advancement. Democracy, which would subject officials to majority will through limiting terms of office and
such devices as recall, is thwarted by progressive bureaucratization.

Weber points out that one way of easing the strain between
democracy and bureaucracy is for a Caesaristic leader to make
himself a trustee of the masses and thereby become an unrestrained
master of the apparatus. He adds, however, that such democratic
Caesarism, or rule of the personal genius, is the very antithesis of the
principle of universally elected officials. For Weber, the essence of
the democratic spirit is found in a remark attributed to an American
worker in the nineteenth century: "We prefer having people in office
whom we can spit upon, rather than a caste of officials who spit
upon us, as is the case with you."[20] The tensions between democracy
and bureaucratization have increased drastically as bureaucracy has
been extended in the twentieth century, and it is not enough to
remark that the experts should be kept on tap and not on top. Even if
bureaucracies are shot through with structural dilemmas, they are
still the most imposing organizations of the modern age.

Weber's Generalization In describing bureaucracy, Weber suc-
ceeds in performing an impressive generalization of preceding
theories of social organization. While organization theorists of the
nineteenth century develop brilliant descriptions of such concrete
types as capitalism and democracy, Weber invents the general
theory of organizations. The key to Weber's innovation is his remark
that "bureaucracy as such is a precision instrument which can put
itself at the disposal of quite varied—purely political as well as
purely economic, or any other sort—of interests in domination."[21]
Thus, Weber divorces the principles of coordinating human activities from specific social contents. The study of organization becomes
the investigation of how human activities are ordered regardless of
the nature of those activities. In this context bureaucracy is the most
efficient and typical form of organization in the modern age. It is a

technique, just like all other forms of organization and just like all human tools. Here the works of Bentley and Weber can be viewed as complementary—bureaucracy is the typical way of organizing cross sections of activity in the modern age.

Interest Groups and Leadership

Dangers Within the System The unity of Weber's political sociology and Bentley's political theory is evidenced by Weber's remark that in contemporary societies politics are managed through parties and that the "management of politics through parties simply means management through interest groups."[22] For Weber, interest groups are the units of effective political power in the contemporary world, and bureaucracies are organized to serve them. In the West bureaucratization has been carried out in "direct alliance with capitalist interests."[23] However, bureaucracies have also appeared as instruments of landed aristocracies, religious groups, workers' groups, and other cross sections of activity. Like Jaspers, Weber was not pleased by this development. He viewed the processes of increasing rationalization and depersonalization with ambivalence.

Ferdinand Kolegar remarks that while Weber viewed rationality as "one of the most signal accomplishments of modern man," he also saw that rationalization, "especially when pursued most systematically and with a singleness of purpose, engenders irrationalities."[24] Kolegar adds that Weber was continually troubled by the question: "What is there that can be done to counteract this 'machinery' and to save the rest of mankind from this 'compartmentalization of soul' and this 'supremacy of the bureaucratic ideals of life.' "[25] The most complete answer that Weber gives to this question is found in the essay "Politics as a Vocation," published in 1921, in which he summarizes his political sociology and discusses the kind of leadership that he prefers.

Qualities of the Leader Weber identifies three qualities of the political leader who could transcend the life order in the twentieth century—passion, a feeling of responsibility, and a sense of proportion. Weber defines each of these qualities in such a way that his description of the leader coincides with existentialist discussions of authentic existence. By passion Weber means devotion to a cause, or a public project beyond political survival or advancement. In working towards the cause a sense of proportion is necessary. Weber holds that the decisive psychological quality of the politician is "his ability to let realities work upon him with inner concentration and calmness."[26]

Among the realities of which the politician should be continually aware is the tragic nature of politics. The final result of political action stands in a paradoxical relation to its original intent. This is bound up with the fact that ultimately politics is power backed up by violence. Confronting the situation that it is impossible to know when the use of violent means is justified by a worthy end, the politician must be responsible both to his cause and to the tragic structure of political action. Weber asserts that "whosoever contracts with violent means for whatever ends—and every politician does— is exposed to its specific consequences."[27] He illustrates these consequences with the example of someone wanting to establish absolute justice in the world by force. To accomplish his goal he must create a political machine and pay off the workers he recruits into it. He will find that his success depends upon the functioning of the machine rather than his own initiatives. Thus, he will have to provide for a steady flow of rewards to his functionaries, and so he will create a stratum of administrators whose sole concern is the maintenance of the organization. Within this administration will be a police force. The domination of private interest, routinization, and depersonalization will necessarily result from his efforts and rather than absolute justice, psychic proletarianization will be realized.

For Weber, psychic proletarians are people who have been forced to surrender their creativity and intelligence in the interests of organizational discipline. The psychic proletarian is Weber's equivalent of Jaspers' and Hocking's mass man and Heidegger's "the One." The psychic proletarian, whose thoughts are the organization's rather than his own, is the opposite of the responsible politician, dedicated to a public project and fully aware of the tragedy of political action.

Kolegar observes that Weber was not confident that such existential leadership would be able to limit the life order. This is not surprising in view of the powerful interest groups and the efficient organizational techniques that he ranges against such leadership in his description of contemporary political systems.

PETER M. BLAU AND W. RICHARD SCOTT

A significant revision of Weber's theory of bureaucracy has been undertaken by the American organization theorists Peter M. Blau and W. Richard Scott. In *Formal Organizations,* Blau and Scott emphasize the idea that every organization is characterized by built-in structural dilemmas and attempt to add a pragmatic aspect to organization theory. Blau and Scott define formal organizations as patterns of social interaction that have been formally established for a specific purpose. They distinguish among types of formal organizations on the basis of who is intended to benefit from the functioning of the organization.

Following this criterion of who benefits, or *cui bono*, they identify four major types of organizations present in contemporary societies. Mutual benefit associations, like labor unions, are supposed to function to benefit their members; businesses are supposed to function to benefit their owners or managers; service organizations, like universities and hospitals, are supposed to function to benefit their clients; and commonweal organizations, like police departments and defense establishments, are supposed to function to benefit the public-at-large. The significance of Blau's and Scott's classification of organizations on the basis of who benefits lies primarily in its use as a tool for uncovering the structural dilemmas present in each type of organization.

Structural Dilemmas

Each major type of formal organization is characterized by a particular dilemma. Mutual benefit associations confront the antinomy of democracy and authoritarianism. In order to provide benefits to members mutual benefit associations must be enabled to act effectively in a frequently hostile environment. The need for unity in a combat organization encourages authoritarian or oligarchic structures of power. However, oligarchies tend to develop an interest in their own persistence and enrichment, leading them to take actions that often defeat the realization of benefits for memberships. Control of oligarchic tendencies among leadership groups in mutual benefit associations requires democracy, but democracy tends to weaken the effectiveness of a combat group. Thus, mutual benefit associations are caught in a vicious circle that is described by their key structural dilemma.

Business concerns are subject to the dilemma that Weber described in his discussion of bureaucracy. While bureaucratic regulations and security of tenure are necessary to the maintenance of an uninterrupted flow of activity towards organizational goals, they militate against individual initiative and discourage ambition. Thus, efficiency is limited by the very mechanism that is supposed to procure it.

Two dilemmas characterize service organizations. The professionals who staff a service organization must

> steer between two dangers: . . . On the one hand, they
> must not lose sight of the welfare of their clients, either
> through concern with their own status and career or

through preoccupation with administrative problems . . . .
On the other hand, the professionals must not become
"captives" of their clientele and surrender to them the
power to determine the nature of the service furnished.[28]

With regard to commonweal organizations, Blau and Scott raise
the most significant problems for political theory. They observe that
the "issue posed by commonweal organizations is that of external
democratic control—the public must possess the means of controlling the ends served by these organizations."[29] The problem of
commonweal organizations is the dilemma explored by Weber in his
discussion of the incompatibility of democracy and bureaucracy.
Blau and Scott argue that while democratic control over the ends
served by commonweal organizations is required in a democratic
society, the internal structure of commonweal organizations must be
bureaucratic and governed by the criterion of efficiency. If commonweal organizations are subject to internal democratic control,
the goals set by majority decision will be not carried out efficiently.
Thus, there must be a strict distinction between goal setting and goal
attainment. Blau and Scott recognize that there is a danger that
bureaucratically organized commonweal organizations will develop
interests in their expansion and perpetuation at the possible expense
of benefits to the public-at-large. However, they do not hold with
Weber that there is a fundamental inconsistency between the requirements of democracy and those of bureaucracy.

Democracy

Blau's and Scott's divergence from Weber with respect to the
interpretation of the place of bureaucracy in a democratic order is
rooted in different conceptions of democracy. While Weber defined
democracy as progressive equalization of power and popular control
over public decisions, Blau and Scott view the democratic state as an
example of a mutual benefit association. This shift is significant in
two ways. First, it shows in bold lines the revolution in political
theory worked by organization theory. Second, it illustrates the
movement from a manipulatory to an assimilatory idea of democracy.

Organization Theory   The effects of organization theory can be
observed by noting that in classical political theory the study of
politics was considered the "master science," and the state or polity
was viewed as the framework for social living. Political philosophy
was a synonym for social philosophy. The study of politics was
deemed so important because the state was considered an all-
inclusive unit of social living and the law was considered the most
rational expression of order in social living. With the rise of

capitalism economics gained a brief priority over political science. Marx, who organized other human activities around the mode of producing goods, represented the eclipse of political science by economics.

In the twentieth century, both economics and political science have been revalued by the general theory of organizations. The democratic state can be discussed as one example of a mutual benefit association and the business concern can be viewed as a kind of bureaucratic organization. The revolution wrought by organization theory was anticipated by Weber, who held that sociologically the state cannot be defined by its function: "There is scarcely any task that some political association has not taken in hand, and there is no task that one could say has always been exclusive and peculiar to those associations which are designated as political ones. . . . "[30] The reduction of the state to a technique for coordinating human activity, which was begun by Weber, has been completed by contemporary organization theorists like Blau and Scott.

Assimilatory Democracy While Weber was not a great partisan for democracy and did not believe that it could be realized in any thoroughgoing way, he interpreted democracy as a process of active control by the public over its conditions of life—the public manipulates the government. The twin ideas of equalization of power and popular direction of public affairs were at the heart of the democratic movement.

For Blau and Scott, the people in a democracy are consumers of political outputs rather than producers of political decisions—the public assimilates the effects of democracy. Since the democratic state is organized like a mutual benefit association, it has the "double purpose of remaining strong enough to survive and yet maintaining the freedoms that permit the democratic establishment of common objectives."[31] In contemporary democracies this dilemma appears in the concrete form of an antinomy between security and civil liberties. In part, democratic states are combat organizations which work to defend members from external threats and advance their interests in external relations. Like other combat organizations they must maintain internal security and a measure of unity. However, their members must be permitted some freedom to oversee governmental actions, or public benefits are likely to be sacrificed to private interest. Blau and Scott remark that no definitive solution of this dilemma is possible and that attempts to resolve it "tend to sacrifice one purpose for the other and thus endanger the very nature of democratic societies."[32]

Perhaps the problem is that the democratic state is not a mutual benefit association. This does not mean that the state must be elevated to a position that makes it superior to other organizations. Rather, it means that William James and Max Weber were correct in insisting that the state, democratic or not, has no intrinsic function. Perhaps the central dynamic of democratic politics is conflict over what functions should be performed by various organizations and how these functions should be performed. The democratic state can be viewed as a mutual benefit association only by stretching the concept of benefit to mean the good life. While Blau and Scott advanced political theory by making the democratic state an example of a type of organization rather than the archetype for all organizations, they erred in according the state a definite function. The democratic state is not necessarily a succession of majorities ordering bureaucrats to perform services while attempting to control abuses of power by their supposed servants. The democratic state, like any state, is an organizational technology which can be used to perform many functions. However, as long as the image of democracy as a confrontation between willful masters and rebellious servants forms the background for discourse, the dilemmas discovered by Blau and Scott will plague political theory.

HERBERT A. SIMON

One of the most impressive developments of organization theory has been undertaken by Herbert A. Simon. Generalizing from Weber's discussion of bureaucracy, Simon writes that "the term *organization* refers to the complex pattern of communications and other relations in a group of human beings."[33] For Simon, this pattern provides each participant in the organization with the information, assumptions, goals, and attitudes which enable him to make decisions. Further, the organization insures a degree of stable behavior among its members, which provides each participant with a ground for his decisions. Simon's view of organizations develops Weber's ideas about bureaucratic rationality rather than his notions of structural dilemmas. The organization itself resembles a process of thought.

Premises of Decisions

Simon states that the basic unanalyzable unit of organization theory is the premise on which a decision is based. A large number of premises determine every significant organizational decision, and the task of the organization theorist is to describe the processes through which premises are limited in organizations. Simon differentiates value premises from factual premises. Every decision involves selection of a goal from the set of all possible goals. Insofar as decisions are oriented toward the selection of goals they are value judgments. Value premises state the goals that administrative activity is supposed to realize. Every decision also involves the selection of means to attain the goals that have been set. Insofar as decisions are oriented towards the selection of means they are factual judgments. Factual premises state the legitimate means to attain organizational goals. Like Weber, Simon strictly distinguishes among value premises and factual premises.

The basic value criteria

> that will be employed in making decisions and choices among alternatives in an organization will be selected for the organization primarily by the controlling group—the group that has the power to set the terms of membership for all participants.[34]

Whatever group controls the organization will attempt to maximize fulfillment of its private interest. Thus, political activity is rooted in private interest rather than public function.

The Business Concern as Paradigm

This position resembles Weber's idea that bureaucracies are controlled by interest groups and diverges from Blau's and Scott's classification of organizations according to the *cui bono* criterion. Rather than attempting to find out who is supposed to benefit from the functioning of an organization, Simon tries to determine who sets the value premises within the organization. Thus, Simon takes the business concern as the paradigm for all organizations. The exploitation of the organization for the private interest of the controlling group is limited by the need of the controlling group to offer incentives for participation in the organization. The controlling group desires to have the organization function according to the criterion of efficiency. Efficiency demands that

> of two alternatives having the same cost, that one be chosen which will lead to the greater attainment of the organization objectives; and that, of two alternatives leading to the same degree of attainment, that one be chosen which entails the lesser cost.[35]

In order to attain efficiency, the controlling group must provide employees with factual premises that are useful in the attainment of organizational goals and motivate employees to act on these premises. This requires a system of authority, or regularized channels of communication and a regularized system of rewards and punishments.

Unlike Weber, Simon does not believe that any one basis of authority is particularly important in contemporary organizations. An authority relation is simply one in which the subordinate "holds in abeyance his own critical faculties for choosing between alternatives and uses the formal criterion of the receipt of a command or signal as his basis for choice."[36] Among the many grounds for obedience are fear of disapproval, psychological identification with a leader, expectation of material reward, unwillingness to accept responsibility, and judgment that obedience will further realization of an organizational goal. The functions of authority are enforcing responsibility of the functionary to the controlling group, securing expertise in decision making, and coordinating activities towards the attainment of organizational goals. Following Weber's description of bureaucracy, Simon states that each authority relation covers a restricted area of acceptance.

Simon and Weber

Simon makes two important revisions of Weber's theory of bureaucracy. First, he recognizes the existence of "informal organizations" within the formal organization. An informal organization is a pattern of interpersonal relations within an organization that affects decisions within it but is omitted from the formal scheme or is inconsistent with that scheme. Informal organizations frequently arise to protect employee interests from the demands of the controlling group. However, they may also be a means for providing more accurate factual premises when the formal organization is inefficient. In either case, the idea of informal organization is a corrective to the distortions contained in the mechanistic image of the life order. The functionary is usually not completely overwhelmed by the organizational structure.

Simon's second revision of Weber's theory comprises an attack on the idea of organizational rationality. Although the groups that control organizations aim at efficient administration, their ability to rationalize operations is severely limited by incomplete information. Simon contrasts the rational man of economic theory with administrative man. Economic man maximizes utility by selecting the most efficient means available to him for the realization of his goals. He requires a consistent hierarchy of goals and complete information about his alternatives of action. Administrative man "satisfices," or selects a course of action that he believes will satisfy some of his desires. He realizes that he has neither complete knowledge of his own goals nor complete information about his alternatives of action. Further, he realizes that there is a basic indeterminacy built into human relations due to the fact his actions are partly determined by his expectations of what others will do, while their actions are partly determined by their expectations of what he will do. While economic man "deals with the 'real world' in all its complexity, administrative man recognizes that the world he perceives is a drastically simplified model of the buzzing, blooming confusion that constitutes the real world."[37]

For administrative man, there will always be limits on the extent to which organizational activity can be rationalized. Simon's discussion of the limits of rationality and the character of administrative man provides a second necessary corrective to images of an inexorable life order. These descriptions of informal organization and administrative man should be kept in mind during the following discussion of existential critics of the contemporary organization.

WILLIAM H. WHYTE AND DAVID RIESMAN

After World War II the critique of existence in large bureaucratic organizations was introduced into American political thought by William H. Whyte and David Riesman. In their works themes from existentialism and political sociology were combined with a concern for the individuality of the functionary. Essentially, Whyte and Riesman democratized the German existentialism of Jaspers and Weber by attempting to make authentic existence or the political vocation accessible to all members of the organization. The cult of the existential leader was replaced by worship of the authentic common man.

The Protestant Ethic and the Social Ethic

In *The Organization Man* Whyte distinguished between the Protestant Ethic and the Social Ethic. The core of the Protestant Ethic is the pursuit of individual salvation through hard work, thrift, and competitive struggle. The Protestant Ethic approved the struggle against one's environment and was founded on the principle that self-seeking results in the greatest good for the greatest number. Whyte observes that the dominance of the Protestant Ethic occurs in periods of early capitalism and industrialization. While in the West it is associated with some varieties of Protestant religious life, its principles are independent of religious thought. The Protestant Ethic functioned to speed the growth of capitalist enterprise. It provided a "degree of unity between the way people wanted to behave and the way they thought they *ought* to behave, and without this ideology, society would have been hostile to the entrepreneur."[38] The Protestant Ethic kept the businessman morally confident. However, as capitalism entered a phase of maturity the Protestant Ethic began to diverge more and more from the facts of social organization and developing currents of thought in the culture. The expansion of bureaucratic organizations created a new environment for work characterized by security of tenure and regularized procedures for promotion and carrying on functions. Thrift, self-reliance, and enterprise are virtues that have little use in contemporary bureaucratic organizations. Thus, as complex organizations created a new reality, a new ethic arose to rationalize the emerging conditions and secure their dominance.

The Social Ethic is "that contemporary body of thought which makes morally legitimate the pressures of society against the individual."[39] It is defined by three major propositions: "a belief in the group as the source of creativity; a belief in 'belongingness' as the ultimate need of the individual; and a belief in the application of science to achieve the belongingness."[40] The Social Ethic deemphasizes conflict and competition, and teaches that the source of conflict is misunderstanding or breakdown in communications. The organization man, who believes this ethic and attempts to act upon it is "imprisoned in brotherhood." Whyte is concerned to point out that the basis of the Social Ethic is not conformity but a sense of moral imperative. Thus, it is not quite equivalent to notions of mass man or "the One." Those who adhere to the Social Ethic believe that one ought to renounce one's independence to secure the integrity of the group. The organization man is less a flaccid conformist than a devotee of the organization.

The Social Ethic Refuted

In opposition to the Social Ethic, Whyte places the idea of "individualism *within* organization life." He remarks that precisely because the contemporary era is an age of organization, resistance to bureaucracies must be emphasized rather than cooperation with them. He regards as the greatest single mistake of the Social Ethic its principle that there is no necessary conflict between the individual and the organization. Belief in this principle robs the individual of his intellectual armor and prevents him from discovering the areas in which he can assert himself against the organization. Whyte diagnoses the problems of organizational life as primarily problems of thought. The faults of an organizational society are not in the organizations themselves, but in human worship of them. At bottom, the organization man is the result of "our vain quest for a utopian equilibrium, which would be horrible if it ever did come to pass; it is in the soft-minded denial that there is a conflict between the individual and society."[41] The tough-minded alternative to the Social Ethic is a heroic adherence to standards independent of organizational maintenance. The individual must fight for his projects within the organization and win his creativity in opposition to the group. The organization man must become Weber's political man.

The severe problem with Whyte's discussion is his assumption that the problems of organizational life are primarily difficulties of thought. While the ideological component of human existence may not be fully reducible to the organizational or technological components, it is certainly related to them in deep-seated ways. It is unlikely that the dominance of the Social Ethic is not functional for the persistence and extension of large bureaucratic organizations. Widespread ideologies usually have structural supports. This insight is the contribution of Dewey's pragmatic sociology of knowledge. Whyte's "individualism *within* organization life" is likely to change very little unless significant structural changes are brought about. Weber and Jaspers may have been too harsh in their descriptions of the inexorable life order and the way it determines thought, but Whyte errs in the other direction. Existentialism cannot be democratized by playing down the importance of bureaucratic organization as an independent variable.

Riesman's Approach

The Other-Directed Man David Riesman and his associates have presented a slightly different existential approach to contemporary society in *The Lonely Crowd.* Riesman distinguishes among tradition-directed, inner-directed, and other-directed characters. The tradition-directed personality acts roughly according to Weber's principle of traditional legitimation; the inner-directed personality is motivated by something similar to what Whyte describes as the Protestant Ethic; and the other-directed personality is influenced by norms resembling Hocking's lateral corroboration. Riesman claims that the kind of person who finds his standards of behavior in the judgments of the groups with which he is associated is becoming more and more prevalent in contemporary societies characterized by high levels of consumption.

For Riesman, the politics of the other-directed man is the politics of veto groups, or interest groups. In the world of the Protestant Ethic, or the inner-directed man, clear-cut power structures create a clarity of goals. The power structure confronted by other-directed man is amorphous. There are neither leadership groups nor groups of the led. The contemporary substitute for leadership is "a series of groups, each of which has struggled for and finally attained a power to stop things conceivably inimical to its interests and, within far narrower limits, to start things."[42] These veto groups engage in monopolistic competition, making sure that they do nothing to endanger their positions. Their rivalries are limited by self-protective codes of fair practice and the few serious conflicts are usually ended by "negotiation, the division of territory, and the formation of a roof organization for the previously split constituency."[43] In Simon's terms, veto groups satisfice rather than maximize, but in the process of satisficing they deaden individual initiative. They are defense groups, not leadership groups, and defense is the appropriate posture for people oriented to adjustment and consumption. The other-directed person has no authentic commitment to a political role or a political cause. He is related to politics through veto groups and he "leaves it to the group to defend his interests, cooperating when called on to vote, to apply pressure, and so on."[44]

The Autonomous Man In opposition to the other-directed person who compulsively adjusts to his social order, Riesman places the autonomous man. He defines autonomous people as "those who on the whole are capable of conforming, to the behavioral norms of their society . . . but are free to choose whether to conform or not."[45] In the present era the autonomous person will realize that his possibilities reside in changing his life style and character within the middle class rather than in entering a new class or working changes in the social structure itself. Riesman compares his notion of autonomy with the existentialist idea of authentic existence, but warns that he does not agree that authentic existence only belongs to the few heroic men. The set of autonomous people is not equivalent to the set of heroic people. The autonomous person is one who is always able to ask, "Is this what I really want?" Riesman pins his hope on a revolution of heightened self-consciousness through which people will come to recognize and respect their own feelings, potentialities, and limitations, and be able to make decisions on the basis of standards independent of shifting group norms. He would attack the deadening effects of satisficing veto groups indirectly. If enough people become autonomous and are not "strait-jacketed before they get started—by the elaboration and forced feeding of a set of official doctrines—people may some day learn to buy not only packages of groceries or books but the larger package of a neighborhood, a society, and a way of life."[46]

Like Whyte, Riesman shows the deficiencies of an existential analysis of political existence. By stressing individualism, autonomy, or authentic existence, existential analysts lose sight of the other two components of the three-sided relationship that makes up political life. Authentic existence will neither banish the indirect consequences of human activity nor dissolve the cultural environment.

Whyte and Riesman use existentialism to make slight correctives in a social order that they consider fundamentally unchangeable. For Whyte, it is not the organization as a cultural technique for organizing power that is at fault, but worship of the organization. For Riesman, the challenge of contemporary existence is to create new and exciting life styles within the middle class. By making the leader into the authentic common man, Riesman and Whyte do not succeed in converting existentialism into a self-sufficient political philosophy. Of course, this does not mean that the quest for autonomy must be abandoned. On the contrary, autonomy remains one of the three requisites—along with harmonious social relations and access to civilization—of a good political existence.

ORGANIZATION THEORY IN REVIEW

Organization theory is one of the four important post-Marxist schools of formal political thought. The significant contribution of organization theorists is to show that the concept of organization itself is more basic than such examples of organization as particular economic systems or types of political order. Organizations contain both dominative and reciprocal relations among human beings. Cross sections of activity are characterized as either organized or disbanded. Organization theory constitutes a revolution in political thought in that traditional political theory distinguishes the state from other associations as the container of all social existence while in organization theory the state is seen as merely one of many organizations, performing functions that cannot be determined prior to observation. Organization theory is closely related to existentialism in that it takes the life order, or the bureaucratic social technology, as a decisive aspect of the contemporary public situation.

Max Weber, the most important organization theorist, combined many themes in his work. Among the most important of these themes are the ideas that organizations confront structural dilemmas, that bureaucratic organization is a technology to rationalize collective activities, and that bureaucratic organization poses a threat to the personal autonomy of both the functionary and the client. In recent American organization theory these three ideas have been developed by different writers. Peter M. Blau and W. Richard Scott have given detailed consideration to the notion of structural dilemmas; Herbert Simon has discussed the limits of bureaucratic rationality; and William Whyte and David Riesman have described the threats to individuality and authentic existence posed by contemporary organizations. One of the most important tasks of future organization theorists will be to resynthesize the aspects of Weber's thought that have become separated.

Like pluralism, organization theory is not self-sufficient. Organizations are grounded in cross sections of activity. In Buchler's terms they are visible communities which depend upon invisible communities for their maintenance and development. Further, organizations are characterized by stratification systems which frequently determine their other characteristics. These stratification systems are the focus of attention for theorists of political elites.

NOTES

1. Edward A. Tiryakian, *Sociologism and Existentialism* (Englewood Cliffs, N.J.: Prentice-Hall, Inc., 1962), p. 152.

2. Herbert Kaufman, "Organization Theory and Political Theory," *American Political Science Review,* 58 (March 1964): 5–14.

3. Karl Jaspers, *Man in the Modern Age* (Garden City, N.Y.: Doubleday & Company, Inc., Anchor Books, 1957), p. 165.

4. Ibid., p. 166.

5. Ibid.

6. Max Rheinstein, ed., *Max Weber on Law in Economy and Society* (New York: Simon & Schuster, Inc., 1967), p. 1.

7. Ibid., p. 2.

8. Karl Marx and Friedrich Engels, *The Communist Manifesto* (New York: Meredith Corporation, Appleton-Century-Crofts, 1955), p. 5.

9. Rheinstein, *Max Weber,* p. 9.

10. David E. Willer, "Max Weber's Missing Authority Type," *Sociological Inquiry,* 37 (Spring 1967): 263.

11. Rheinstein, *Max Weber,* p. 9.

12. H. H. Gerth and C. Wright Mills, *From Max Weber* (New York: Oxford University Press, Inc., 1958), p. 199.

13. Ibid., p. 228.

14. Ibid.

15. Ibid.

16. Ibid.

17. Ibid.

18. Ibid., p. 203.

19. Ibid., p. 231.

20. Ibid., p. 110.

21. Ibid., p. 230.

22. Ibid., p. 94.

23. Ibid., p. 230.

24. Ferdinand Kolegar, "The Concept of 'Rationalization' and Cultural Pessimism in Max Weber's Sociology," *The Sociological Quarterly,* 5 (Autumn 1964): 370, 365.

25. Ibid., 365.

26. Gerth and Mills, *From Max Weber,* p. 115.

27. Ibid., p. 124.

28. Peter M. Blau and W. Richard Scott, *Formal Organizations* (San Francisco: Chandler Publishing Co., 1962), p. 52.

29. Ibid., p. 55.

30. Gerth and Mills, *From Max Weber,* p. 77.

31. Blau and Scott, *Formal Organizations,* p. 253.

32. Ibid.

33. Herbert A. Simon, *Administrative Behavior* (New York: The Macmillan Company, 1960), p. xvi.

34. Ibid., p. 118.

35. Ibid., p. 122.

36. Ibid., pp. 126–127.

37. Ibid., p. xxv.

38. William H. Whyte, Jr., *The Organization Man* (Garden City, N.Y.: Doubleday & Company, Inc., Anchor Books, 1957), p. 18.

39. Ibid., p. 7.

40. Ibid.

41. Ibid., p. 14.

42. David Riesman, with Nathan Glazer and Reuel Denney, *The Lonely Crowd* (New Haven: Yale University Press, 1961), p. 213.

43. Ibid., p. 214.

44. Ibid., p. 223.

45. Ibid., p. 242.

46. Ibid., pp. 306–307.

SUGGESTED READINGS

Barnard, Chester I. *The Functions of the Executive.* Cambridge, Mass.: Harvard University Press, 1938.

Blau, Peter M. *Exchange and Power in Social Life.* New York: John Wiley & Sons, Inc., 1967.

Durkheim, Emile. *The Division of Labor in Society.* Glencoe, Ill.: Free Press of Glencoe, Ill., 1947.

Etzioni, Amitai, ed. *Complex Organizations.* New York: Holt, Rinehart & Winston, Inc., 1961.

Gouldner, Alvin W. *Studies in Leadership.* New York: Harper & Bros., 1950.

Martindale, Don. *Institutions, Organizations, and Mass Society.* Boston: Houghton Mifflin Company, 1966.

Merton, Robert K. *Social Theory and Social Structure.* Glencoe, Ill.: Free Press of Glencoe, Ill., 1957.

Parsons, Talcott. *Structure and Process in Modern Societies.* Glencoe, Ill.: Free Press of Glencoe, Ill., 1960.

Presthus, Robert. *The Organizational Society.* New York: Alfred A. Knopf, Inc., 1962.

Thompson, Victor A. *Modern Organization.* New York: Alfred A. Knopf, Inc., 1961.

CHAPTER SEVEN

THE THEORY
OF POLITICAL ELITES

The movement in political theory that corresponds most to civilized humanism is the theory of political elites. While pluralist theories introduced the notion of cross section of activity into contemporary political thought and existentialist theories described how these cross sections of activity are organized, theories of political elites contribute discussions of human differentiation within organized cross sections of activity.

EARLY THEORY OF POLITICAL ELITES

Saint-Simon

The origins of the modern theory of political elites can be traced to the work of the French political philosopher Saint-Simon in the early nineteenth century. Gaetano Mosca remarks that the principles of the modern theory of political elites are first "traced in a fairly definite and clear-cut fashion . . . in the writings of Saint-Simon."[1] Mosca observes that Saint-Simon makes two particularly important contributions to the theory of political elites. First, he distinguishes among medieval and industrialized societies on the basis of the character of their ruling classes. In medieval society priests and military leaders controlled decision-making processes, while in industrialized societies scientists and managers gained ascendancy. Second, Saint-Simon asserts that the ruling class in a society "has to possess the requisites and aptitudes most necessary to social leadership at a given time and in a given type of civilization."[2] Sereno observes that Saint-Simon was the first Western intellectual to state that control of the instruments of production in a society is the basic determinant of political power.[3]

Aside from his contributions to descriptive political science, Saint-Simon also enunciates a political ideal that has actuated many people in the modern world, particularly civilized humanists. He urges the formation of a new social order in which capacity to perform social functions rather than birth or possession of property would entitle one to share control in the management of public services. Saint-Simon uses the term "political science" to characterize the systematic description of social existence. In the final analysis, he recommends rule by political scientists. He advocates "the placing of the control of the material destiny of society in the hands of technological experts, of social engineers who could master and apply the dictates of the new social science."[4] The idea that experts should rule recurs frequently in Western intellectual history after Saint-Simon. At present, it is best represented by civilized humanists who call for increasing the autonomy of professionals in all sectors of the society. Of course, Saint-Simon's idea that an elite of experts should rule can be detached from the goal of a systematic political science and the doctrine that every society has a ruling class. Just such a separation was carried out at the turn of the twentieth century by theorists of political elites who accepted much of Saint-Simon's descriptive theory while rejecting his hierarchical socialism.

Karl Marx

Apart from Saint-Simon, who may be considered one of the founders of modern political science, the intellectual who exerted the greatest influence on modern elite theory was Karl Marx. Like the existentialists and the pluralists, theorists of political elites generalized some of Marx' concepts. While one of the prime motivations behind elite theory at the turn of the twentieth century was opposition to Marxist ideology, this opposition did not prevent theorists of political elites from using Marx' writings as a basis for their own constructive work. As in the case of Saint-Simon, it is vital to distinguish between descriptions and prescriptions. While theorists of political elites took over much of Marx' descriptive analysis, they abhorred his preference for socialism.

Class Struggle The elements of Marx' theory of political elites are found in *The Communist Manifesto,* first published in 1848. In the preface to the English edition of 1888, Friedrich Engels states that the fundamental proposition of the Manifesto is that "the whole history of mankind (since the dissolution of primitive tribal society, holding land in common ownership) has been a history of class struggles, contests between exploiting and exploited, ruling and oppressed classes."[5] For Marx, these classes were defined by the mode of economic production and exchange that prevailed in a society. The history of struggles between classes formed "a series of evolutions" in which ruling classes were successively displaced by classes representing progressive modes of production and exchange.

Marx held that in modern society, the bourgeoisie, which owned productive property, had "conquered for itself, in the modern representative state, exclusive political sway." In a famous passage, Marx and Engels assert that the "executive of the modern state is but a committee for managing the common affairs of the whole bourgeoisie."[6] Past historical movements consisted in one minority replacing another minority as the ruling class in a society. However, the movement of the proletariat against the bourgeoisie is a movement of the immense majority in the interest of the immense majority.

Marx and Engels take a strong position in deriving political activity from private interest. They claim that political power, "properly so called, is merely the organized power of one class for oppressing another."[7] Thus, in the past ruling classes have not performed a public function. They have governed in their various private interests. Marx and Engels argue that when class distinctions have been eliminated "and all production has been concentrated in the hands of a vast association of the whole nation, the public power will lose its political character."[8] The rational coordination of things will replace the exploitation of people. Marx and Engels do not dispute that elites in the past have provided social coordination. However, they argue that this coordination was principled towards maximizing socially available values for the ruling class.

Political Ideas   For Marx and Engels, political ideas are expressions of class interest. In the *Manifesto,* they pose a question that has disturbed political thinkers ever since: "Does it require deep intuition to comprehend that man's ideas, views, and conceptions, in one word, man's consciousness, changes with every change in the conditions of his material existence, in his social relations and in his social life?"[9] They answer the question succinctly: "The ruling ideas of each age have ever been the ideas of its ruling class."[10] Ideas do not revolutionize society. Rather, ideas are born of social conditions and express both the goals and legitimations of contending social classes.

Marx and Engels recognize one fact that underlies the various ideas about society that have appeared in the past—one part of society has always exploited the others. In light of this fact, the social function of political ideas can be stated. Political ideas are either weapons of an ascending class bidding for power or tools of a regnant class extending or defending its claims to socially available values.

As an extension of this concept of political ideas, Marx derives political activity from private interest. Theorists of political elites, however, maintain a tension between public function and private interest. They hold that political elites must perform some actual social functions to maintain their rule. At a minimum they must maintain order within the society. In fact, by definition, if they do not maintain order they will cease to rule. Much of the work of theorists of political elites is devoted to discovering how elites manage to maintain order within societies.

Public Function and Private Interest

Among the early theorists of political elites, Robert Michels placed the greatest emphasis on the social functions performed by ruling classes. Michels argued that ruling classes, or oligarchies, were inevitable in modern complex societies simply to perform the function of coordinating activities widely extended in space and time. He claimed that the "extensive division of labor in modern civilized society, which renders it more and more impossible to embrace in a single glance the totality of the political organization of the state and its ever more complicated mechanism," and the "profound differences of culture and education among the members" of contemporary societies, "give to the need for leadership felt by the masses a continually increasing dynamic tendency."[11] While Michels stated the oligarchies tend to acquire an overriding interest in the continuation and extension of their dominance, he also cautioned that the ground of this dominance was in the performance of the social functions of maintaining order and providing coordination of disparate activities. Thus, the structural analysis presented by theorists of political elites looks two ways. One can study elites with a view toward determining their contributions to maintaining order and coordinating activities within a society, and one can also study elites with a view toward determining how they extend and maintain their control over socially available values.

The duality in the structural analysis of theorists of political elites is present as a fundamental distinction throughout twentieth-century political theory. In Dewey it takes the form of a tension between the ideas of the contemporary state as instrument of dominant economic interests and as tender of the indirect consequences of human activity. In the civilized humanists it takes the form of a tension between the ideas of the contemporary state as instrument of powerful interest groups and as defender of civilization. The existentialists follow the civilized humanists in their treatment of the duality between public function and private interest. For theorists of political elites, the duality is presented as a tragic dilemma that is ever present in political life. The description of the dilemma follows the outlines of Michels' discussion of the social functions of oligarchy. In complex societies, characterized by extensive division of labor and specialization, there is a need for specialized structures and groups through which the functions of maintaining order and coordinating diverse activities can be performed. However, that group which has the power to perform the functions of maintenance and coordination will tend to use that power to extend its control over socially available values. It will use force, exchange, and fraud to maintain and enhance its advantages, and it will attempt to make these advantages cumulative. If the elite scrupulously fulfills its social functions it will sacrifice some opportunities for gaining socially available values. If the elite uses its power strictly for extending its advantages it will fail to perform its social function. This tension between private interest and public function is not resolved by theorists of political elites. However, by fixing attention on the duality of political activity they avoid the mistakes of seizing either horn of the dilemma.

ELITE THEORY AND MARXISM

Monistic Theory

Marxian analysis provided theorists of political elites with two central ideas. First, theorists of political elites adopted the idea that every society is characterized by a ruling class which attempts to maximize control of socially available values. Second, they developed the conception that political ideas are weapons in the combat between contending social groupings. However, the differences between Marxian analysis and theories of political elites are even more significant than the similarities. In his essay about Vilfredo Pareto, who was one of the leading theorists of political elites, S. E. Finer remarks that it is best to regard Pareto's work "not as the last of the 'great systems', but as an anti-system: a system to kill all systems."[12] Finer observes that Pareto was instrumental in defeating the quest for monistic theories of social change, such as that of Marx. He notes that both Pareto and Bentley were key figures in developing a modern political analysis marked by "a model of classes, groupings, sections and strata interacting upon one another, with policies as the result."[13]

While Finer is correct that theorists of political elites abandoned the search for monistic theories of society and joined with the pluralists in adopting the cross section of activity as a fundamental unit of analysis, they did much more than rebel against systems and argue in favor of multivariate causation. Like Bentley and Weber, the theorists of political elites formalized important parts of Marxist theory.

Cross Section, Social Type, and Political Formula

Rejecting the centrality of economic variables for a general theory of political activity, the theorists of political elites developed three important concepts. Their idea of ruling class as a dominant and organized cross section of activity resembles elements in the theories of Bentley and Weber. Theorists of political elites did not assume a priori that the dominant activity in a society is always economic. They left the content of the dominant cross section or cross sections of activity open to empirical investigation. However, they preserved the Marxist ideas that the history of mankind has been a history of struggles between ruling and ruled classes, and that past historical movements have consisted in one minority replacing another minority as the ruling class in a society. While the primary contribution of pluralism is the concept of cross section of activity and the significant contribution of existential sociology is the concept of organization, theories of political elites contribute the idea of the dominance of one or more cross sections of activity over others.

The second important concept developed by theorists of political elites is that of social type. While Marx and Engels held that each mode of organizing the means of production in a society gave rise to a different range of personality types, theorists of political elites argued that each set of dominant cross sections of activity conditioned a different range of social characters. The social type, or the character adapted to and typical of a specific mode of social organization, represents a formalization of Marx' suggestions about the relations between culture and personality.

The third significant concept developed by theorists of political elites is that of political formula. Here the Marxian idea that the "ruling ideas of each age have ever been the ideas of its ruling class" was transformed into the doctrine that ideas legitimating the dominant cross sections of activity in a society tend to be the most important political ideas in that society. As the idolon of the civilized humanists was the compact way of expressing the central values of a civilization, the political formula of theorists of political elites is a concept denoting the essence of justifications of dominance presented by ruling classes. In developing the ideas of dominant cross sections of activity, social type, and political formula, theorists of political elites completed the formalization of political science undertaken independently by pluralists and theorists of organizations.

Reaction to Marx

While Bentley and Weber revised Marx' work, the theorists of political elites reacted against it with vehemence. Jean-Paul Sartre has claimed that we live in the age of Marx, and that no one can surpass his political analysis. Under this interpretation, theorists of political elites are reactionaries. They represent a bourgeoisie in the posture of defense. Their doctrine of the multivariate causation of political events is an attempt to disguise the class struggle with trivial complexities. Their firm distinction between elite and mass is a way of discouraging progressive social action. Their structural dilemma between public function and private interest is a way of justifying the status quo. Their formalism is an attempt to eternalize a moment in the history of class struggles.

This kind of analysis is at variance with the central ideas of the present study. While theorists of political elites clearly reacted to Marx, they did not merely restate the claims of bourgeois theorists who preceded and followed Marx. Their reaction was special in that it adopted both structural analysis and the sociology of knowledge. In one important way, theorists of political elites surpassed Marx. They rejected the idea that economic class is the primary variable in political analysis and proposed, along with pluralists and existential sociologists, that political theorists study the general principles of all organization. While Marx proclaimed the centrality of property ownership, theorists of political elites stressed the importance of domination and coordination of human beings and resources what-ever the mode of property ownership. Marx organized around the economic system all the other zones of social existence, but theorists of political elites found in each zone of social existence the unifying factor of organization. Furthermore, unlike Marx—who was oriented toward the content of a particular historical period—theorists of political elites attempted to isolate the ultimate forms of political relation.

In emphasizing their attempts to create a political phenome-nology, one should not conclude that theorists of political elites believed that all cross sections of human activity are equally important in determining political events or that political scientists cannot justify investigating some cross sections of human activity rather than others. For the purposes of a pure phenomenology of politics hair styling is just as important as munitions manufacturing. Both are cross sections of activity and both can be represented in political activity. However, while the naïveté of the pure phenome-nologist is indispensable for describing the fundamental units of political analysis, the same naïveté is fatal in the empirical investi-gation of political events. The political scientist who believes that he can take any set of cross sections of activity and investigate their interrelations has missed his calling. The formalization of political science is not a carte blanche for irresponsibility in the choice of subject matter for investigation.

GAETANO MOSCA

Gaetano Mosca was the seminal theorist of political elites. In his writings, he developed all of the themes characteristic of the theory of political elites and coined the terms *social type* and *political formula.* Mosca based his theorizing on the principle that in

> all societies—from societies that are very meagerly developed and have barely attained the dawnings of civilization, down to the most advanced and powerful societies—two classes of people appear—a class that rules and a class that is ruled.[14]

The ruling class is always a minority, performs all political functions, monopolizes power, and maximizes its enjoyment of socially available values. The class of the ruled, or the mass, is controlled by the rulers and supplies them with their means to dominance.

Ruling Class

Mosca compares the principle that all societies are divided into ruling class and mass with two other principles that appear to be important in political existence. The first principle is that in every political system one member of the ruling class is chief among the other leaders. Mosca remarks that this principle is relatively unimportant because no single person can govern a state without the support of a class that enforces respect for his orders and administers his policies. The second principle is that in every political system pressures that stem from the masses exert some influence on the policies of the ruling class. Mosca observes that even if the masses are in some cases powerful enough to depose one ruling class, a new ruling class will take the place of the old one. Demonstrating his affinity to civilized humanism, Mosca holds that from the viewpoint of

> scientific research the real superiority of the concept of the ruling, or political, class lies in the fact that the varying structure of ruling classes has a preponderant importance in determining the political type, and also the level of civilization, of the different peoples.[15]

Organization Mosca bases the dominance of ruling classes over masses on superior organization. While it may superficially appear as though majorities rule in contemporary industrialized societies, the ascendancy of organized minorities, actuated by single principles, over unorganized majorities is inevitable. Mosca observes that the power of organized minorities is employed against single individuals in the majority. The common man "who stands alone before the totality of the organized minority" is helpless.

The importance that Mosca accords to organization relates his work to that of Weber and the other organization theorists. However, Mosca's work also resembles pluralist theories in its emphasis on the cross section of activity as a fundamental unit of analysis. Mosca notes that organization itself is not sufficient to account for the dominance of one kind of ruling class rather than another. He calls upon the notion of political forces to complete his general theory. In every society there are various sources of wealth, different kinds of knowledge, various currents of ideas and religious beliefs, and other means to activity. Around each means to activity, a "political force" or interest group appears.

Balance of Political Forces   Mosca holds that ruling classes represent the "balance of political forces" in a society. He asserts that whenever there is a shift in the balance of political forces in a society, the composition of the ruling class changes. This is equivalent to Bentley's principle that political activities represent or reflect underlying social activities. However, Mosca adds one significant claim to pluralist thought. He observes that the balance of political forces changes when "a need is felt that capacities different from the old should assert themselves in the management of the state, when the old capacities, therefore, lose some of their importance or changes in their distribution occur." [16]

Here Mosca introduces the tension between public function and private interest characteristic of theories of political elites. While ruling classes monopolize political power and attempt to maximize access to socially available values for their members, they also gain dominance through performing a public function or expressing a capacity in action. Mosca remarks that the

> whole history of civilized mankind comes down to a conflict between the tendency of dominant elements to monopolize political power and transmit possession of it by inheritance, and the tendency toward a dislocation of old forces and an insurgence of new forces. [17]

Ruling classes lose their power when they no longer have a field in which to exercise their capacities, when they have no opportunity to perform the "social services" that they once rendered or when their particular talents and services lose importance in comparison with other capacities.

Public Function   The relationship between public function and private interest is quite subtle. There is a circulation of elites controlled by two social processes working in opposite directions. Already constituted ruling classes that are organized and have channels of access to socially available values attempt to maintain their dominance by marginalizing performance of social function. They are opposed by counterelites that appear in the masses, representing new definitions of social function. However, these new definitions of social function represent particular cross sections of activity around which special interest groups form.

The line between public function and private interest is hopelessly blurred. In their efforts to marginalize performance of public function, ruling classes are blocked by the promises of competitors. This competition forces them either to co-opt members of the opposition and thereby share their dominance, or to perform more public functions. According to this hypothesis, the more competition the more public functions will be performed. This hypothesis can be restated: The performance of public function is maximized when such performance is in the private interest of the ruling class.

Strata Within the Ruling Class   Mosca divides the ruling class into two groups. The first group is the small political elite which makes concrete decisions and declares policy. This elite may be composed of those in the highest formal positions, those who exercise great informal power, or both types. This governing elite is rooted in a second and larger stratum of the ruling class which supports it and from which it is recruited. The people who occupy the highest posts are "more or less imbued with the ideas, sentiments, passions and, therefore, policies of the social strata which come just below them, the strata with which they are in continuous and immediate contact and without which they could not govern."[18]

The second and larger stratum of the ruling class both represents and forms the social type dominant in the particular society. The concept of social type is grounded in the idea of cross section of activity. Mosca holds that every group of persons "that is engaged in a special function has a certain homogeneousness of spirit, education and, especially, interests."[19] The most important cross sections of activity within a society determine the social type dominant in that society.

Social Types   Mosca defines the state as "nothing more than the organization of all social forces that have a political significance."[20] In periods of stability, ruling classes tend to produce a single social type. Every social type has a tendency to form a political system and once a political system has been organized it is used to spread the social type that it expresses. Mosca remarks that when a state is made up of several social types, the ruling class should be recruited only from the dominant type. Where several social types compete for rule, there is likely to be instability. This observation runs counter to Mosca's idea that competition tends to maximize the performance of public function. This inconsistency is perhaps due to Mosca's failure to define clearly any content for public function.

Since public function varies with the social forces that can be represented at a particular place and time, Mosca tends to judge the consequences of human activity in terms of their effects upon the stability of the given political system. The reference to political stability does not logically follow from the historical relativity of public function. Perhaps it is possible to grasp the public functions appropriate to a particular place and time and refer the consequences of human activity to their realization. In any case, even if political stability is the standard of reference for consequences, it is not clear that the ruling class should be recruited only from the dominant social type. Mosca remarks that a civilization can "literally speaking" be immortal if it learns how to transform itself continually without losing a basic integrity. In view of the circulation of elites, this requirement would seem to mean operationally the recruitment of new social types into the ruling class.

The Bureaucrat Like Weber, Mosca holds that the dominant social type of the twentieth century is the bureaucrat, or salaried employee performing specialized services. In terms reminiscent of descriptions of the life order, Mosca remarks that never before in history "has the material life of each single individual been so directly dependent upon the perfect functioning of the whole social mechanism as it is today."[21] In contemporary societies, the functioning of each part of the life order is entrusted to a particular group of specialists. Each one of these groups of specialists, representing a cross section of activity, performs a public function and seeks maximization of private interest. Given this principle, Mosca concludes that the normal functioning of society as a whole is dependent upon the good will of specialized groups organized around cross sections of activity. In view of the rest of Mosca's theory, good will seems to be a weak reed on which to rest political stability. The bureaucrat is actuated less by good will than by specialized competence, and there is no assurance that the activities of different groups of specialists will harmonize. This is the insight of existential sociology and the ground of its emphasis on the leadership of generalists.

In the notion of the bureaucrat as social type is the synthesis of pluralist theory and existential sociology. The bureaucrat expresses a specific cross section of activity, but he expresses it in a way similar to bureaucrats who represent other cross sections of activity. This does not mean that functionaries representing different cross sections of activity do not come into conflict with one another. Instead, it illustrates the point that while Marx organized around the economic system all the other zones of social existence, theorists of political elites found in each zone of social existence the unifying factor of organization.

Ideology

Political Formulas For Mosca, dominant social types that are organized into ruling classes do not "justify their power exclusively by de facto possession of it, but try to find a moral and legal basis for it, representing it as the logical and necessary consequence of doctrines and beliefs that are generally recognized and accepted."[22] The legal and moral basis on which the power of the ruling class is rationalized is the political formula. Political formulas vary according to the level of civilization. Thus, some political formulas give religious justification for rule, while others appear to embody principles of positive science. In neither case is the political formula an accurate representation of the realities of political rule. Mosca remarks that if

> no one has ever seen the authentic document by which the Lord empowered certain privileged persons or families to rule his people on his behalf, neither can it be maintained that a popular election, however liberal the suffrage may be, is ordinarily the expression of the will of a people, or even of the will of the majority of a people.[23]

Despite the fact that political formulas do not accurately represent the facts of political rule, Mosca argues that they are not "mere quackeries aptly invented to trick the masses into obedience." Political formulas function to meet the universally felt need of knowing that one is governed "not on the basis of mere material or intellectual force, but on the basis of a moral principle."[24] Mosca opines that universal illusions are instrumental in unifying whole civilizations. Political formulas have both cognitive and evaluative components. They explain the political organization of society through a myth at the same time that they justify it. Political formulas describe the capacities for social service characteristic of the members of the ruling class and emphasize the virtues typical of the dominant social type.

Mosca believes that the dominant political formulas of the twentieth century are democracy and socialism. Both democracy and socialism serve to legitimate the rule of bureaucratized interest groups. Through the symbols of democracy and socialism bureaucrats can claim that they are experts acting to carry out the orders of the people. Mosca holds that democracy and socialism present absolute political formulas which cloak despotism. He asserts that "the strictly logical application of any single principle in all public law" is an essential element in despotism because it enables "anyone who is in power to exploit the advantages of a superior position more thoroughly for the benefit of his own interests and passions."[25]

Political Science In opposition to the absolute political formulas of democracy and socialism, Mosca places the idea of a political science. Mosca argues that a "realistic" social science must be deployed to demolish the pretensions of socialist metaphysics. Political scientists must discover and demonstrate great constant laws of political activity so that knowledge of the impossibility of realizing the democratic idea will become widespread. In a statement reminiscent of current appeals for an ideology to combat communism, Mosca declares: "A whole metaphysical system must be met with a whole scientific *system.*"[26] Among the fundamental principles of Mosca's purified social science are the doctrine of the inevitability of a ruling class, the plural causation of political events, and the idea that public function is inextricably bound up with private interest.

In addition to a purified social science, Mosca lists three strategies to combat democratic totalitarianism. First, he calls for the creation of a moral and intellectual aristocracy in contemporary societies, whose members would mold the minds of their fellows in the principles of the new social science. Second, Mosca embraces interest group liberalism. He argues that the

> only demand that it is important, and possible, to make of a political system is that all social values shall have a part in it, and that it shall find a place for all who possess any of the qualities which determine what prestige and what influence an individual, or a class, is to have.[27]

In place of rule according to a single principle Mosca favors the adjustment of many principles within the state. Third, Mosca calls for a constitution that would enable all of the important cross sections of activity within contemporary societies to perform public functions maximally. Here Mosca favors a Madisonian regime in which social forces reciprocally check one another through a legal system. Only through such reciprocal checks could responsibility be enforced.

Civilized Humanism

Mosca's doctrine of "juridical defense" and much of his theory of political elites is founded on a philosophy of civilization. For Mosca, the hallmark of civilization is variety. Accompanying the growth of civilization is an increase in the number of cross sections of activity which are capable of becoming social forces and organizing to gain representation in the political system. In order to gain political influence commensurate with its social importance an activity must be organized by an interest group. Attempts to subject the many activities characteristic of advanced civilizations to control in accordance with a single principle will usher in barbarism. Public administration becomes the great civilized art:

> That art, in the last analysis, comes down to enabling a great society, with the least possible constraint, to see to it that the activity which each individual carries on spontaneously for his own advantage shall be useful to the group as a whole.[28]

In this comment, Mosca shows himself to be more than a defender of classical liberal doctrines. Like other twentieth century writers, his work is marked by a repudiation of the classical liberal doctrine that there is an unseen hand assuring that human activities will result in public benefits.

Early in *The Ruling Class* Mosca remarks that the great fallacy of nineteenth-century social theory was the assertion that "an action that is useful to society is generally useful to the individual who performs it and vice versa."[29] Like other twentieth-century political theorists, Mosca holds that the current era must be one of self-conscious realization of collective projects and the barriers to their fulfillment. While his proposals for alleviating the tension between private interest and public function are not original and have been criticized in the discussion of pluralism, his statement of the problem remains significant.

VILFREDO PARETO

The second important theorist of political elites who wrote at the turn of the twentieth century is Vilfredo Pareto. Much of Pareto's political thought is similar to Mosca's speculations, and the two Italian theorists carried on a running conflict over who had discovered the basic principles of the theory of political elites. Like Mosca, Pareto carries out an important revision in Marxist theory. While he writes that the "struggle of some individuals to appropriate the wealth produced by others is the great factor dominating all human history," he is quick to point out that he does not mean that the class struggle as interpreted by Marx is the correct description of political dynamics.[30] Although he recognizes the importance of the class struggle in determining political decisions, he observes that the "struggle is not confined only to two classes: the proletariat and the capitalist; it occurs between an infinite number of groups with different interests, and above all between the elites contending for power."[31] Thus, Pareto makes the cross section of activity a primary unit in his political theory.

Political interest groups, which represent underlying activities, are organizations primarily devoted to spoliation, or forcefully and fraudulently acquiring goods produced by others. Pareto calls the system of interest group domination of contemporary political systems "bourgeois socialism." Under a regime of bourgeois socialism interest groups attempt to influence legislation in such a way that they can "exact tribute from other citizens."[32] Pareto's description of bourgeois socialism is equivalent to Lowi's discussion of interest group liberalism, only it was written more than sixty-five years earlier. This is less proof that writers like Lowi are unoriginal than it is evidence that the basic structure of contemporary Western societies has not altered drastically since the turn of the twentieth century. With respect to political thought, post-Marxist formalism is still regnant.

Elites

Like Mosca, Pareto emphasizes the importance of elite-mass relationships as fundamental to an understanding of contemporary political existence. He begins his discussion with the supposition that in every branch of human activity a grade can be assigned to every individual in the same way that marks are accorded for performance in school. For example, the best doctor might receive a score of ten, while the physician who could not get any clients might receive zero. Or, the confidence man who made a fortune and evaded legal punishment would receive a ten and the "wretched pilferer who snaffles the cutlery in a restaurant and bumps redhanded into the nearest policeman" would receive one.[33] Pareto proceeds to call those people who have the highest indices in a particular branch of activity the elite with respect to that activity. The social elite is made up of all those who have the highest indices in any activity.

Governing and Nongoverning Elites Within the social elite, Pareto distinguishes between governing and nongoverning elites. The governing elite includes the people who directly or indirectly play a significant role in political affairs, and the nongoverning elite includes the people who do not play significant roles in political life. Thus, there are two strata in all populations—the nonelite class and the elite class. The elite class is further divided into governing and nongoverning elites. Pareto remarks that the notion of an elite is dependent upon the qualities that one looks for in it. There are elites of murderers as well as aristocracies of saints. However, he adds that the "totality of qualities promoting the well-being and domination of a class in society constitutes something which we will call simply *the elite.*"[34]

Critique Pareto's discussion of elites is far more ambiguous and defective than Mosca's analysis. In Pareto's argument there is a fundamental ambiguity at the very beginning. The process of assigning an index number to each person performing an activity cannot be done in any clear-cut way for many activities. In the case of activities where success is merely judged by wealth acquired, power exercised, or deference gained, there is no problem. However, in the case of activities where performance of a social function is a criterion of excellence, there is a fatal ambiguity. Is that doctor who gains the most patients or the one who exercises the most skill to be given a "ten"? One cannot assume that skillful performance of social function always gains a just reward. Even in political affairs judgment is not clear-cut. As long as one recognizes a public function for politics one must admit the possibility of a difference between those who gain the most power over decision making and those who are best fit to perform the public function assigned.

A further difficulty in Pareto's discussion follows from his making all cross sections of activity equal for the purposes of empirical analysis rather than theoretical clarification. The social elite of a society cannot be a useful concept if it is defined as that group composed of individuals who rank the highest in the performance of each kind of activity. The elite of house painters can in no way be counted as socially equal with the elite of industrialists. In fact, the least important industrialist is likely to be more socially significant than the most important house painter. Thus, Pareto's failure to define politically relevant cross sections of activity makes his theory even more defective.

The distinction between governing and nongoverning elites is much less useful than Mosca's distinction between two strata in the ruling class. Mosca's elite of the politically powerful is equivalent to Pareto's governing elite. However, the second stratum of Mosca's ruling class is defined by representatives of politically relevant social forces. This stratum supports the elite of the politically powerful and provides the base for its recruitment. Pareto's nongoverning elite does not perform either function of Mosca's second stratum. In fact, one would be hard pressed to discover what function it does serve. While Mosca holds public function and private interest in delicate tension, Pareto fails to distinguish between them. The weakness of his discussion of elites is the penalty that he pays for failing to make this distinction.

Circulation of Elites

Pareto's major contribution to the theory of political elites is his discussion of the circulation of elites. Pareto observes that society "is harmed not only by the accumulation of inferior elements in upper strata but also by the accumulation in lower strata of superior elements which are prevented from rising."[35] He remarks that whenever inferior elements coalesce in the upper strata at the same time superior elements aggregate in the lower strata a violent revolution is likely to occur. Revolutions are, therefore, only one manifestation of the appearance of new elites which, "through an incessant movement of circulation, rise up from the lower strata of society, mount up to the higher strata, flourish there, and then fall into decadence, are annihilated and disappear."[36]

The circulation of elites can take place by either of two means. First, new members can infiltrate constituted elites and thereby participate in a process of peaceful change. Second, established elites can refuse to co-opt new members in sufficient quantity and, as a result, be deposed through revolution or war. Normally, established elites attempt to stop the infiltration of new members and thereby contribute to their own ruin. While it may appear that significant changes are continually taking place in political affairs, there is never more involved than the struggle between one aristocracy and another. Pareto remarks that "outside the vain agitations of politicians" there is one important movement in world history— "the slow transformation and improvement of social conditions."[37]

Pareto's disdain for politics separates him from Mosca and weakens even his discussion of the circulation of elites. As Mosca implied, one cannot separate superior and inferior elements in a population from the social forces active in that population. Social change is not a matter of decadent elites confronting healthy and vigorous counterelites. It is much more a matter of groups organized around new elements in a civilization bidding for political representation against groups organized around older elements in a civilization. In his recognition of the sociality of political change Mosca was a far superior political theorist to Pareto.

ROBERT MICHELS

The third important theorist of political elites who wrote at the turn of the twentieth century was Robert Michels. Michels' contributions to the theory of political elites consists in generalizing the theory to cover all complex organizations rather than just the state, and in developing the "iron law of oligarchy" as a summation of the conclusions of theorists of political elites. Essentially, Michels' thesis is that the requirements of complex organizations militate against the attainment of democracy in those organizations. Thus, Michels did not believe, as Blau does, that in mutual benefit associations there is a dilemma between effectiveness of function and control by membership. He holds that control by membership is impossible in any meaningful sense of that term. In an attempt to demonstrate the truth of his thesis, Michels studies the internal political system of the German Social Democratic Party. He chooses this particular organization for his case study because the social democratic parties in Europe before World War I were the organizations that appeared to be most dedicated to the principles of democracy. Michels hypothesizes that if the German Social Democratic Party was not democratic, no other complex organization was likely to be democratic.

Influence of Mosca and Marx

Michels acknowledges the importance of Mosca as a seminal influence on the theory of political elites. In *Political Parties,* he approves of Mosca's idea that the "social classes which under our eyes engage in gigantic battles upon the scene of history, battles whose ultimate causes are to be found in economic antagonism, may thus be compared to two groups of dancers executing a chasse croise in a quadrille."[38]

Michels also recognizes Marx as a key figure in the development of political sociology. Like Mosca and Pareto, Michels was a revisionist of Marx' work. He seizes upon Marx' idea that a proletarian revolution would eliminate antagonisms between classes and end the political character of public power. Michels objects most to Marx' claim that human affairs could be managed without politics and domination. He attacks the thesis that after a proletarian revolution the rational coordination of things would replace the exploitation and domination of people. He argues that social wealth could not be administered efficiently in the absence of a complex bureaucratic organization. By definition, that necessary bureaucracy would embody the principle of hierarchy and thereby create classes. Anticipating the structure of bureaucratic socialist organization in the twentieth century, Michels remarks that the "administration of an immeasurably large capital, above all when this capital is collective property, confers upon the administrator influence at least equal to that possessed by the private owner of capital."[39] He observes that Marx' idea of a dictatorship of the proletariat bridging the gap between capitalist and socialist economic orders implies the creation of a new ruling class. Michels doubts that the party which ruled in the name of the proletariat would voluntarily allow the state to wither away. A self-perpetuating dictatorship manned by those who had been "sufficiently astute and sufficiently powerful to grasp the scepter of dominion in the name of socialism" would dominate the state.

IRON LAW OF OLIGARCHY

Michels bases his critique of Marxism on a "universally applicable social law" that he formulated—the "iron law of oligarchy." He holds that "every organ of the collectivity, brought into existence through the need for the division of labor, creates for itself, as soon as it becomes consolidated, interests peculiar to itself."[40] Further, he asserts that these interests are in necessary conflict with the interests of the collectivity. Social strata fulfilling particular functions tend to become isolated from control by membership and to develop an organizational apparatus adapted to defending their special interests. In their most complete development, these strata are transformed into distinct classes or ruling oligarchies.

Dialectics The dynamics of oligarchic rule are dialectical in form and turn on the duality of public function and private interest. For Michels, politics is grounded in public function. Organizations are set up to administer affairs that cannot be managed by the entire membership of the collectivity. Once the organizational apparatus is functioning, those who control access to resources and decision-making centers develop an interest in the maintenance and extension of their control. In the final analysis, public function is swamped by private interest. Michels observes that the aim of ruling minorities, or oligarchies, is to "impose upon the rest of society a 'legal order,' which is the outcome of the exigencies of dominion and of exploitation of the mass of helots effected by the ruling minority, and can never be truly representative of the majority."[41]

Michels holds that the iron law of oligarchy is far from a wholesale attack on Marxist political sociology. Instead, he sees it as a completion and a vindication of the materialist interpretation of history. Even the Marxist dialectic stands. Michels remarks that the essential content of Marxism as a philosophy of history is the principle that the dominance of ruling classes arises as a result of the "relationships between the different social forces competing for supremacy, these forces being of course considered dynamically and not quantitatively."[42] In his study of the German Social Democratic

Party, Michels finds that even in voluntary associations the same kinds of political dynamics take place that are found in states. The Party's administrative apparatus became a self-perpetuating oligarchy. The iron law of oligarchy and its range of application to all organizations marked by appreciable division of labor is the primary example of how theorists of political elites found in each zone of social existence the unifying factor of organization.

The Role of Education Michels was concerned with how the social consequences of oligarchy might be alleviated. Like Bentley and many other twentieth-century political theorists, he put his hope in increased educational opportunities for masses of people. He observed that the intellectual and cultural inferiority of the masses makes it impossible for them to judge the significance of a leader's actions. Thus, he held that "the great task of social education" is to "raise the intellectual level of the masses, so that they may be enabled, within the limits of what is possible, to counteract the oligarchical tendencies of the working-class movement."[43]

In view of the structural determinants of oligarchy, stressed in Michels' theory, increased education would seem to hold little promise of effectively alleviating the tendencies for ruling classes to dominate and spoliate masses of people. Further, and perhaps even more important, in a highly bureaucratized social order the chances for education in criticism of society deteriorate. When education is mediated through powerful bureaucracies which have intimate relationships with other dominant organized interest groups, the body of independent critical standards upon which Michels' proposal rests is unlikely to be widely disseminated or even to appear. What takes the place of criticism is a series of propaganda wars between competing interest groups that are bureaucratically entrenched. While such ideological conflict sometimes gives the appearance of independent criticism, the description of political existence is distorted as a result of its function as an apology for a cross section of activity organized as a political interest group. Enlightenment is the great means that twentieth-century political theorists oppose to force, bribery, and fraud as weapons for attaining social change. It is ironic that their own theories show the limitations and obstacles to enlightenment in the contemporary world.

HAROLD D. LASSWELL

The foremost theorist of political elites in the United States is Harold D. Lasswell. In his *Politics: Who Gets What, When, How*

Lasswell introduces the principles formulated by Mosca, Pareto, Michels, and Weber into American political science. In his theory of political elites, Lasswell carries out a pragmatic shift of emphasis from attention to decision making to concern with consumption. For Lasswell, the elite is composed of those people who "get the most of what there is to get."[44] The influential are those who receive the greatest share of socially available values. This simple definition of elite led Lasswell to the task of specifying the most general types of values that can be sought by human beings. After several attempts he settled on a list of eight values including power, wealth, respect, well-being, rectitude, skill, enlightenment, and affection. Each of these values can become politically relevant, and at different places and times political elites have been concerned with maximizing attainment of different combinations of the eight values.

Lasswell's specification of the values sought by human beings can be viewed as an attempt to add content to the formal categories of the early theories of political elites. While elite is still defined formally as that group of people in a society who attain the greatest share of socially available values, social type and political formula are given a measure of content. The social types that compose elites can be classified according to the values with which they are associated. The warrior, the businessman, the aristocrat, the youthful leader, the priest, the technocrat, the demagogue, and the politician are all social types associated with different sets of values sought by human beings. Similarly, political formulas can be classified according to legitimating values. Protection, growth and prosperity, stability, dynamism, salvation, competence, truth, and popularity are political formulas that legitimate the rule of the various elite groups identified by Lasswell.

Like the other theorists of political elites, Lasswell acknowledges a debt to Marxian analysis. He observes that the "most important political analysis of modern times (the Marxist) has concentrated attention upon the class results of social change."[45] While recognizing the importance of class in the determination of political events, Lasswell argues that Marxist theory must be revised to take account of the many other "equally relevant ways of viewing the results of social life, such as the fate of skill, personality, and attitude groups."[46] Like other twentieth-century political theorists, Lasswell here proposes to adopt the cross section of activity as the primary unit of political analysis. He holds that emphasis on class as a unit of analysis should be interpreted as a "methodological contrivance of systematic thinkers, a selected frame of reference to be held constant during the course of a *particular* act of analysis."[47] From this phenomenological perspective, there are innumerable other frames of reference through which to interpret political affairs.

Skill

Lasswell advocates that political scientists experiment with several perspectives in their work so that they would not become bound to a single and biased interpretation of political existence. However, he does not imply that all ways of interpreting political existence are equally useful. In his own work he gives primary attention to the construct of skill, and uses categories of skill groupings to describe historical trends and to predict future developments. He traces the

> decline of skills of violence (military, police) while industrialism and capitalism spread during the nineteenth century, giving prominence as they rose to the specialized skills of business, of mass political party organization and propaganda; and giving ground in the twentieth century to a renewed wave of specialists on violence as world crises continue.[48]

He has predicted increased power for scientifically sophisticated technicians and has remarked that traditional class formations like landed aristocracies, the bourgeoisie and proletariats are giving way in importance to skill groups in contemporary Western societies. Lasswell's emphasis on skill in contemporary politics is consistent with, if not implied by, the extension of bureaucratic organization in the West. Lasswell's major error lies in the overemphasis on specialism common to most political theories derived from civilized humanism. However, if Lasswell neglects the importance of publics and generalists, in favor of the significance of functionaries, he does not take all cross sections of activity as equal. Rather, he presents one of the three important perspectives of contemporary political analysis.

Modes of Domination

The Four Modes   One of Lasswell's contributions to the theory of political elites has been to systematize the ways in which ruling classes maintain dominance within societies. He divides the means through which ruling classes manipulate their environments into four categories: symbols, violence, goods, and practices. All elites defend and assert themselves "in the name of symbols of the common destiny."[49] Such symbols of the common destiny are the elements of political formulas legitimating elite rule. As long as the masses believe in the righteousness of elite rule and venerate the symbols communicated by the elite, spoliation of the masses proceeds with relatively little hindrance. Lasswell observes that the use of symbols is one of the favored strategies of counterelites, because counterelites do not have access to the means to violence or goods, and are systematically injured by the operation of constituted practices.

Control of the means to organized violence and the exercise of such violence is, of course, another weapon of elite domination. Like Bentley and unlike Weber, Lasswell does not argue that violence is in any way an ultimate weapon in politics. Violence, though important, must take its place beside the other means to maintaining and extending dominance.

Control of goods and the means to producing goods is the aspect of elite dominance emphasized by the Marxists. Lasswell points out that the "use of goods in elite attack and defense takes the form of destroying, withholding, apportioning."[50] Elites have used both pricing mechanisms and rationing strategies in their attempts to keep and extend dominance. As in the case of violence, Lasswell does not give any special preeminence to the control of economic goods.

Practices, or those procedures comprising "all the ways by which elites are recruited and trained, all the forms observed in policy-making and administration," compose the final means to elite control.[51] Practices, which include constitutional laws, can be used by elites for defense by "catharsis and minor readjustment." For example, when confronted by revolutionary threats, elites can alter details in the system of representation and perhaps placate dissident elements with form rather than substance. Lasswell observes that the struggles over democratization in the nineteenth century functioned to divert attention from "the underlying property system." Suffrage was substituted for socialism. A strict distinction must be made here between the actual social consequences of the struggles over democratization and the intentions of elite groups in the nineteenth century. Lasswell does not make this distinction and thereby confuses a latent (unintended and unrecognized) function with a manifest (intended and recognized) function.

Consequences of Activity   Many difficulties in the theory of political elites hinge on lack of careful attention to the different types of consequences of human activity, as do difficulties with criticisms of theories of political elites. Many aspects of elite dominance may be unintended and unrecognized, while others may be intended and unrecognized, unintended and recognized, and recognized and intended. Just because one cannot point out a specific decision made by notables in an elite one is not warranted to deny the existence of an elite. The civilization and social processes may be structured so that a small group gains a large proportion of socially available values and possibilities for new values are closed off. Also, just because one can show that certain events have differentially favored a small group, one is not warranted to affirm the existence of a tightly organized ruling class. In discussions of political elites one must pay attention to both latent and manifest functions, as well as those intermediate between the two.

THE THEORY OF POLITICAL ELITES IN REVIEW

Theorists of political elites added the third major dimension to the formal political theory that was developed at the turn of the twentieth century. While the pluralists in America defined the cross section of human activity as the basic unit of political analysis and the organization theorists showed that cross sections of activity could be organized or disbanded, theorists of political elites showed that the relation of domination-subordination characterizes cross sections of activity. Within each human activity some individuals exercise domination over others, and some human activities claim resources at the expense of other activities. To the interest group of pluralist theory and the bureaucracy of organization theory is added the ruling class, elite, or oligarchy of the theory of political elites. When synthesized these three aspects of formal theory define the political system. Thus, systems theories of political existence are the culmination of formalism in political thought.

Like pluralism and organization theory, theories of political elites are revisions of Marxist political analysis. While pluralists generalized Marx' economic class into the group as cross-sectional activity, and organization theorists generalized Marx' capitalist system into the organization as a means of coordinating collective projects, theorists of political elites generalized Marx' ruling economic class into the ruling class as dominative social element. The key to all of these transformations of Marxist analysis is the operation of discovering organization within each social content. While Marx organized human existence around the content of the economic act, pluralists, organization theorists, and theorists of political elites found structure in each type of human act. They were enabled to grasp this structure by refusing to make any particular content of human existence more significant than any other prior to observation. Thus, pluralism, organization theory, and the theory of political elites are not regressions from Marxism to a previous era of bourgeois theory—despite Sartre's claim to the contrary. They are advances in political analysis that preserve the progressive features of nineteenth-century political sociologies and add the characteristic of universality. While formalism has run its course in the twentieth century, it constitutes a necessary preparation for an existential political theory.

NOTES

1. Gaetano Mosca, *The Ruling Class* (New York: McGraw-Hill Book Company, 1939), p. 329.

2. Ibid., pp. 329–330.

3. Renzo Sereno, *The Rulers* (New York: Frederick A. Praeger, Inc., 1962), p. 22.

4. Howard Becker and Harry Elmer Barnes, *Social Thought from Lore to Science,* Volume 2 (New York: Dover Publications, Inc., 1961), p. 502.

5. Karl Marx and Friedrich Engels, *The Communist Manifesto* (New York: Meredith Corporation, Appleton-Century-Crofts, 1955), p. 5.

6. Ibid., pp. 11–12.

7. Ibid., p. 32.

8. Ibid.

9. Ibid., pp. 29–30.

10. Ibid., p. 30.

11. Robert Michels, *Political Parties* (New York: The Macmillan Company, Collier Books, 1962), p. 88.

12. S. E. Finer, ed., *Vilfredo Pareto: Sociological Writings* (New York: Frederick A. Praeger, Inc., 1966), p. 82.

13. Ibid.

14. Mosca, *The Ruling Class,* p. 50.

15. Ibid., p. 51.

16. Ibid., p. 65.

17. Ibid.

18. Ibid., p. 430.

19. Ibid., p. 480.

20. Ibid., p. 158.

21. Ibid., p. 480.

22. Ibid., p. 70.

23. Ibid., p. 71.

24. Ibid.

25. Ibid., p. 134.

26. Ibid., p. 327.

27. Ibid., p. 258.

28. Ibid., p. 347.

29. Ibid., p. 37.

30. Finer, *Vilfredo Pareto,* p. 118.

31. Ibid., p. 140.

32. Ibid., p. 138.

33. Ibid., p. 248.

34. Ibid., p. 155.

35. Ibid., p. 159.

36. Ibid., p. 134.

37. Ibid., p. 137.

38. Michels, *Political Parties,* p. 342.

39. Ibid., p. 348.

40. Ibid., p. 353.

41. Ibid.

42. Ibid., p. 354.

43. Ibid., p. 369.

44. Harold D. Lasswell, *Politics: Who Gets What, When, How* (Cleveland: The World Publishing Company, 1958), p. 13.

45. Ibid., p. 167.

46. Ibid.

47. Ibid., p. 168.

48. Ibid., p. 196.

49. Ibid., p. 31

50. Ibid., p. 62.

51. Ibid., p. 80.

SUGGESTED READINGS

Bachrach, Peter. *The Theory of Democratic Elitism.* Boston: Little, Brown and Company, 1967.

Baltzell, E. Digby. *The Protestant Establishment.* New York: Random House, Inc., 1964.

Berle, Adolf A. *Power Without Property.* New York: Harcourt Brace Jovanovich, Inc., 1959.

Durkheim, Emile. *Socialism.* New York: The Macmillan Company, Collier Books, 1962.

Keller, Suzanne. *Beyond the Ruling Class.* New York: Random House, Inc., 1963.

Mannheim, Karl. *Man and Society in an Age of Reconstruction.* London: Kegan Paul, 1946.

Meisel, James H. *The Myth of the Ruling Class.* Ann Arbor, Mich.: The University of Michigan Press, 1962.

Mills, C. Wright. *The Power Elite.* New York: Oxford University Press, Inc., 1956.

Sartori, Giovanni. *Democratic Theory.* New York: Frederick A. Praeger, Inc., 1967.

Sereno, Renzo. *The Rulers.* New York: Frederick A. Praeger, Inc., 1962.

CHAPTER EIGHT

SYSTEMS THEORY
AND DAVID EASTON

Since World War II, the major themes present in the diverse movements of pragmatism and pluralism, existentialism and the theory of organizations, and civilized humanism and the theory of political elites, have been brought together in systems theories of political affairs. Under the concept of political system have been ranged the ideas of cross-sectional activity, organization, and elite, as well as the guiding conceptions of social consequences and social process, the human condition and culture. In the most general sense, in the second half of the twentieth century the various approaches to formalizing Marxism and other nineteenth-century political theories have been consolidated in theories of the political system. This consolidation represents the culmination and triumph of formalism in political theory, and may signal the advent of new approaches in the last quarter of the twentieth century.

GENERAL SYSTEMS THEORY

In *Politics and Social Science,* W. J. M. Mackenzie points out that "general systems theory" is a contemporary movement that arches over many sciences. Current theorists of the political system usually claim some affiliation with general systems theory, which began within the discipline of biology in the 1920's. Mackenzie traces the origins of general systems theory to biologists who

> opposed reductionism, that is to say an analysis of living things merely as a sum of parts (a view contradicted by observation), and yet also rejected vitalism as being an unscientific appeal to a mystical substance (a 'phlogiston'), with no properties except that of answering the question put.[1]

In place of reductionism and vitalism, biologists like von Bertalanffy substituted the concept of system. For von Bertalanffy, a system is defined abstractly as a "set of units with relationships among them."

He attempted to employ the concept to characterize diverse biological situations, such as the processes of organisms and ecological phenomena. Concurrent with the development of the systems idea in biology was its adaptation to the science of cybernetics, the growth of structural-functional analysis in social anthropology, and the *gestalt* school in psychology.

While it appears to have the virtues of abstraction, von Bertalanffy's definition of a system as a set of units with relationships among them is fraught with conceptual difficulties. Analyses of the concept "system" have opened up many fundamental debates, and systems theory has fast become as complicated as scholastic theology and Marxist social criticism in its diversity of approaches and positions. With respect to political theory, David Easton, the most prominent exponent of systems analysis among contemporary political scientists, has attempted to clarify the issues at stake in applying general systems theory to political phenomena.

TYPES OF SYSTEMS

In *A Framework for Political Analysis,* Easton attempts to answer the question: "What kinds of commitments might be inadvertently undertaken if political life is characterized as a system of behavior and the implications of this description are pursued diligently?"[2] In responding to this question, Easton discusses four general premises upon which his systems analysis of political life is based. The first two premises link theories of the political system to general systems theory. They state that it is useful to view political life as a system of behavior and that a system is "distinguishable from the environment in which it exists and open to influences from it."[3] The second two premises are peculiar to Easton's approach. They state that variations in "the structures and processes within a system may usefully be interpreted as constructive or positive alternative efforts by members of a system to regulate or cope with stress flowing from environmental as well as internal sources," and that the capacity of a system "to persist in the face of stress is a function of the presence and nature of the information and other influences that return to its actors and decision-makers."[4] Having defined the elements of his theory of political systems, Easton discusses the different ways in which the concept "system" can be developed.

Empirical and Symbolic Systems

First, with respect to the scientific enterprise, there are empirical and symbolic systems. The term *empirical system* refers to the set of units that the scientist observes and the set of relationships that the investigator aims at describing. Complementing empirical systems are symbolic systems that consist of sets of symbols through which scientists hope to explain the behavior of relevant empirical systems. For example, Einstein's theory of relativity describes a symbolic system referring to the empirical system of the order of the universe. Easton points out that for the scientist the adequacy of a symbolic system is measured by its ability to explain the relationships present in an empirical system. In deductive disciplines such as mathematics and symbolic logic, the adequacy of a symbolic system is measured by its consistency and its economy. Easton states that when he uses the term *political system,* he refers to an empirical system of political behavior. This commits him to the position that there is some order to the appearances that scientists observe. Easton's cosmos is not a sheer chaos into which human beings put meaning. This commitment is not demonstrated by Easton as logically necessary, and it is possible to take the position that only symbolic systems occur in the universe or the stand that skepticism about the occurrence of empirical systems is warranted.

Natural and Constructive Systems

Second, with respect to the interpretation of empirical systems, one can speak of natural and constructive systems. Unlike the concepts "empirical system" and "symbolic system," the concepts "natural system" and "constructive system" are not complementary. To speak of natural systems involves not only the commitment to the view that appearances have some order, but the stand that "whether or not a set of interactions constitutes a system will depend upon the extent to which they naturally cohere."[5] For those who interpret empirical systems as natural systems, the systems investigated by scientists are given in nature. The scientist must discover the systems that actually exist and then observe them in operation. Opposed to the naturalistic interpretation of empirical systems is the constructivist perspective. Easton states that the constructivist position is defined by the claim that all systems are constructs of the mind. Constructivists maintain that it is "pointless to try to distinguish so-called natural from nonnatural or nonexistent systems," that "any aggregate of interactions that we choose to identify may be said to form a system," and that it is "solely a matter of conceptual or theoretical convenience" which interactions are chosen by the scientist.

Advantages of Constructivism   Easton argues that while naturalism has great commonsense appeal, constructivism is the only foundation adequate to support a rigorous political science. He claims that the naturalistic position has three crucial defects. First, he argues that interpreting empirical systems as natural systems does not aid the investigator in identifying such systems. In other words, the statement that political scientists should study natural systems is more a metaphysical assertion about the nature of reality than a scientific assertion about the relationships among sets of phenomena.

Second, Easton argues that interpreting empirical systems as natural systems involves the difficulty of determining where systems begin and end in the world. Where the elements of a system are tightly connected, the identification of the system is not difficult. However, in cases where the elements of a system are loosely connected, identification of the system may be quite difficult. Easton states that the naturalist is faced with the problem of determining when systems disappear and random collections begin. He implies that while this problem may be amenable to scholastic logic-chopping, it is not subject to scientific solution.

Third, Easton claims that naturalists confront the problem of "whether the existence of what is only an apparent interdependence would thereby transform the elements into a system of some kind."[6] This problem is similar to the second difficulty of determining at what point natural systems begin and end. According to Easton, naturalists must be prepared to decide under what conditions apparent relationships among elements become real connections. Presumably, this problem is a result of the metaphysical character of the naturalistic interpretation of empirical systems.

Interesting and Trivial Systems Easton claims that the constructivist perspective avoids all of the difficulties of the naturalistic interpretation of empirical systems. The position that all systems are constructs of the mind does not force the abandonment of science to chaos. Constructivists distinguish among interesting and trivial systems. Where

> the selected parts of political life are relevant, show some
> degree of interdependence, and seem to have a common
> fate, we can say that we have an interesting and useful
> system from the point of view of understanding the way in
> which political systems are likely to operate.[7]

However, where the selected units are not tightly connected, they may still be called a political system; but the only useful statement to make about such a system is that its elements are independent of one another. Easton states that the constructivist position has two significant advantages. First, it avoids interminable debate about the reality of systems. Second, it is flexible enough to allow for the creation of new systems and the alteration of old ones whenever new relationships are discovered.

Ambiguities There are several major ambiguities in Easton's discussion of natural, symbolic, and constructive systems. The central problem resides in his claim that all systems are merely constructs of the mind. If empirical systems are composed of observable units and if interesting systems are empirical systems which evince theoretically significant relationships, then systems are not merely constructs of the mind. At most, symbolic systems are constructs of the mind. However, even this statement is questionable after a thorough consideration of Bentley's observation that symbols are defined in and through a social process. With respect to empirical systems, the notion that systems are merely constructs of the mind is clearly untenable. Are the observations that define empirical systems merely constructs of the mind? An affirmative response to this question would seem to be impossible given Easton's definition of an interesting empirical system.

Empirical systems may be interesting when two conditions are met. First, the observed elements must cohere in some way. Second, this coherence must be of a kind that is relevant to some human purpose. Through the concept of an interesting empirical system Easton imports the notion of natural systems into his political theory. Easton embraces constructivism so that he can avoid debates about the reality of systems and retain the flexibility to create and alter descriptions of systems when the evidence warrants such actions. He could better attain these objectives by refining the idea of natural systems.

One can accept the notion of a world characterized in part by natural systems without embracing an arid dialectic of concepts or bending data to fit a Procrustean bed. Full description of the dynamics of natural systems can function as a regulative ideal for investigation. Once description of natural systems is made a regulative ideal rather than a present reality, any particular description of a system can be altered when new evidence suggests a better description. Treating natural systems as a regulative ideal for investigation allows the scientist to avoid the difficulties brought out by Easton's discussion of natural systems and saves him also from the absurdities of constructivism.

Closed and Open Systems

Besides treating the differences between empirical and symbolic systems, natural and constructive systems, and interesting and trivial systems, Easton discusses the distinction between closed and open systems. A closed system is one that is isolated from all environmental influences. Any of its dynamics are internally generated. Open systems are influenced by their environments and a study of their dynamics must take account of exchanges between system and environment. According to Easton, political systems are open systems. He argues that although it is "entirely possible to conceive of a mode of analysis that would follow some models of physical systems and interpret political life as a closed system, one that conceived it to be isolated from the influences of its environment," this decision would involve the commitment to describe how the system moves toward maximal social entropy.[8] He claims that political scientists would find it difficult to define what is implied in the idea of a political system running down.

The interpretation of political systems as open systems has been challenged by Morton Kaplan, a political theorist who has applied systems analysis in the field of international relations. In *Macropolitics* Kaplan states: "A system consists of a set of variables related by one or more functions. Although the world is open, the systems model is always closed."[9] Thus, Kaplan holds that all empirical systems are open systems. Scientists make symbolic models of functionally related parts of experience, and these symbolic systems are closed to all influences not specifically included in them. In this debate, Easton seems to make the stronger case. There is no reason why the scientist should not define a system and trace the effects on it of selected stimuli from the environment. When a physiologist studies the consequences of ingesting a drug for bodily functions he is showing the impact of an environmental influence on the operation of a system. Kaplan seems to be objecting more to the notion of creative systems than to the concept of open systems.

Adaptive and Repetitive Systems

Besides stating that the political system is an open system, Easton claims that it is also a constructively adaptive system rather than a repetitive system. Unlike biological organisms, political systems have the possibility of restructuring themselves when they are under stress. They are the only such creative systems known to human observers, and far surpass human beings in their capacity for flexible response.

For Easton, political systems are defined by the performance of the function of authoritatively allocating values for a society. They persist as long as they perform this function, and they may perform it through a wide variety of different structures. Only other social systems are similarly creative. Kaplan calls the concept of a creatively adaptive system unscientific. He claims that scientists can only study empirical regularities. Insofar as political phenomena are irregular, they are not amenable to the procedures of scientific investigation. Even here, however, Easton seems to have the better of the argument. Perhaps the ways in which political systems are constructively adapted are not completely irregular. The weakness of Easton's concept of constructive adaptation does not reside in the idea of structural transformation. Rather, it lies in the implication that political systems transform themselves in some way. Human beings transform political systems; political systems do not transform themselves. This judgment is all the more important in the light of Easton's final distinction among the various kinds of systems.

Membership and Analytic Systems

With respect to the fundamental units of political analysis, Easton distinguishes among membership systems and analytic systems. Membership systems are composed of concrete human beings, while analytic systems are defined by types of human interaction, or, in Bentley's terms, by particular cross sections of activity. For Easton, all social systems are analytic systems defined as cross sections of activity or sets of interactions. For example, the political system of a society is defined as that set of interactions which has relevance to the authoritative allocation of values for the society. Social systems are not membership systems because they neither exhaust all of the activities of human beings nor capture the entirety of significant cross sections of activity in organizations. In the first sense, much human activity is nonpolitical in that it is not concerned with the authoritative allocation of values for a society. Thus, the political system cannot engulf the complete human being. In the second sense, formal political organizations such as parties and interest groups do not contain all of the activities involved in the authoritative allocation of values for a society. Thus, formal membership organizations cannot engulf the political system. Easton remarks that in a strict sense, organizations are analytic systems. No organization contains all of a human being's activity, and so-called membership systems are less systems of biological persons than systems of specialized roles.

In defining the political system as an analytic system, Easton is consistent with the formalist tradition of twentieth-century political theory. The idea that politics is a certain kind of interaction is consistent with the conclusions of Bentley, Weber, and Mosca. Thus, beginning with von Bertalanffy's notion of a system as a "set of units with relationships among them," Easton makes successive qualifications in his view of system. First he defines the political system as an empirical system and distinguishes it from a symbolic system. Second he defines the political system as a constructive empirical system and distinguishes it from a natural system. Third he argues that political scientists are concerned with discovering interesting constructive systems rather than trivial constructive systems. In his distinction among interesting and trivial systems he smuggles in the notion of natural system. Fourth Easton defines the political system as an open system and distinguishes it from a closed system. Fifth he makes a further distinction among open systems and argues that the political system is a constructively adaptive system rather than a repetitive system. Finally Easton defines the political system as an analytic system and distinguishes it from a membership system. Thus, the political system is a set of observable units, selected by a political scientist, which is open to influences from an environment, has the possibility for constructive adaptation, and is defined by interactions rather than concrete human beings. The political system is also that social system which has the function of authoritatively allocating values for a society. The definition of this function must now be clarified.

CRITIQUE OF POLITICAL THEORY

Like Bentley, David Easton originally made his mark on political theory by publishing a critique of the work done by the leading political scientists of his time. In *The Political System,* published in 1953, Easton criticizes the major intellectual tendencies present in the discipline of political science immediately after World War II and appeals for a rebirth of political theory. For Easton, work in political science at midcentury was divided between hyperfactual empirical research and studies in the history of political ideas. Easton calls for causal theory to inform empirical research and imaginative value theory to replace the mere history of political thought.

Trends at Midcentury

By hyperfactualism Easton means the tendency of political scientists to select highly particularized problems in their research and to ignore the relationships of these problems to other questions and to the operation of the entire political system. Joined to hyperfactualism was a premature policy science. Easton pointed out that a strong reformist tradition existed in American political science. Political scientists continuously made recommendations about how to make the operation of liberal democratic institutions more efficient. However, these recommendations were usually not based upon empirically verified causal relations among key variables or rigorously clarified systems of value. Instead, they were relatively uncritical in both the empirical and normative senses.

While Easton appreciates the appeal that policy-oriented research had for political scientists, he cautions that recommendations that were not backed up by reliable knowledge would have little ultimate influence on policy.

Parallel to a hyperfactual and policy-oriented political science, Easton finds a political theory that had been engulfed by the history of ideas. With respect to American political theory, the history of ideas was a variant of the sociology of knowledge. Easton identifies three major tendencies of thought in the subdiscipline of political theory at midcentury. In the first tendency, represented by Dunning, political theory is viewed as an enterprise in discovering the conditions under which political ideas appear and the consequences that political ideas have for institutional development. Jurispruden-tial ideas are at the center of attention and ethical theories are relatively ignored. The hallmark of Dunning's approach to political theory is the idea of an interplay between political thought and institutional structure in the flow of political events.

In the second tendency, represented by McIlwain, political theory is viewed as an enterprise in describing political ideas as effects of social conditions. McIlwain holds that political ideas are epiphenomena of the social process; they do not influence the pattern of political activity. However, McIlwain stresses the im-portance of ethical theory in his writings, perhaps because it is a good summation of the more particular political thought of a time.

In the third tendency, represented by Sabine, Dunning's idea of an interplay between political ideas and political institutions in the flow of political events, and McIlwain's notion of the importance of ethical theory are synthesized. Easton points out that each of the three tendencies in political theory at midcentury was historicist in that it exemplified the idea that "very little more can be said about values except that they are a product of certain historical conditions and that they have played a given role in the historical process."[10]

Moral Relativism

For Easton, the majority of American political theorists of the twentieth century had surrendered the quest for imaginative visions of human possibilities in favor of the study of history. However, beneath the sociology of knowledge and historicism lurked a fallacy. Easton argues that the political theorists of the twentieth century had embraced equalistic relativism. Equalistic relativism involves the moral position that "because no value judgment can be proved superior, all values must be treated as equally good."[11] Easton opposes moral relativism to equalistic relativism. Moral relativists argue merely that all value judgments are responses to historical conditions. They make no judgment that all values must be treated as equally good. While equalistic relativism involves a surrender of work towards a creative value theory, moral relativism leaves the field open for a reconstruction of values in line with changing historical circumstances.

Thus, after World War II, Easton found the discipline of political science divided between hyperfactual research and studies in the history of ideas. In order to remedy this situation he recommended a revival of theory in the classical sense of inquiry into what criteria ought to be used "in evaluating the variety of social programs offered by groups competing for political power," and the creation of a body of empirically testable general theory that would outline the causal links between political events.[12] In clearing the ground for such an empirically testable general theory of political life, Easton's first task was to define the scope of political science. At this point he introduced the guiding idea of the political system as that set of interactions relevant to the authoritative allocation of values for a society.

THE AUTHORITATIVE ALLOCATION OF VALUES

Easton begins his discussion with a description of the common-sense idea of political life. He states that if we can "recapture for a moment our original and unembellished naivete about matters political" we will find two basic insights. First, wherever "we find a group of people, whatever their purposes or form of organization, there we usually encounter maneuvering for position and power."[13] Second, we find "an activity related in some vague way to problems of government or the making of policy for the whole society in which we live."[14] It is from these two insights that the definition of political science as the study of the authoritative allocation of values for a society is derived.

Policy

The term *allocation of values* is related to the insight that political life has reference to the making of policy for a human group. For Easton, the essence of a policy lies in the fact that through it values (or desirable properties) are denied to some people and made accessible to others. Thus, a policy is really a set of decisions and actions through which values are allocated to individuals and groups.

Easton claims that policies become peculiarly political when they allocate values for an entire society. He defines a society as "the broadest grouping of human beings who live together and collectively undertake to satisfy all the minimum prerequisites of group life."[15] A society is composed of human beings who continually interact with one another and possess a consciousness of belonging together. This common consciousness is grounded in similar culture and social structure. However, societies are not the only groups whose members possess a common consciousness. Ethnic groups, for example, may be characterized by a strong sense of community. Societies are distinguished from other groupings by the fact that they seek to solve all of the problems that relate to the maintenance of a group of people. Thus, societies are defined by the performance of functions that are necessary for the survival of a group of people. Among the functions that are necessary for the survival of a group of people, Easton identifies the authoritative allocation of values as the primary concern of political scientists.

Authority

The final aspect of Easton's definition of the scope of political science is the idea of authority. Easton argues that all social institutions and practices are means for allocating values. However, we do not give the name "political" to all social institutions and practices. Political institutions and roles are relevant to the authoritative allocation of values, where authoritative refers to the binding nature of a policy. Easton remarks that a policy is authoritative "when the people to whom it is intended to apply or who are affected by it consider that they must or ought to obey it."[16] He makes a sharp distinction between the grounds on which a person accepts a policy as authoritative and the sheer acceptance of that policy as authoritative. For the purposes of defining the scope of political science, Easton believes that the wider conception of authority is the more useful one. He maintains, however, that research into the grounds of obedience is legitimate and even important.

Easton attempts to justify each aspect of his definition of the scope of political science. He argues that if the political scientist were to attempt to study all allocations of values he would end up investigating all social activity. Even if he were to attempt to study all authoritative allocations of values his work would overlap with that of sociologists and economists who study binding allocations of values in organizations such as families, business firms, universities, and hospitals. Only the authoritative allocation of values for an entire society is adequate to carve out a special area of inquiry for political scientists. This is convenient, because the authoritative allocation of values for a society is, according to Easton, one of the functions that must be performed if a society is to persist:

> Every society provides some mechanisms, however rudi-
> mentary they may be, for authoritatively resolving differ-
> ences about the ends that are to be pursued, that is, for
> deciding who is to get what there is of the desirable
> things. An authoritative allocation of values is unavoid-
> able.[17]

Despite brave words like these, Easton does not succeed in proving
that this function must be performed.

The supposed necessity of Easton's function is founded on the
Hobbesian judgment that the human condition is one of conflict
among human beings over the distribution of scarce resources. In the
Hobbesian vein, he claims that it is

> patent that without the provision for some means of
> deciding among competing claims to limited values, soci-
> ety would be rent by constant strife; the regularized
> interaction which distinguishes a society from a random
> mob of individuals could not exist.[18]

Thus, Easton's claim to have identified a functional prerequisite for a
society is neither logically nor phenomenologically necessary. From
the idea of interaction does not logically follow the need for
authoritative allocations of value. Phenomenologically, the discussion is even more interesting. One can imagine a society in which no
roles for authoritatively allocating values were present. Such societies have already been envisioned in the literature of utopian social
criticism. The idea of anarchy cannot simply be assumed away with
a bow to the Hobbesian description of the human condition. However, if Easton's description of the necessity for performing the
allocative function makes neither logical nor phenomenological
sense, can it be given a reasonable interpretation? At most it is a
hypothesis that can be tested empirically.

PUBLIC FUNCTION

Easton recognizes that there is a tension between public function and private interest in the study of political affairs. However, he
interprets that tension in a different way from Bentley, Weber, or
Mosca. For Bentley, public function is engulfed by private interest.
In fact, one could argue strongly that Bentley does not recognize the
existence of a public domain in his work. For Weber, private interest
precedes public function. Organizations function to serve the interest of dominant groups. However, unlike Bentley, Weber allows for
the existence of a public domain in his discussion of how the

fulfillment of human needs has become increasingly bureaucratized in the modern age. The relationship between public function and private interest in Weber's work is, therefore, quite complex. While organizations function to serve private interests, these interests can only be satisfied if the organizations perform some public functions. Mosca and Michels provide interpretations that are similar to Weber's account. However, they reverse the order of precedence between public function and private interest.

Necessary Existence of Public Function

For theorists of political elites, organizations arise to serve public functions. Each organization is characterized by a subsystem which functions to coordinate activities towards the realization of the public function. However, those individuals who perform the function of coordination within the organization gain an interest in the perpetuation and extension of their power. They become a power elite and attempt to make the organization operate to serve their private interest. Thus, while Bentley reduces political activity to the pursuit of private interest and Weber holds that the pursuit of private interest is limited by the need to perform some public functions, theorists of political elites hold that political activity itself includes the public function of coordination toward collective goals.

Easton's discussion goes even further in the direction of providing a public function for political activity. For Easton, political activity arises from the social need to resolve disputes among members of a society about the distribution of scarce values. While this need is a result of the pursuit of private interest, the function itself is public because Easton argues that if it is not performed no social life at all will be possible. It is important to note that the public function identified by theorists of political elites is primarily administrative. Complex tasks require coordination. However, the function assigned to politics by Easton is more traditionally political. Differences must be resolved. Most political theorists of the twentieth century have assimilated dispute settling to private interest rather than public function. They have assumed that since allocations of values invariably favor the fulfillment of only some group interests, private interest governs the authoritative allocation of values.

Maintaining Order

By stating that regardless of standards of justice or standards for good collective projects, the authoritative allocation of values is a public function, Easton has returned to a Hobbesian interpretation of political activity. He does not deny that any set of authoritative allocations of values for a society benefit the most powerful groups in that society. He claims that whether or not ruling classes gain disproportionate benefit from the application of public policies, the authoritative allocation of values remains a public function because if it is not performed no social life at all will be possible. Thus, Easton embraces order as the essence of politics.

Easton's view of the public function of political activity also distinguishes his thought from that of the important political philosophers of the twentieth century. While Easton identifies a minimal function for political activity, contemporary political philosophers have attempted to describe a maximal function for political activity. Thus, Dewey wrote that the function of politics is intelligent care for the secondary consequences of human activity; Jaspers stated that the function of politics is the encouragement of authentic existence and cultural contribution; and the civilized humanists maintained that the function of politics is the maintenance and extension of civilization. By positing a minimal function for political activity Easton has taken another step on the way to the culmination of formalism in twentieth-century political theory.

THE ELEMENTS OF SYSTEMS ANALYSIS

In defining the political system as that set of interactions which are relevant to the authoritative allocation of values for a society, Easton both marked off a field for political inquiry and made the concept of system the basic unit of analysis for the scientific study of political life. While Easton's *A Framework for Political Analysis* was primarily devoted to an explication of the concept "system," and his *The Political System* was a critique of traditional political science in the United States and an attempt to define a new scope for the discipline, Easton's chief work, *A Systems Analysis of Political Life,* comprises his effort to develop a general theory of political activity. *A Systems Analysis of Political Life* poses in the sharpest form the issue of how adequately a functional analysis of political activity can synthesize the major contributions to political theory that were made in the first half of the twentieth century.

The Political System

The fundamental elements of Easton's systems analysis have already been presented in the earlier phases of this discussion. Formally, a system is defined as a set of units with relationships among them. The political system is an empirical system in the sense that it refers to a set of observable units. According to Easton, it is also a constructive system, devised by him for purposes of inquiry. However, he also hopes that it will be an interesting system which will illuminate significant aspects of political life. The political system is an open system in that it is subject to influences from its environment, which includes physical systems, biological systems, personality systems, and other social systems. Further, the political system is a constructively adaptive system with the capacity of having its internal structure transformed. Finally, the political system is an analytic system rather than a membership system. It is not composed of individuals, but is defined as a set of interactions which share a common attribute.

Substantively, the political system is defined as that set of interactions relevant to the process of authoritatively allocating values for a society. The authoritative allocation of values is considered a public function that must be performed if social life is to persist at all. The necessity for the performance of this function is grounded in the Hobbesian judgment that without an authoritative means for settling disputes about the distribution of values in a society, a war of all against all will ensue. Thus, the political system is described by a public function that mediates the conflicts among private interests. If each of these aspects of Easton's earlier discussion is kept in mind, the nature of his systems analysis of political life will be understood clearly.

The Political System as Ego Easton states that the basic question he wishes to answer in *A Systems Analysis of Political Life* is: "How does it come about that any type of system can persist at all, even under the pressures of frequent or constant crises?"[19] He considers this question the most general query that can be raised in political theory and argues that it includes all of the previous relevant questions discussed in descriptive political theory as special queries. A close analysis of Easton's basic question shows its unique nature. In *The Political System* Easton demonstrated to his satisfaction that the political system is necessary to the continuance of social life. However, the function performed by the political system is different in kind from the functions of other social systems, in which disputes originate that cannot be resolved through customary modes of settlement. These disputes enter the political system and are acted upon through an authoritative allocation of values. Thus, the political system is uniquely reflexive. It is like the ego in the individual personality, which settles conflicts among impulses and plans future activities.

In *A Systems Analysis of Political Life* Easton does not ask the commonsense question: How does the political system perform its function of authoritatively allocating values for a society? He considers this a question for special theories in political science. Instead, Easton is concerned with answering what he deems a prior question: How is the political system maintained? If the political system is reflexive in the sense that it acts upon materials provided by other systems, Easton opens up inquiry into a double-reflexive process. If the political system is instrumental in preventing a war of all against all, it must itself be maintained in such condition as to enable performance of its function. The processes through which political systems are maintained Easton calls the life processes of political systems. Easton's idea of studying the ways in which political systems are enabled to persist is analogous to the psychiatrist's idea of inquiring into the processes through which the ego is maintained in such condition that it is enabled to prevent dissolution of the personality through disastrous conflicts among impulses. Both Easton's question and the psychiatrist's question are legitimate.

Project Orientation It is doubtful, however, that Easton is correct in claiming that the question—How does it come about that any type of system can persist at all, even under the pressures of frequent and constant crises?—is the most general query that one can make about political life. Perhaps it is the case that Easton's question is the most abstract query that can be raised in political science. It amounts to having political science turn upon itself and results in the culmination of formalism. One must investigate how the system which maintains order is itself maintained in order. However, this is certainly not the most general question that can be asked by a political theorist, because it excludes all questions about the ways in which political systems perform their function rather than including them. It fixes attention on the small but critical sphere of processes which keep intact the processes involved in authoritatively allocating values for a society. It turns attention away from what a political system does and how it does it, and turns it towards what makes it possible for a political system to do anything.

In the terms of the phenomenologist Friedrich Baerwald, Easton is devising a theory of project rather than object orientation. For Baerwald, social existence is fundamentally ambiguous. In every socially relevant action two things are intended: "the achievement of explicit objectives and at the same time the maintenance or change of the social position of the persons engaged in such an activity."[20] Baerwald calls concern with the achievement of explicit objectives "object orientation" and concern with the maintenance or change of social position or social relations "project orientation."[21] Political activity is peculiarly concerned with project orientation.

Translating Easton's discourse into Baerwald's language, the authoritative allocation of values for a society is the project orientation of that society. Thus, in Baerwald's terms, Easton is engaged in devising a theory of the project orientation of the project orientation of a society. It is doubtful that political theory has ever been as formal as this in the past, or that it will be as formal in the future. Similarly, it is clear that while Easton has perhaps posed the most abstract question possible in political theory, he has not raised the most general question.

Stress

In responding to the question—How does it come about that any type of system can persist at all, even under the pressures of frequent or constant crisis?—Easton deploys a set of concepts derived from his discussions of general systems theory and the scope of political science. Easton begins his discussion of the life processes of political systems by clarifying the notion of disturbance. A disturbance refers to any influences from the total environment of a political system that "act upon it so that it is different after the stimulus from what it was before."[22] Some disturbances are such that they strengthen the political system. However, other disturbances pose the danger that the essential variables of the political system will be pushed beyond their critical range and thereby cause the system to dissolve. In this case, dissolution is defined as the failure of the political system to perform the functions of allocating values for the society and inducing the members of society to accept these allocations as binding. Those disturbances which endanger the persistence of the political system constitute stress on the system.

Inputs

Easton's description of the life processes of political systems centers on the identification of the ways in which political systems cope with stress. Having defined stress, Easton is ready to define the three summary variables that describe the general outlines of the political system: inputs, outputs, and feedback. Inputs "serve as *summary variables* that concentrate and mirror everything in the environment that is relevant to political stress."[23] Looking back, there is a close relation between Easton's concept of inputs and his discussion of why the political system is a functional prerequisite for the maintenance of social existence. In *The Political System* Easton argued that every society must have some regularized process for settling disputes that arise over the allocation of values. In *A Systems Analysis of Political Life,* these disputes are reflected in the concept of inputs.

Demands Easton divides inputs into demands and supports. Political demands arise when an effort is made by an individual or group to gain a particular authoritative allocation of values. Easton remarks that conflicts over demands constitute the "flesh and blood of all political systems," and that if "we could find a political system in which the input of demands shrank to zero, we could be certain that the system was in the process of disintegrating."[24] Without conflicts over demands, or disputes, society would not need a system for authoritatively allocating values to persist.

However, while a flow of demands is required for the very existence of a political system, demands are also the major source of stress on a political system. Demand stress may be a function of either content or volume (quality or quantity). A system functions in a context of limited space and time. Volume stress refers to the fact that any political system is capable of processing only a finite number of demands. If the volume of demands exceeds a certain limit, the political system will either dissolve, find ways of decreasing the volume, or develop new capacities to handle increased volume.

Content stress refers to the fact that in any political system demands may appear which are either incompatible with the satisfaction of other demands or impossible for the political system to satisfy. In the case of incompatible demands, if two powerful groups are in irreconcilable conflict over a set of significant issues, the political system may dissolve. Easton remarks that private interest plays a key role in the persistence of political systems. While political systems perform a public function, they must perform this function in accordance with the interests of powerful groups: " . . . the failure to meet the demands of at least the politically powerful members in a system will undermine the basic support for the system."[25] If powerful groups make demands that the political system cannot physically meet, the political system may dissolve. Thus, both the quantity and quality of demands may be sources of stress upon the political system. The political system is continuously imperiled by the possibility that either the volume or the content of demands will exceed critical limits.

Supports Despite the seriousness of demands, political systems are not helpless. First, the political system can structurally regulate demands by providing limited channels for their expression, reducing them through combination, modification, or elimination, and transforming them into procedural issues. Demands are also regulated through cultural norms that specify what kinds of wants an individual or group should attempt to satisfy politically. However, the most important way in which political systems cope with volume and content stress is through the mobilization of support.

Support is the second major kind of input and it refers to a favorable orientation towards the political system. Easton states:

We can say that *A* supports *B* either when *A* acts on behalf of *B* or when he orients himself favorably toward *B*. *B* may be a person or group; it may be a goal, idea or institution. I shall designate supportive *actions* as overt support and supportive *attitudes* or sentiments as covert support.[26]

With respect to the political system, support may be given to any or all of the three basic political objects—the political community, the regime, and the authorities. The political community is the most general political object and it refers to "that aspect of a political system that consists of its members seen as a group of persons bound together by a political division of labor."[27] Support of the political community refers to support of any political system for a given group of people.

The regime is the next most general political object and it refers to the basic procedures through which values are allocated for a society. Easton remarks that even if a group of people was characterized by a strong sense of community, it would still have to devise particular ways in which the authoritative settlement of disputes could take place. Support of the regime refers to support of the system of procedures by which values are allocated for a society and support of the most general values sought in the political system.

The authorities constitute the least general political object. They are the occupants of the roles through which values are allocated authoritatively for a society. Support of the authorities refers to support for those who make political decisions.

For Easton, support is grounded in consensus or agreement on the desirability of a given political community, the rightness and goodness of a given regime, and the rectitude and beneficence of given authorities. Thus, the most general answer to Easton's question—How does it come about that any type of system can persist at all, even under the pressures of frequent or constant crises?—is: In most instances there is widespread support, grounded in consensus, for the political community, the regime, and the authorities.

Outputs

The study of inputs constitutes only a third of Easton's systems analysis of political life. In response to stress, political systems produce outputs. The most important outputs are binding allocations of values. Easton views outputs from the perspective of his basic question. They are less attempts to meet demands than they are efforts to cope with stress:

> If we view outputs as the mechanism through which the authorities in a system reach out to cope with problems

created by external changes as they are reflected through changing demands and support, we are led to see the outputs, in their true, dynamic terms.

Through producing outlets, the political system is enabled to exert some influence on the level of support by satisfying demands. Just as Easton holds that no political system can persist in the absence of consensus on fundamental norms and values, he also maintains that no political system can persist which does not satisfy a certain number of demands, or convince people that it is satisfying a certain number of demands. However, if outputs are to perform their function of maintaining support, the authorities must have knowledge of the consequences of authoritative allocations of values on the support of relevant actors in the political system.

Feedback

The requirement of knowledge of consequences leads Easton to discuss the last major element in the political system—feedback. Easton remarks that the "dominant and most fertile intellectual innovation of our own age has been that of information feedback."[29] He observes that political systems can be usefully classified according to the variety or limitations of their responses to stress. Easton points out that for political systems, which are constructively adaptive, feedback "can be shown to be fundamental both for error-regulation, that is, to keep a system pointed in an established direction—preservation of the *status quo*—or for purposive redirection, that is, to move off in search of new goals to conquer."[30] Thus, another way in which political systems are enabled to persist is through the provision of adequate processes, mechanisms, and channels for information feedback. By collecting and ordering information about the consequences of authoritative allocations of values and other outputs, the authorities are given the opportunity to change the character of outputs so that support will be increased. Easton does not maintain that the political system is a completely self-regulating mechanism which will automatically adjust to disturbances in a way which will maximize support. Rather, he claims that the authorities have the option of using information feedback to further the survival of the political system.

SYSTEMS THEORY IN REVIEW

In *A Systems Analysis of Political Life* Easton discusses the various ways in which the political system can be most generally characterized. He states that at the most general level it is "highly useful to depict a political system as a set of interactions through which valued things are authoritatively allocated for a society."[31] However, in addition to this definition, he also provides three other interpretations of the political system. The political system can be usefully depicted as a means for resolving differences, a set of interactions through which demands are processed into outputs, and, from another perspective, "a means through which the resources and energies of society are mobilized and oriented to the pursuit of goals."[32]

Easton also attempts to depict the political system metaphorically. He states that "we might compare a political system to a huge and complex factory in which raw material in the form of wants in our generalized sense, are taken in, worked upon and transformed into a primary product called demands."[33] Alternatively, Easton suggests that the political system can be compared to a gigantic communications network. Elsewhere he states that the political system can be visualized as a vast conversion process. Through each of these definitions and analogies runs a common thread. The concept of the political system gathers together the major tendencies in descriptive political theory in the twentieth century and synthesizes them.

Influence of Earlier Theories

Climax of Post-Marxist Theory   While the synthesis is formal, it also represents the culmination of post-Marxist political theory in the West. Of all of the three major working political theories of the first half of the twentieth century, Easton is most closely allied with the pluralist tradition. In *The Political System* he undertakes a critique of American political science and even feels it necessary to remark that his discussion of James Bryce is relevant in this context. Thus, Easton's greatest debt is to political theorists like Arthur Bentley.

Unlike Bentley, Easton does not recognize any special debt to Marx. In *The Political System* he represents a later generation of political theorists who have already absorbed the phenomenological generalization of writers like Bentley, Weber, and Mosca. Thus, in his brief discussion of Marx, Easton maintains that "Marx's attempt to isolate the influence of social classes on policy is a search for the role of class groupings in the situation."[34] He reduces Marxist theory to the hypothesis that

> in the relationship of forces in a society, groupings formed
> around expectations with regard to the mode of produc-
> tion and property relations confront the policy-makers

with a power situation in which they must meet the needs
of the dominant class or lose their positions of authority.[35]

With respect to political theory, Marx is merely an early theorist of
interest groups who seized upon a particular cross section of activity
as specially important in determining the authoritative allocation of
values for a society. Later theorists improved upon Marx by showing
that a wide variety of cross sections of activity could become
politically relevant. Thus, from the pluralists, Easton takes the
concept of cross section of activity and the idea of the importance of
interest groups.

Easton uses the idea of cross-sectional activity in two ways.
First, his definition of the political system is itself in terms of a cross
section of activity. The set of interactions relevant to the process of
authoritatively allocating values for a society describes a particular
cross section of activity. In his notion of representative activity,
Bentley was working towards a definition of the political system
similar to Easton's proposal. However, it is the functionalist perspective adopted by Easton which enables him to base the definition
of the political system on a cross section of activity.

Second, Easton uses the idea of cross section of activity in the
traditional pluralist way. Like Bentley, Easton distinguishes underlying activities from representative activities. Out of the mass of
activity that constitutes society, only some actions are politically
relevant. Political relevance here is not defined in terms of content,
but with reference to form. Social activities become politically
relevant when they involve demands for certain authoritative allocations of value for the entire society. Any want that appears in society
can be converted into a demand as long as it can be represented in
the political system. Of course, this does not mean that all wants can
be satisfied, but that all cross sections of activity can become
politically relevant. Through his concept of demand, Easton also
integrates interest groups into his systems analysis of political life.
Interest groups are demand-making activities and, as in Bentley, are
coextensive with politically relevant activities.

Organization Theory While Easton is most usefully considered
in his relation to the pluralist tradition of twentieth-century political
thought, his work also incorporates the contributions of organization
theorists and theorists of political elites. With respect to organization theory, in the *Political System* Easton distinguishes between
groups and groupings. These units are the result of a distinction
within cross sections of activity. The grouping is a pattern of activity
or relation of individuals to one another that is not formally
organized, that requires no close interaction among the members,

and that is not deliberately directed to the pursuit of specified purposes. It is a collection of individuals "who are classed together as a result of the fact that they have specified characteristics in common."[36] Groupings are defined by a common characteristic rather than a collective purpose.

The group is an organized pattern of activity directed to the achievement of a particular purpose or set of purposes. In the terms of this study, the group is an organization. Like Buchler, James, and others in the pragmatic tradition, Easton claims that social groupings are analytically prior to social groups "in the sense that the activity and even the interpretation of goals of a formal organization reflect the fundamental social groupings from which its members come."[37] However, in his discussion of the importance of the structure of the regime, Easton recognizes the importance of organization.

The Theory of Political Elites Easton's relation to the theory of political elites is even closer than his relation to organization theory. Besides stating that a political system cannot persist unless a significant proportion of the demands of powerful interests are met, Easton argues that his systems analysis of political life includes the theory of political elites. He holds that the question posed by theorists of political elites—"Who gets what, when, and how?"—takes for granted the "actual and continued existence of some kind of political system."[38] Elites only function within a political system, and political conflicts are bounded by the norms that help define a political system.

While Easton may be correct that elites only function within a political system, he is not correct that questions about the persistence of the political system are prior to questions about elites. If the political system arises to process demands, then the question— "Who gets what, when, and how?"—is just as fundamental as the question—"How does it come about that any type of system can persist at all, even under the pressures of frequent or constant crisis?" However, even if Easton fails to solve the problem of the relations between public function and private interest, his idea of system constitutes a framework in which the major developments of twentieth-century descriptive political theory can be placed.

Components of Analysis

The systems analysis of David Easton consists of two separable components. The first component is the formal concept of the political system as an empirical, constructively adaptive, and analytic system. The second component is the definition of the political system as that set of interactions through which values are authoritatively allocated for a society. The first component represents the culmination of formalism in twentieth-century political theory. It provides a framework for the next major development in political theory. The second component represents the introduction of content into twentieth-century political theory through the approach of functional analysis. The political system is given an arbitrary public function and political analysis is directed to state the conditions in which that function is performed. This type of functional analysis, separable from systems theory as a set of formal categories, raises the problem of methodology in its broadest sense of a philosophy of political science. The next development in political theory will substitute the methods of existentialism for those of functionalism. In order to understand this statement it is necessary to devote some discussion to the problem of method.

NOTES

1. W. J. M. Mackenzie, *Politics and Social Science* (Baltimore: Penguin Books, Inc., 1967), p. 96.

2. David Easton, *A Framework for Political Analysis* (Englewood Cliffs, N.J.: Prentice-Hall, Inc., 1965), p. 23.

3. Ibid., p. 24.

4. Ibid., p. 25.

5. Ibid., p. 27.

6. Ibid., p. 30.

7. Ibid.

8. Ibid., pp. 61–62.

9. Morton A. Kaplan, *Macropolitics* (Chicago: Aldine Publishing Company, 1969), p. 26.

10. David Easton, *The Political System* (New York: Alfred A. Knopf, Inc., 1953), p. 236.

11. Ibid., p. 262.

12. Ibid., p. 260.

13. Ibid., p. 127.

14. Ibid.

15. Ibid., p. 135.

16. Ibid., p. 132.

17. Ibid., p. 137.

18. Ibid.

19. David Easton, A *Systems Analysis of Political Life* (New York: John Wiley & Sons, Inc., 1965), p. vii.

20. Friedrich Baerwald, "A Sociological View of Depersonalization," *Thought*, 21 (Spring 1956): 70.

21. Friedrich Baerwald, "Humanism and Social Ambivalence," *Thought*, 42 (Winter 1967): 554.

22. Easton, *A Systems Analysis*, p.22.

23. Ibid., p. 26.

24. Ibid., p. 48.

25. Ibid., p. 60.

26. Ibid., p. 159.

27. Ibid., p. 178.

28. Ibid., p. 346.

29. Ibid., p. 367.

30. Ibid., p. 372.

31. Ibid., p. 153.

32. Ibid.

33. Ibid., p. 72.

34. Easton, *The Political System*, p. 189.

35. Ibid.

36. Ibid., p. 186.

37. Ibid., p. 187.

38. Easton, *A Systems Analysis*, p. 475.

SUGGESTED READINGS

Almond, Gabriel A., and Sidney Verba. *The Civic Culture.* Princeton, N.J.: Princeton University Press, 1963.

Apter, David E. *Some Conceptual Approaches to the Study of Modernization.* Englewood Cliffs, N.J.: Prentice-Hall, Inc., 1968.

Deutsch, Karl. *The Nerves of Government.* New York: The Free Press, 1966.

Easton, David. *A Systems Analysis of Political Life.* New York: John Wiley & Sons, Inc., 1965.

Eulau, Heinz. *The Behavioral Persuasion in Politics.* New York: Random House, Inc., 1963.

Kaplan, Morton. *Macropolitics.* Chicago: Aldine Publishing Company, 1969.

Lipset, Seymour M. *Political Man.* Garden City, N.Y.: Doubleday & Company, Inc., 1963.

Mitchell, William C. *The American Polity.* New York: The Free Press, 1962.

Parsons, Talcott. *The Social System.* Glencoe, Ill.: The Free Press of Glencoe, Ill., 1951.

Wiseman, H. V. *Political Systems.* New York: Frederick A. Praeger, Inc., 1967.

PART FOUR

KEY METHODS
OF POLITICAL INQUIRY

CHAPTER NINE

THE SEARCH
FOR A METHOD

Sheldon Wolin has remarked that in the modern age the adoption of a method of inquiry is not "equivalent to buying a new suit, to a transaction in which only the external appearance of the purchaser" is altered. Rather, it is "a profound personal choice, perhaps the closest functional equivalent to conversionary experience that the modern mind can achieve."[1] With respect to political theory, the history of methodic choice in the twentieth century has been the history of debates about the correct interpretation of the scientific method and its application to political phenomena.

It is indisputable that the project of making the study of political affairs scientific has been central to the enterprise of political theory in the twentieth century. We have already remarked that theorists of political elites—Mosca, Pareto, and Michels—believed that only a scientific study of politics would prove adequate to the task of refuting socialist and democratic ideas. American pluralists—particularly John Dewey, Sidney Hook, and their followers—have proposed the development of a political science that would vindicate democracy and aid the extension of democratic practices in all phases of social existence. Most contemporary political theorists in the United States do not believe that the scientific study of politics will aid the development of any particular political regime. Like Lasswell, they hold that all sciences have various policy branches. The biological sciences include medicine, which is organized knowledge in reference to health, and biological warfare, which is organized knowledge in reference to harm. Similarly, political science has policy branches "suggested by such phrases as 'the political science (or policy science) of democracy' or of despotism."[2] Thus, political science includes the policy sciences of death as well as of life. However, whether or not political theorists in the twentieth century maintain that the scientific study of politics will support the claims of a given regime, the idea of a science of political activity has been a guiding ideal for them.

CIVILIZED HUMANISM AND THE HISTORICAL METHOD

The first phase of the debate over scientific method in the study of political activity concerns the use of the historical method. The foremost twentieth-century political theorist to identify the scientific study of politics with the historical method was Gaetano Mosca. In *The Ruling Class*, Mosca asserts that "if political science is to be grounded upon the observation and interpretation of the facts of political life, it is to the old historical method that we must return."[3] For Mosca, progress in the field of political science will be based upon the study of social facts, and social facts are only available in the history of the various nations of the world. He recognizes that there have been many objections lodged against the historical method as a scientific approach, but believes that they can be refuted.

Mosca's Defense

Mosca discusses the argument that while political theorists from Aristotle to the present have used the historical method, no truly scientific system has arisen from it. He responds to this objection with the claim that the historical method has not yet been properly applied. Before the historical method can yield scientific knowledge one must have a wide and accurate knowledge of history, but only in the nineteenth century did the data which are a prerequisite of such knowledge become available to scholars.

Mosca is impressed with the results of modern historical scholarship for two reasons. First, in the nineteenth century history became an exact discipline. Standards of documentation and evidence became rigorous and, therefore, knowledge of past events became more reliable. Second, and more important, during the nineteenth century the scope of historical knowledge became much broader than it had been previously. This increase in scope itself had two facets. First, European scholars became aware of the details of life in past civilizations throughout the world and in contemporary non-Western societies. Thus, for the first time scholars could undertake serious comparative studies of social existence that ranged across cultures. Further, the development of statistics made it possible to carry through such comparisons with exactitude. Second, historians began to collect and systematize data about social custom and political and administrative organization among different peoples. Such data about social structure were far more fundamental for the development of political science than information about the personal accomplishments of rulers which made up the content of chronicles. Thus, for Mosca, at the turn of the twentieth century a scientific study of political affairs had become possible due to the reliability and scope of historical data. The historical method of political study was scientific because it applied comparison to social structural data. Mosca remarked optimistically: "There can be no doubt about it: where the student of the social sciences could once only guess, he now has the means to *observe* and the instruments and the materials to *demonstrate.*"[4] The inaccuracies and mistakes of classical political theorists like Aristotle, Machiavelli, and Montesquieu could be traced not to their method but to their lack of reliable and comparative data.

A second objection to the historical method is more fundamental than the argument that no body of systematic theory has yet arisen from it. Here the critics argue that no historical data are reliable:

> It is commonly alleged that, for all of their many efforts, historians often fail to discover the truth: that it is often hard to determine with any exactness just how things which have happened in our own towns within the year actually came to pass; so that it is virtually impossible to obtain accounts that are worthy of belief when faraway times and places are concerned.[5]

Mosca claims that this objection misunderstands the objective of a scientific study of politics. He observes that the historical facts which are the least reliable are those that concern individual biography and the "vanity or profit" of an individual or a group. With respect to these facts, commentators are likely to let their passions get in the way of objectivity. However, the scientific study of politics is not concerned with such issues as whether a general won a battle because of his sterling character or because of his competence as a tactician. Political scientists use structural data and ignore information about individuals. For the political scientist, "there are facts that concern the social type and organization of the various peoples and the various epochs; and it is about such facts, which are of the greater interest to us, that historians, spontaneously and without bias, often tell the truth."[6] Further, the most important barrier to learning the truth about social affairs arises when interest groups oppose the quest for knowledge. Mosca states optimistically that where interest groups do not interfere, anyone who is willing to spend enough time and money can always, through intensive inquiry, discover the circumstances surrounding a given event. With respect to historical facts about past civilizations, the interference of interest groups in the conduct of inquiry is unlikely.

Mosca concludes his discussion with the observation that the "great psychological laws that are manifested in the lives of nations" reveal their operation "in administrative and judicial institutions, in religions, in all the moral and political customs of the various nations."[7] The political scientist should not set up rigid standards of preference with regard to such structural data. Any detail of information about the institutions of a civilized people may be useful.

Mosca's Advice

Parochialism Mosca will make only one recommendation about the use of historical data: the political scientist should not derive all of his observations from a single group of regimes representative of only one historical period and one civilization. A restricted scope of data selection will lead the scholar to mistake patterns of activity that are peculiar to a particular historical period for great and universal laws of social structure. Parochialism, in fact, is the most subtle danger present in political inquiry. It is not enough for the political scientist to recognize his political, national, and religious prejudices. He must also know how to lift his "judgment above the beliefs and opinions which are current in [his] time or peculiar to the social or national type" to which he belongs.[8] Such knowledge can only be gained through the study of the history of mankind as a whole.

Anthropology With this principle in mind, Mosca remarks that scholars who study the social life of bees, apes, and primitive peoples have relatively little to contribute to the scientific study of politics. Especially with respect to investigations of primitive social institutions, Mosca holds that the reports of observers are likely to be much less objective than the data provided by historians about past civilizations. Mosca wrote these passages before anthropologists had fully developed the method of participant observation to correct for cultural bias. Twentieth-century anthropologists agree with Mosca that mere recognition of one's prejudices is not sufficient to insure objective observation. The anthropologist must also be prepared to learn the categories of social relationships that are fundamental to the people that he studies.

However, even if he had known about the method of participant observation, Mosca would not have been satisfied with the investigation of primitive social existence. He remarks that in the small group "the political problem hardly exists, and therefore cannot be studied." For Mosca, the political problem is the formation, character, and maintenance of ruling classes. Only in complex organizations do the phenomena associated with political domination appear clearly: "Psychological social forces cannot develop, and cannot find scope, except in large political organisms, in aggregates, that is, where numerous groups of human beings are brought together in a moral and political union."[9] While the study of primitive societies might show in embryo all of the structures that develop in advanced societies, the scholar can best describe these structures when he observes them in their most differentiated state. For Mosca, the questions of how a small ruling class can impose itself on a mass of people and how millions of people can come to share an intense national feeling, cannot be resolved in the study of small groups.

The Civilized Human Being

The historical method is the methodological expression of civilized humanism in political theory. For Mosca, as for all of the major political theorists of the twentieth century, Wolin's remark that the choice of a method is the closest functional equivalent to conversionary experience that the modern mind can achieve expresses a fundamental truth. As a civilized humanist, Mosca maintains that in order to become a good political scientist one must become a civilized human being. It is impossible to separate strictly the education of a political scientist from the education of a civilized person. In both cases, correct education consists in learning to transcend one's parochial situation by studying the history of mankind as a whole. Only through such a study will the person be able to distinguish what is universal in social existence from what is peculiar to a particular place and time. For the political scientist, in search of generalizations that apply to all social structures, the necessity of distinguishing universal from particular is obvious. The civilized man must also have this ability. It defines his judgment and ability to transcend his prejudices without succumbing to a shallow relativism.

Science and History

The good political scientist is only one kind of civilized human being. He is a scientist. For Mosca, a

> science is always built up on a system of observations which have been made with particular care and by appropriate methods on a given order of phenomena and which have been so coordinated as to disclose incontrovertible truths which would not have been discovered by the ordinary observation of the plain man.[10]

Mosca identifies mathematics as the most perfect science. Mathematics begins with a small number of axioms whose truth is apparent even to the plain man. From the coordination of these axioms are derived proofs of simple theorems, and from the coordination of the simple theorems are derived proofs for complex theorems whose truth could not be anticipated by nonmathematicians.

The procedure in the natural sciences is not different in essentials from that in mathematics. However, the definition of principles equivalent to mathematical axioms can only be accomplished after long periods of observation and experimentation. Of course, mere observation and experimentation does not assure scientific results. The activity of generalizing, or coordinating observations under principles, is equal in importance to observation. A political science founded on the historical method will provide a wealth of observations for classification. The general theory of political elites will provide the most promising set of axioms upon which to base further research. For Mosca, the activity of political science is a civilized activity. There is no rift between the scientist and the humanist, because the good scientist must be a good humanist.

Weaknesses of Mosca's Approach Mosca's view of the nature of a science should be distinguished from his account of the historical method. The philosophy of science expressed by Mosca is open to serious question. It is doubtful that mathematics can be made a useful model for all of the other sciences. Not all mathematical systems begin with a small number of axioms whose truth is apparent even to the plain man. There are geometries in which the axiom appears that parallel lines converge, as well as geometries in which the axiom appears that parallel lines remain equidistant. Neither geometry is more true than the other one. Truth value in mathematics is accorded to propositions that have been correctly deduced from axioms. Contrariwise, the truth value of statements in the natural sciences is dependent on the accord of hypothesized relationships with observation, as well as upon correct deduction from theoretical premises.

Current literature in the philosophy of science would also cast doubt upon Mosca's statement that science discloses incontrovertible truths. If the truth value of scientific statements is dependent on the accord of hypothesized relationships with observation, future observation may always disconfirm a hypothesis. One can never be sure that a scientific statement is an incontrovertible truth. One can be sure that many hypothesized relationships are not true. Some mathematical propositions may be incontrovertibly true in the sense that they have been correctly deduced from other mathematical statements.

Merits of the Historical Method If Mosca's account of the philosophy of science is faulty, the historical method that he suggests does not necessarily fall with it. In fact, the historical method, as the contribution of civilized humanism to the study of political activity, is one of the three significant methods in contemporary political inquiry. The historical method is also the method of comparison of social structures. Guided by a set of general categories, such as cross section of activity, interest group, organization, elite, social type, political formula, and political system, the scholar classifies data available from a wide range of civilizations and attempts to discover relationships among them that overarch particular civilizations. The weakness of the historical method is that it does not provide any guidance about the kinds of relationships that one should seek, or the way in which one should go about organizing the data with respect to the categories. This weakness is remedied by the other two important methods that arose in the twentieth-century—the functional method, which is derived from pragmatism, and the method of totalization, which is derived from existentialism.

The great strength of the historical method is its response to the insight that it is not enough for the political scientist to recognize his political, national, and religious prejudices. It is fashionable for contemporary political scientists to announce their social preferences and proceed to do their research as if they had absolved themselves from bias. Mosca shows that bias in the social sciences is not primarily a matter of fudging the data in favor of one's preferences, or even of serving powerful interest groups, but of having a parochial perspective. In a world in which linkages among cultures are increasing in number and intensity, the only good data base for comparative studies of social structure is in historical literature. In the modern age, to become civilized, one must go to the past. And if Mosca is correct that a good political scientist must be civilized, the historical method is necessary to political science. For Mosca and other civilized humanists, history is the content that makes form meaningful.

PRAGMATISM AND THE FUNCTIONAL METHOD

As the historical method is the expression of civilized humanism in the study of politics, the functional method is the expression of pragmatism in political inquiry. In its most rudimentary sense, the functional method involves discovering and describing the consequences of a human activity or practice on the continuation or change of another human activity or practice. In this context, the functional method does not necessarily mean the analysis of the effects of human activities and practices on the maintenance of the political system as a whole, although such analysis is included within the definition. Interpreting the functional method simply as the study of the consequences of some human activities on the performance of other human activities allows one to appreciate the centrality of this method to all forms of pragmatic political study. The functional sociology of knowledge traces the effects of political rhetoric on the satisfaction of group interests, the study of public problems describes the indirect consequences of human activities, and the investigation of the political system involves discovering the effects of activities and practices on the persistence of the political system. Even in organization theory, Blau and Scott use the functional method when they classify organizations according to who benefits from their operation and describe the central dilemmas of organizational life in terms of prime beneficiaries.

Marx and Easton

Interpreted broadly, the functional method is implied in all studies of social structure. While the data for structural studies are historical, the kinds of relationships sought in these studies are functional. For example, Marx used the functional method in his study of capitalist society. He described the consequences of a wide variety of human activities for the maintenance of capitalist institutions. With respect to political affairs, the idea of the state as the executive committee of the ruling class is a result of using the functional method. For Marx, the state has consequences for other institutionalized human activities. Formally, this claim is not different from Easton's idea that the political system is the set of interactions through which values are authoritatively allocated for a society. While Marx refers the consequences of human activities to the persistence of the economic system, Easton refers the consequences of human activities to the political system, and indirectly, to the maintenance of the entire society.

The functionalisms of Easton and Marx are different in their relative emphases on form and content. Marx organized his functional analysis around the study of specific historical types of economic systems and gave economic activity priority over other human activities. Easton has organized his functional analysis around the study of how any political system persists and, in the tradition of Bentley, Weber, and Mosca, has not given any human activity a priori precedence over any other. Of course, Easton has brought content into his system through his definition of the function of the political system as the authoritative allocation of values for a society. In view of the many functions that have been proposed for the political system, this is perhaps the weakest part of his analysis. However, despite the particular problems that are present in the discussions of Marx and Easton, both writers adopt a functional method in the broad sense defined here.

Kinds of Functional Approaches

Eclectic Functionalism William Flanigan and Edwin Fogelman have made a set of useful distinctions among the various kinds of functional approaches. They define "eclectic functionalism" as the most rudimentary form of functional analysis. The eclectic functionalist attempts to describe the purposes served by a phenomenon X, and may either "only provide a list of activities in which X is engaged, or . . . may provide answers to more or less explicit questions with respect to how X contributes to the performance of certain purposes or activities."[11] Flanigan and Fogelman point out that eclectic functionalists have no commitment to functionalism as a distinctive method of analysis which defines the kinds of relationships sought by political scientists. They do not make function the focus of analysis, but make the study of consequences only one aspect of their research. Further, they do not integrate systematically the functional method with other methods of analysis.

Empirical Functionalism A more rigorous approach is "empirical functionalism," identified with the work of the sociologist Robert K. Merton. Flanigan and Fogelman define empirical functionalism as the study of the purposes or consequences of human activities with special reference to their bearing on the satisfaction of demands. For Merton and other theorists, like Blau, functions are performed to the extent that human activities satisfy demands. However, beyond initial demand satisfaction, the political scientist must analyze the indirect consequences of human activity:

> Functional analysis requires an elucidation not only of manifest functions, the obvious and intended purposes and consequences, but also of latent functions, the more covert and unintended consequences that are equally important and enlightening as subjects for analysis.[12]

Flanigan and Fogelman point out that there are severe limitations to empirical functionalism. Empirical functionalists do not attempt to define the functional requisites for the persistence of society, or the conditions in the absence of which societies would not persist. Even more important, empirical functionalists isolate particular elements within social existence and do not clarify the significance of these elements for social existence as a whole. Whether or not these limitations are critically damaging to empirical

functionalism is partly dependent upon one's theoretical perspective. Flanigan and Fogelman assume that there is a concrete social
system to which the consequences of human activities and practices
can be referred. If such a social system is more an idea whose content
is continually changing than a concrete entity, then some form of
empirical functionalism is the most ambitious mode of analysis that
one can attempt.

Structural-Functional Analysis For Flanigan and Fogelman,
the most ambitious and rigorous application of the functional
method appears in structural-functional analysis. *Structural-
functional analysis* is defined as the attempt to state the activities in
the absence of which societies would not persist and then to
describe the structures within particular societies that perform these
activities. David Easton's theory of the political system is an example of a partial structural-functional analysis. Easton argues that no
society could persist in the absence of structures for authoritatively
allocating values for the society. While the authoritative allocation
of values for a society is not the only functional requisite for the
persistence of a society, it is the function appropriate to investigation by political scientists.

While we have already criticized Easton's particular structural-
functional analysis by showing its Hobbesian assumptions, this
critique would not necessarily be applicable to every example of
structural-functional analysis. However, it is likely that any attempt
to specify a function for political activity that is also a functional
requisite for the persistence of society would involve assumptions
about an invariant human condition. Of course, this judgment does
not apply to all attempts to provide a function for politics. Efforts to
show that a certain function for politics is within the scope of human
possibility do not assume an invariant human nature.

It is only when a theorist attempts to show that a particular
function is a requisite for the persistence of society that the functional method becomes unalterably opposed to the insights of
existentialists into the human condition, in the sense that structural-functional requisite analysis assumes a substantive description of
human nature. Failure to distinguish between the claims of structural-functional requisite analysis and empirical functionalism have
led some scholars to set up a false contradiction between all forms of
the functional method and all forms of existentialism. Suggested
functions for politics, such as Dewey's idea that political actors
should care for the indirect consequences of human activity and
Jaspers' idea that political actors should make cultural contribution
possible, do not contradict the requirements of authentic existence.
Rather, they are available as goals for human projection.

Logic of Functional Analysis

Structural-functional analysis has sparked a lively debate in political theory over the meaning of scientific explanation. Flanigan and Fogelman have summarized the basic form of the structural-functional argument in two syllogisms. The first syllogism states that if "system s is to be maintained adequately under conditions c, then requisite functions $f1, f2 \ldots fn$ must be performed;" and if "system s is being maintained adequately;" then "requisite functions $f1, f2 \ldots fn$ are being performed."[13] The second syllogism states that if "requisite functions $f1, f2 \ldots fn$ are being performed;" then "requisite functions are being performed by existing structures."[14] They point out that the structural-functionalist argument leaves many problems unresolved. First, the argument does not specify criteria for determining when a system is adequately maintained. Second, the argument does not relate changes in structures to changes in the ways in which functions are performed. Third, the argument does not provide any criteria for determining what functions are requisite for the persistence of the system.

In principle, each of these defects could be remedied if one assumed the existence of a social system. Criteria of systems maintenance could be derived empirically with the guidance of such concepts as political community, regime, and authorities. Special theories could be devised to account for the interaction between structure and function in particular regimes. The assumptions of requisite analysis could be clarified through a rigorous analysis of the human condition. However, all of this assumes that it is useful to undertake structural-functional requisite analysis in the first place. Are there empirical social systems defined through functional requisites? This ontological question is prior to questions about the refinement of the logic of inquiry.

While Easton attempts to base his systems analysis of political life on the notion of constructive systems that appear only in the mind of the investigator, he is led eventually to justify his analysis in terms of natural systems that appear in observation. It is legitimate to question the appearance of political systems characterized by single functions in observation. However, if one answers the ontological question in favor of structural-functional analysis, it is clear that functional explanations are, in principle, scientific explanations. James Gregor argues that functional analysis "serves primarily as an exhortation to conceive the entity, entities, process or processes under scrutiny as teleological, that is, as having some systemic properties."[15] Thus, he holds that functional analysis is merely a recommendation to consider human activities as part of a system, an exhortation to "entertain hypotheses concerning the existence of functional systems, self-regulating and goal-directed entities, and the occurrence of functional relationships among the objects of research."[16] Jerone Stephens challenges Gregor's interpretation and argues that structural-functional analysis is an attempt "to provide an explanation of an item of behavior by showing that it contributes to maintaining a functional requisite within a given range."[17] Stephens points out that this kind of statement makes an empirically verifiable truth claim rather than a recommendation to consider certain kinds of data.

In our earlier criticism of Easton's systems analysis, we remarked that it is neither logically nor phenomenologically possible to show that the authoritative allocation of values for a society is a requisite function for the persistence of a society. However, if the authoritative allocation of values is neither logically nor phenomenologically necessary, it can only be empirically observable. Thus, in the debate between those who characterize structural-functional analysis as a heuristic device and those who characterize this kind of analysis as an attempt at an empirical theory, the second position seems to be the stronger one. Stephens points out cogently that while the explanations offered by structural-functional analysts are often inadequate, "it must be emphasized that an inadequate explanation does not thereby turn a functional or systems analysis into a useful heuristic device or make the statements appearing in the purported explanation analytical ones where no truth claim is made."[18] The only important consideration to add to Stephens' argument is that as a source of explanations structural-functional analysis is probably defective for ontological reasons. It attempts to identify a minimal function for a political system when the entire tendency of twentieth-century political philosophy—represented by the pragmatic, existentialist, and civilized humanist movements—is to keep the attribution of functions as open as possible.

Functional Analysis and Social Criticism

Structural-functional analysis does not exhaust the functional method. In fact, it is merely the most defective example of that method. At its best, the functional method, like the historical method, is a moral discipline as well as a mode of empirical inquiry. While the proper use of the historical method requires one to be a civilized human being, the proper use of the functional method requires one to be a socially conscious human being. The requirement of social consciousness is apparent in the two fundamental expressions of the functional method—the analysis of indirect consequences of human activity and the functional sociology of knowledge.

Expressions of the Functional Method The analysis of the indirect consequences of human activity, as it is found in Dewey, Merton, Blau, and many other pragmatists, fixes the attention of the investigator on the social dimension of action. As Dewey recognizes in *Individualism Old and New,* the functional method is as much a critique of narrow individualism and privatization as it is a means to describing social structures. Human activities can be described in terms of their effects on a multitude of other activities and practices. The political scientist should be aware particularly of intense consequences for groups of human beings which are either unintended and unrecognized, or intended and unrecognized. He should describe private actions in terms of their public effects and show that private problems may be conditioned by public circumstances. For Dewey, the political scientist using the functional method cannot help but be a social critic. Part of his vocation involves describing consequences of human activity that may be extremely embarrassing to powerful interest groups.

The second typical expression of the functional method is the sociology of knowledge. Bentley's idea of a socioanalysis that would function political rhetoric in terms of group activity was both a serious proposal for political inquiry and the analogue in sociology of psychoanalysis in psychology. In *Relativity in Man and Society,* Bentley equates the education of the competent political scientist with the education of the socially conscious human being. He distinguishes between education and training. Training fits the individual for effective action in a particular groupal complex. One is trained to be a podiatrist, a survey researcher, or a computer programmer. For Bentley, there is nothing despicable about training. Without specialization modern society would be impossible. However, the mere learning of techniques ignores education, or the loosening of the individual from his special attachments so that he can be widened for other and more profitable attachments. Bentley remarks that even "our universities with the broadest cultural claims often stop that culture, even restrict it and hamper it before it gives comprehension of the real groupal aspects of the coming young man's and young woman's life."[19] The role of education is not to satisfy people with their positions in society, but to free people to comprehension "of their own position's value in terms of all the positions around them."[20] Thus, socioanalysis is both a primary tool of inquiry for the political scientist and a requirement of the socially conscious individual.

The Socially Conscious Human Being The competent political scientist is inseparable from the socially conscious human being. The good political scientist is also a free human being in the sense that he does not unreflectively assume the perspective of his social position. While Mosca's civilized human being was enabled to raise his level of judgment by study of the history of mankind, Bentley's and Dewey's socially conscious human being is enabled to raise his level of judgment by relativizing his social position in terms of other positions and appreciating the secondary consequences of human activities. The socially conscious human being is the highest result of the use of the functional method. For political science, the most important result of the functional method is an awareness of the kinds of relationships that are sought in political inquiry.

EXISTENTIALISM AND THE METHOD OF TOTALIZATION

While the strength of the historical method for political inquiry is the identification of a body of data and the strength of the functional method is the identification of the kind of relationship sought, the importance of the method of totalization for political science lies in its identification of the way in which one should go about organizing political data with respect to the formal categories defined in twentieth-century political theory. The method of totalization is the expression of existentialism in political inquiry. Like the civilized humanist historical method and the pragmatic functional method, the method of totalization requires moral discipline as well as the mastery of technique. While the product of the historical method is the civilized human being and the product of the functional method is the socially conscious human being, the product of the method of totalization is the freely creative human being.

Freedom to Create

The method of totalization is special in that it demands more than merely raising the level of judgment of the investigator. The freedom of thought gained by the study of the history of mankind and the relativization of one's own social position in terms of other positions is only preparatory to a freedom of creation. The method of totalization comprises an attempt to give some structure to the act of creation in political science and political theory. It also makes political inquiry more of what is usually considered an art than a science. However, properly understood, the method of totalization uses mathematical analysis or techniques of deliberate and structured investigation in political science. It also admits the goal of functional generalizations and their coordination into deductive systems for descriptive political theory. Finally, the method of totalization allows rigorous empirical testing of functional generalizations.

Like the other key methods of contemporary political theory, the method of totalization is concerned with neither matters of technique nor matters of verification. It is only indirectly concerned with the logical structure of descriptive political theory. Questions of technique and verification are not likely to drive human beings to the closest functional equivalent to conversionary experience that the modern mind can achieve. However, the decisions to apply seriously the historical method and the functional method are likely to have profound ramifications for an individual's entire mode of existence. One must become a certain kind of human being to apply these methods correctly. The same judgment is even more accurate with respect to the method of totalization, which requires the person to make his decisions about social existence in a particular way. While the method of totalization does not oppose the use of mathematical analysis, techniques of deliberate and structured investigation, systems of deductive theory, and precise empirical tests of hypothesized generalizations, it interprets these elements of political inquiry as parts of a larger project and attempts to show their limitations.

Critique of Contemporary Analysis

The method of totalization can be best understood as an application of existentialism to political inquiry and as a revolt against approaches like structural-functional requisite analysis. In its most fundamental sense, the method of totalization is an attempt to describe the character of authentic existence for a political scientist. Like existentialism, the method of totalization is defined initially by its opposition to architectonic systems of political thought. In its American version, best represented by the works of C. Wright Mills, it is a criticism of thought-structures like David Easton's systems analysis of political life. In its European version, best represented by the works of Jean-Paul Sartre, it is a criticism of orthodox Marxism and Soviet ideology.

Answer to Inauthentic Methods The method of totalization is a response to the inauthentic method that Mills, Sartre, and other humanistic social theorists find dominant in the social sciences. Sartre names the inauthentic method of political science *placing.* Sartre holds that contemporary political theories, especially Soviet Marxism, are made up of formalized abstractions that he calls *general particularities.* Abstractions such as the authoritative allocation of values for a society in Easton's political theory pretend to refer to concrete human situations, but are actually timeless sets of relations. Armed with a set of general particularities, the contemporary systematic political theorist goes about denuding particular historical events of their detail and of their relations with other events, and placing them as instances of one or another of the formalized abstractions. For Sartre, the method of placing violates experience because its "sole purpose is to force the events, the persons, or the acts considered into pre-fabricated molds."[21]

Similar to Sartre's critique of the method of placing is Barrington Moore's discussion of the method of illustrating. Moore, an American political sociologist, associates the method of illustrating with systems theories characterized by "logically watertight" analytical categories. Systems theorists tend to support their category systems by detaching particular historical events from their context in time and space and subsuming them under one or another of their concepts. Moore observes that "any concept can be 'illustrated' somehow or other, and facts picked up off the table and put into pigeon holes."[22]

For Sartre and the American humanist political sociologists, the methods of placing and illustrating are totalitarian as well as unscientific. Social existence does not appear as a set of examples of timeless ideas. Any attempt to describe social existence in this way will result in ignoring human possibility and choice, and the relational contexts in which political events take place. In brief, the methods of placing and illustrating make society appear as though it is simply a life order in which political activity appears merely as the performance of one function among others.

Openness to Possibility The opposition of proponents of the method of totalization to the methods of placing and illustrating does not involve a commitment to view social existence as a succession of utterly unique occurrences. The core of the methods of placing and illustrating is defined less in terms of a penchant for universalizing than in terms of a tendency to force the facts to fit predetermined categories. Sartre and the American humanists object primarily to the tendency of contemporary systematic political theorists to define in advance the content of what they will observe about political existence. An example of the existentialist critique of structural-functional requisite analysis is the criticism undertaken here in the section concerning the functional method. Structural-functional requisite analysis is antiexistential because it specifies in advance the functions that must be performed for societies to persist. Each system is given a particular function, and no other functions or systems are permitted.

Such attribution of functions involves assigning a particular content to political activity in advance of observation. Once this is done, human activities can be taken out of context and judged politically relevant or politically irrelevant on the basis of whether or not they are related to the particular function. Political analysis is frozen around a content that pretends to be a universal form. Making the authoritative allocation of values for a society or some other function the essence of political activity runs counter to the existential observation of Max Weber that "there is scarcely any task that some political association has not taken in hand, and there is no task that one could say has always been exclusive and peculiar to those associations which are designated as political ones"[23] and William James' equally existential remark that if

> we should inquire for the essence of 'government', for example, one man might tell us it was authority, another submission, another police, another an army, another an assembly, another a system of laws; yet all the while it would be true that no concrete government can exist without all these things, one of which is more important at one moment and others at another.[24]

This argument does not imply that formal definitions of the scope of political inquiry are not useful. The notions of cross-sectional activity, organization, and dominance are essential concepts in the investigation of political activity. However, none of them fix once and for all the purposes that political activity must serve. They do not renounce possibility. The openness to possibility is particularly apparent in the most useful formal category of all—system. Once the attribution of a particular function has been separated from the notion of system, the importance of the concept of system can be understood. The notion of a natural, open, and creatively adjustive system provides a ground for Bentley's idea that "we have a great moving process" to study in which the interlacing of cross-sectional activities "itself is the activity," and for Weber's observation that no "usable concept of domination can be defined in any way other than by reference to power of command; but we must never forget that here, as everywhere else in life, everything is 'in transition.'"[25] The method of totalization can be considered the appropriate way in which to study a natural, open, and creatively adjustive system.

Sociological Imagination

Although the term *totalization* was coined by Sartre, the clearest exposition of the method of totalization has been given by C. Wright Mills under the name *sociological imagination.* Contrary to systematic political theorists, Mills states that political inquiry must be historically specific in that "any given society is to be understood in terms of the specific period in which it exists."[26] He maintains that the "institutions, the ideologies, the types of men and women prevailing in any given period constitute something of a unique pattern."[27] Further, he holds that within this pattern the different mechanisms of social change reach a specific type of intersection. The task of the political scientist is to identify the pattern that characterizes his age and understand the dominant mechanisms of change. For Mills, the social structure must be studied as a whole. The political scientist should attempt to relate various aspects of human activity to one another so that he can gain a conception of the whole. Clearly, there is nothing about this activity of relating that is prejudicial to the use of mathematical analysis, structured observation, and rigorous verification. It is likely that sets of functional generalizations will define the conception of the whole. However, Mills' conception of the whole does not include the idea of an integrated organism or a grid of preconceived substantive categories. For Mills, the patterns of political activity are continually changing and the political theorist should attempt to grasp major trends as "moving parts of the total structure of the period."[28] Thus, no set of functional generalizations will ever adequately account for political affairs. Political events always outrun attempts to describe them in functional patterns. Sets of functional generalizations are ideal types that highlight certain aspects of the social relations of a period and describe human possibilities.

The social scientist committed to the sociological imagination is always attempting to catch up with the pattern of social relationships characteristic of his time and then to project ahead of them the possibilities for future action. The sociological imagination is the methodological result of Bentley's vision of the political process in which the interlacing of cross sections of activity itself is the activity. As a natural, open, and creatively adjustive system, patterns of political activity are continually in the making. The sociological imagination represents an authentic encounter with the data of political science. The method of placing or the method of illustration represents an inauthentic encounter with this data because, despite protestations to the contrary, it encapsulates the data of political science in a substantively defined and closed system. From the point of view of the proponents of a natural science of politics, the method of totalization is, perhaps, the price that one must pay for considering the political system as a constructively adaptive system. For those who are satisfied with a distinctively social science, the method of totalization is less a cost than an opportunity.

Wholes-in-the-Making

Sartre's discussion of the method of totalization parallels the account of Mills. Sartre remarks that the "ruling principle" of his inquiry is "the search for the synthetic ensemble, each fact, once established, is questioned and interpreted as a part of a whole."[29] However, this whole is again not the predefined totality of systematic political theory. Instead, it is a "unity in the process of being made." Wholes-in-the-making are the only social wholes. New activities that appear in social existence tend to be expressed in old vocabularies, while new vocabularies are ambiguous because the actions that they signify have not yet realized their possibilities. For Sartre, all significant political activities should be defined in terms of their incomplete development and their *deviated objectification.* By the latter term he means that in society no activity ever reaches the full development envisioned for it in the projection of human beings. Each new activity is resisted by other projects, the world, and the set of cultural objects that have already been created. Further, the results of activity always escape from the originators of activity. Part of the human condition is to be plagued by the indirect consequences of human activity. This aspect of the human condition is most poignant when the indirect consequences that one suffers are the results of one's own activity. Sartre defines political activity as a struggle in the dark which can only be partially illuminated by the method of totalization. Thus, the synthetic ensemble is never complete.

The "whole-in-the-making" sought by the method of totalization does not assume the belief that everything in the universe, or social existence, is interconnected. The synthetic ensemble does not imply that social organization is organic or that human relations can be deduced from a single master principle. Due to the projecting activity of human beings political life is characterized by an irreducible element of surprise. Just as the individual human being can surpass any particular definition of human nature, specific social organizations cannot be defined once and for all with respect to their functions. The method of totalization does not allow the individual to take control of the complex public situation in which he is embedded. However, it does help him to comprehend his contribution and relation to that public situation. In the twentieth century, the individual confronts James' pluralistic universe, in which he can never be sure that the disparate parts fit together with any final meaning. In order to make provisional sense out of this pluralistic experience the method of totalization introduces the notion of wholes-in-the-making. In each period the public situation shows a number of central characteristics. It is the task of the existential political scientist to identify these characteristics, relate them to one another and draw out their possibilities for future action.

The Moral Aspect

Like the historical method of civilized humanism and the functional method of pragmatism, the existentialist method of totalization has an important moral aspect. The existential political scientist is the free human being who also treats others as free human beings in his analysis. The existential political scientist exists authentically because he refuses to attribute a final essence or function to political activity that once and for all defines political possibility. He describes the major projects in a society as they appear and derives the major functions of political activity from a study of the interlacing of projects. He defines political activity formally as activity concerned with the maintenance or extension of other human activities. Thus, the political system is a set of interactions concerned with the maintenance or extension of other interactions. Political systems appear wherever such reflexive or representative activities form a pattern. They are not specifically identified with any particular kind of collectivity. Thus, the existential political scientist does not reduce the human being to a function in a predetermined life order.

The status of the human being in social existence is determined by a study of ongoing projects as they are mediated through social processes and related to cultural objects. The existential political scientist recognizes that the possibilities of social existence outrun the pattern of activities that appear at any given place and time. Part of his function is to discover these possibilities and to inform others about them. In order to perform this function he must be free enough of predefined thought structures to apprehend new tendencies. The method of totalization makes the political scientist a creator as well as a civilized and socially conscious observer. Among the requirements for such creation are authentic existence and respect for the freedom of human beings under study.

Basic Assumptions

Like the historical method and the functional method, the method of totalization is not self-sufficient. It makes three assumptions that are not included in the idea of totalization itself. First, the claim that totalization applies to specific historical periods assumes a definition of historical period that transcends the description of particular historical periods. In this essay, the units of analysis applicable to all historical periods are found in the formal concepts of the post-Marxist political theorists. Sartre and Mills have developed their own sets of formal concepts that are less critically elaborated than the analyses of Bentley, Weber, Mosca, and Easton. For example, Mills proposes the concepts of history, biography, and milieu as frames for analysis. Sartre makes a similar proposal in arguing for a synthesis of Marxism and psychoanalysis.

The second important limitation of totalization as an independent method is its failure to specify the type of relationship sought by political theorists. While Mills remarks that the sociologist should attempt to understand the contemporary function of human activities, he does not provide a detailed discussion of the notion of function. The same judgment holds true for Sartre's work, in which the concept of synthetic ensemble is not fully explicated.

The third important limitation of totalization as an autonomous method is its failure to account for the importance of the historical method as a means to discovering what aspects of a historical period are peculiar to it. Totalization tends to be a future-oriented method, concerned with the discovery of current possibilities for future action. Thus, as a corrective for the tendency to dignify the banal, it must be supplemented by the historical method. Thus, the method of totalization assumes transhistorical units of analysis, functional relations, and history without including them. The political science of the future will be a synthesis of the historical, functional, and totalizing methods, bounded by a formal theory.

The Synthesis of Methods

The discussion of the key methods of political inquiry has drawn heavily upon the concept of method outlined by Justus Buchler in his metaphysics of the human process. Buchler, whose ideas were considered in the chapter on pragmatism as a political philosophy, based his discussion of method on the insight that the human being is "the animal that tries deliberately to limit his world in some respects and to make it more abundant in others." For Buchler, method arises in human existence when people recognize that they are manipulators of the world. Along with this self-consciousness comes the knowledge that one can repeat an action previously performed. Repetition is the ground of methodic action, which is further defined as a mode of conduct, directed in a given way, to a particular set of circumstances, for the attainment of a result. In Buchler's theory there is a close connection between method and policy. Policy is an inclination toward a specific kind of activity and method provides a policy with its identity through recurrent instances of application. Buchler holds that method must be adapted to policy rather than policy to available method. He maintains that no one method is adequate to the fulfillment of all significant human purposes. If method is not constantly criticized in terms of its adequacy to the realization of human purposes it becomes habit, and, for Buchler, habitual existence is unreflective and borders on death. With respect to political theory, we have considered method as an orientation to the data, relationships sought, and modes of organization in political inquiry. Thus, we have viewed method as the set of principles that gives identity to the political scientist's policy toward his work.

Compatibility of Goals

The key methods of political inquiry suggested by twentieth-century political theorists are complementary and, therefore, are amenable to synthesis. Each one of them can be defined as a mode of conduct, directed in a given way, to a particular set of circumstances, for the attainment of a result. Each one of them is also adapted to a policy and oriented to the fulfillment of a purpose. To state that the key methods of political inquiry are amenable to synthesis is to maintain that they are not contradictory as modes of conduct. The use of one method to attain the goal to which it is adapted does not exclude the attainment of the goals set by the other two methods. Rather than leading to contradictory results, concurrent use of the three methods leads to more efficient realization of each goal. This is the meaning of the claim that the methods are complementary. Together, the historical, functional, and totalizing methods comprise a program for contemporary political science and political theory.

It is not difficult to show that the goals of the historical, functional, and totalizing methods are compatible. With respect to political science, the goal of the historical method is the discovery of general principles of political activity. Proponents of the historical method assume that the only way to apprehend high-level generalizations about political activity is to undertake a comparative study of political institutions. Such a comparative study will separate out what is peculiar to particular civilizations from what is common to all of them. Through a historical study, the political theorists of civilized humanism expect to add substantive principles to the formal concepts of political theory. Insofar as they hold that these substantive principles will bind future political activity, they are in conflict with existential theorists. However, if they confine their claim to the statement that such principles have characterized political activity in the past and will continue to characterize it as long as present trends continue, their work is compatible with existential principles. Theorists of political elites are correct in making the phenomenological point that dominance is always a possibility in human relationships. They are stepping beyond the logic of their position if they claim that dominance must always be an actuality in human relationships. Thus, interpreted in terms of the principle that a hypothesized empirical relationship can never be proven true in all cases, even though it can be falsified, the goal of the historical method is compatible with the goals of the functional method and the method of totalization.

With respect to political science, the goal of the functional method is the discovery of functional generalizations. As in the case of the historical method, the goal of the functional method is not incompatible with existential principles as long as the functional generalizations are not considered binding for future human action because they belong to a sociological level of analysis that is independent of the effects of concrete human projects.

With respect to political science, the goal of the method of totalization is the description of the major functional relationships within a historical period and the identification of possibilities for new relationships. Here the compatibility of the method of totalization with the historical and functional methods is apparent. The historical method provides knowledge of the distinctive character of a historical period and the functional method provides the generalizations that make up the description of it. The identification of possibilities is the unique contribution of the method of totalization. Thus, with regard to political inquiry, the goals of the three key methods are complementary.

The Contemporary Situation

A modest example of the use of the historical, functional, and totalizing methods is the description of the public situation presented in the first chapter of this study. According to this description, the central features of political existence in the contemporary world are the increasing importance of the indirect consequences of human action, the organization of human relations into bureaucratic forms, and the threat to systems of civilized objects posed by various fanatical barbarisms.

From the viewpoint of the historical method, the disruptions caused by the indirect consequences of human action, the emergence of bureaucracies, and the rise of pseudoscientific and fanatical barbarisms are historically specific occurrences with various antecedents in previous eras.

From the perspective of the functional method, these aspects of the public situation are closely related to one another. Bureaucratic organizations are responsible for important indirect consequences like environmental pollution and the appearance of masses of refugees. These organizations are also readily turned to the ends of fanatical barbarians who manage to attain power. Pseudoscientific barbarism is likely to flourish in a world in which human beings suffer indirect consequences which they cannot understand.

From the viewpoint of the method of totalization, the aspects of the public situation form a whole-in-the-making with possibilities for future action. Among these possibilities are more intelligent control of the indirect consequences of human action, the creation of strategies for maintaining autonomy in complex organizations, and the devising of measures to protect systems of civilized objects. For political theorists, appreciation and use of the historical, functional, and totalizing methods is one possibility for action in the contemporary public situation.

Definition of an Ideal

Even more important than the bearing of the historical, functional, and totalizing methods on the practice of political science is their significance for the conduct of life. Besides providing insights into the character of political inquiry, the three methods define an ideal for the political actor in the contemporary world. Each method is characterized by a moral discipline and each moral discipline is complementary to the others. The historical method can be applied correctly only by a civilized human being. Its application demands a person whose judgment has been tempered by a study of the history of mankind. Excluded from practice of the historical method are barbarians whose perspectives are confined to the cultures of single places and times. The ideal for political action—exemplified and expressed in the works of Northrop, Sorokin, and other civilized humanists—rests on the insight that in the modern age it is not enough to recognize one's biases. It is also necessary to surmount them and become first of all a human being and only secondarily a member of a more partial collectivity. However, surmounting one's biases cannot be accomplished simply through a wave of emotion, the expression of good intentions, or attendance at group therapy sessions. One's judgment must be broadened through the study of human history.

The functional method can be applied correctly only by a socially conscious human being. Its application demands a person who can relativize his own social position in terms of other positions and can recognize the indirect consequences of human activity. Excluded from practice of the functional method are bigots who absolutize the interests of the groups of which they are members. Thus, the functional method embodies an ideal for political action; the socioanalyst does not veil the pursuit of group interest behind rhetoric about the public interest. The historical method allows one to relativize his own historical period in terms of other periods, while the functional method allows one to relativize his own social position in terms of other positions. In both cases biases are surmounted.

Finally, the method of totalization can be applied correctly only by a freely creative human being. Its application demands a person who does not attribute a predetermined essence to human activity. Excluded from the practice of the method of totalization are the inauthentic human beings who ascribe responsibility for human actions to the operation of iron laws of human nature, social structure, or divine will. Thus, the method of totalization embodies an ideal for human action—authentic existence and the recognition of human possibility. The goal of the method of totalization is compatible with the ideals of the historical and functional methods. Among the conditions of authentic existence are freedom from barbarism and bigotry.

Goals for the Modern Age

A civilized and socially conscious existentialism presents a philosophy of political action viable in the modern age. This does not mean that acceptance of such a philosophy will be widespread. The judgment on the vitality of civilized and socially conscious existentialism in concrete political action will only be rendered after the present period in history has ended. Throughout the world, human beings are becoming "existentialized" in the sense that they no longer accept traditional definitions of social roles and they reject specific definitions of human nature. In this condition people need not accept the values of civilized humanism, social consciousness, and authentic existence. These values are not a necessary consequence of sloughing off traditional modes of thought and behavior. However, these values are appropriate to the contemporary public situation. Their acceptance is a project to be worked at rather than a dictate of historical dynamics. If twentieth century thought is characterized by a rejection of the notion that an unseen hand guides human destiny, it is also marked by a call for human responsibility. Only responsible human beings will make a civilized and socially conscious existentialism a vigorous force shaping the public situation.

NOTES

1. Sheldon S. Wolin, "Political Theory as a Vocation," *The American Political Science Review,* 63 (December 1969): 1067.

2. Harold Lasswell, *Politics: Who Gets What, When, How* (Cleveland: World Publishing Company, 1958), p. 211.

3. Gaetano Mosca, *The Ruling Class* (New York: McGraw-Hill Book Company, 1939), p. 41.

4. Ibid., p. 42.

5. Ibid., p. 43.

6. Ibid.

7. Ibid., p. 46.

8. Ibid., p. 47.

9. Ibid., p. 48.

10. Ibid., p. 3.

11. James C. Charlesworth, ed., *Contemporary Political Analysis* (New York: The Free Press, 1967), p. 73.

12. Ibid., p. 74.

13. Ibid., p. 80.

14. Ibid.

15. A. James Gregor, "Political Science and the Uses of Functional Analysis," *The American Political Science Review,* 62 (June 1968): 434–435.

16. Ibid., 435.

17. Jerone Stephens, "The Logic of Functional and Systems Analysis in Political Science," *Midwest Journal of Political Science,* 13 (August 1969): 369.

18. Ibid.

19. Arthur F. Bentley, *Relativity in Man and Society* (New York: G. P. Putnam's Sons, 1926), pp. 197–198.

20. Ibid., p. 198.

21. Jean-Paul Sartre, *Search for a Method* (New York: Random House, Inc., Vintage Books, 1968), p. 37.

22. Barrington Moore, *Political Power and Social Theory* (Cambridge, Mass.: Harvard University Press, 1958), p. 100.

23. H. H. Gerth and C. Wright Mills, eds., *From Max Weber* (New York: Oxford University Press, Inc., 1946), p. 77.

24. William James, *The Varieties of Religious Experience* (London: Longmans, Green & Co., Ltd., 1929), p. 26.

25. Max Rheinstein, ed., *Max Weber on Law in Economy and Society* (New York: Simon & Schuster, Inc., 1967), p. 329.

26. C. Wright Mills, *The Sociological Imagination* (New York: Grove Press, Inc., 1961), p. 149.

27. Ibid.

28. Ibid., p. 153.

29. Sartre, *Search For a Method,* p. 26.

SUGGESTED READINGS

Bentley, Arthur F. *Relativity in Man and Society.* New York: G. P. Putnam's Sons, 1926.

Durkheim, Emile. *The Rules of Sociological Method.* Glencoe, Ill.: The Free Press, 1950.

Gottschalk, Louis. *Understanding History.* New York: Alfred A. Knopf, Inc., 1969.

MacIver, Robert M. *Social Causation.* Boston: Ginn and Company, 1942.

Mills, C. Wright. *The Sociological Imagination.* New York: Grove Press, Inc., 1961.

Mosca, Gaetano. *The Ruling Class.* New York: McGraw-Hill Book Company, 1939.

Sartre, Jean-Paul. *Search for a Method.* New York: Random House, Inc., 1968.

Weber, Max. *The Methodology of the Social Sciences.* Glencoe, Ill.: The Free Press of Glencoe, Ill., 1949.

Wolin, Sheldon S. "Political Theory as a Vocation." *The American Political Science Review,* 63 (December 1969), pp. 1062–1082.

Znaniecki, Florian. *The Method of Sociology.* New York: Farrar and Rinehart, 1934.

CONCLUSION

NEW DIRECTIONS
IN POLITICAL THEORY

The primary need of contemporary political thought is for a reintegration of master political philosophies and empirical political theories. A major aspect in the history of empirical political theory in the twentieth century is a movement toward formalism and a consequent detachment of descriptions of political existence from problems in the public situation. The formalist tendency in political theory has reached its culmination in the works of systems theorists of political existence, particularly in theories such as the one developed by David Easton. However, at the same time that systems theorists bring formalism to its completion through the concept of system as a set of units with relationships among them, they also introduce content into political theory through definitions of the social functions of political systems. Thus, for the systems theorists, the data of political affairs are ordered with reference to the performance of various postulated functions. For example, Easton maintains that political analysis is concerned with the reference of human interactions to the authoritative allocation of values for a society.

The choice of social function as the ground to which cross sections of human activity should be referred is decisive for all aspects of contemporary empirical political theory. When human activities are judged in terms of their contributions to the performance of a social function not only does political study deal with a separate level of analysis from the personal and relational, it also becomes concerned with a unique kind of reality. Split off from a ground in the unified contributions of existentialism, pragmatism, and civilized humanism, empirical political theory is inevitably split off from human beings and their activities. Systems theories of political existence that are based on the attribution of particular social functions to political activity are dehumanized political theories. However, in addition to depreciating human activity, they also make unwarranted assumptions about the character of political reality. A systems theory of political existence grounded in the

PART FIVE
CONCLUSION

description of the human act derived from the contributions of existentialism, pragmatism, and civilized humanism would represent a distinct advance over current systematic political theories. The essential description of such a theory must be preceded by a critique of systems theories of political existence as they have been described. The next advance in political theory will not destroy the successive contributions of nineteenth- and twentieth-century political theorists and political philosophers to the description of the public situation. It will unify the master political philosophies of the twentieth century and provide a humanistic ground for theories of the political system rather than a ground in structural-functional requisite analysis.

CRITIQUE OF SYSTEMS THEORIES WITH FUNCTIONAL GROUNDS

The Concept of Society

In *The Political System* David Easton defines a political system as the set of interactions that is relevant to the authoritative allocation of values for a society. For the purposes of this critique, the most important element of this definition is the notion of society. Only by first presuming the concrete existence of a social system composed of full human beings can Easton study analytic systems composed of interactions. For Easton, society is an "all-embracing suprasystem," which "calls attention to the gross mass of conceptually unorganized social interactions that we might perceive if we were able to take in the whole of a society, literally, in one glance."[1] Society is defined as "the social behavior of a group of biological persons, conceived in their totality."[2] Thus, in Easton's view, society is a concrete and self-sufficient unit of collective existence. There is a special object for political scientists, political theorists, and political philosophers to study. Ultimately, political theorists do not describe human beings acting, but investigate, instead, societies. However, while most people are used to speaking in terms of societies as concrete units, this mode of interpreting human existence does not really make sense.

The first difficulties in the commonsense notion of society which underlies Easton's analytical categories are encountered in the difficulties of marking off the boundaries of a society. Easton claims that it is imperative for the systems analyst to distinguish precisely the system under study from its environment. However, in observing the present public situation one finds that it is impossible to distinguish any concrete and self-sufficient unit of collective existence but living humanity. Easton, of course, does not claim that there is only one political system for political scientists to study in the contemporary world. He distinguishes among parapolitical systems through which values are allocated for partial associations and authentic political systems. He remarks that the "governing body of no parapolitical system has such a capacity to speak in the name of society, the most inclusive social system, unless it happens to coincide with the authorities of the societal political system."[3] It is clear in this case that Easton is defining a society as a territorial unit administered by a government. Thus, political systems do not appear in societies. The only identifiable badge of a society is a government. However, except in a purely arbitrary sense, governmental institutions do not define the authoritative allocation of values for a society. In switching his definition of society from a concrete and self-sufficient unit of collective existence to a territory administered by a government, Easton has rendered his definition of the political system circular. In effect, he claims that a political system is defined as a political system.

The Concept of the State

Many political theorists have defined the study of political activity as the study of government. Why should Easton be criticized for this move? Easton himself has provided the tools for criticizing his view. In *The Political System* he remarks that one of the traditional schools of political analysis is the discussion of the nature of the state. He observes that the "truth is" that the notion of the state "was originally less an analytical tool than a symbol for unity." He adds that it "offered a myth which could offset the emotional attractiveness of the church and which later could counteract the myths of internationalism and of opposing national units."[4] Primarily an element in modern ideologies, the state is a deficient concept for empirical political analysis. Easton claims that undue attention to the state by political theorists deemphasized the study of underlying functions in favor of the analysis of particular institutions:

> Basically the inadequacy of the state concept as a definition of subject matter stems from the fact that it implies that political science is interested in studying a particular kind of institution or organization of life, not a kind of activity that may express itself through a variety of institutions.[5]

The Concept of the Political System

This excellent criticism of theories based on the notion of the state can be turned against Easton's own definition of the political system. If the political system is defined as the set of interactions relevant to the authoritative allocation of values for a society, and society is defined in terms of a political system identified by governmental institutions and a system of law, Easton is actually presenting another theory of the state. He may be accused justly of substituting the analysis of particular structures for the study of underlying functions or human activities. However, if the political system is defined as the set of interactions relevant to the authoritative allocation of values for a society, and society is defined as a concrete and self-sufficient unit of collective existence, there is only one political system in the world. Political scientists must study the authoritative allocation of values for living humanity. This definition would restrict greatly the activity of political scientists, because there are presently relatively few authoritative allocations of values made for living humanity.

There is no objection to political theorists making humanity the relevant collectivity to which human activities should be referred. As early as 1912, the Indian political theorist Benoy Kumar Sarkar observed that "for a proper understanding of any of the conditions of a single people, it is absolutely necessary to realise the whole situation of the human world at the time and minutely study the array of world-forces that has been the result of mutual intercourse between the several peoples in social, economic, intellectual, and political matters."[6] However, political theorists would not have the aim of providing general descriptions of the authoritative allocation of values for humanity. Instead, they would study the consequences of activities oriented to the maintenance and/or extension of other human activities for the eventual attainment of an organized humanity.

Arieli's Classifications

The major defect of Easton's political theory is that it is grounded in a phantom collectivity. There is no concrete unit for political study corresponding to Easton's definition of a society as a self-sufficient collectivity. If by society Easton means nation states, tribes that have not yet been organized into nation states, or an international society whose members are nation states, he has simply expanded the traditional study of government to include two other kinds of institutional patterns. He has not identified self-sufficient collectivities. Easton's normal society is the nation state, or territory administered by a differentiated government. In adopting this conception of normal political life he has not only substituted the study of particular structures for the investigation of underlying functions, he has founded his political theory on an element in the dominant contemporary ideologies.

In his penetrating study, *Individualism and Nationalism in American Ideology,* Yehoshua Arieli remarks that the "focus of all ideological endeavors has been the state, which has been the ultimate framework of social obligation, social order, and coercive power."[7] He identifies three major types of ideological orientation in Western political history. The first ideological orientation to appear was political ideology which

> defines the structure and functions of the state, the nature and limit of its sovereign will, and its relationships to all other forms of social life, [and] aims to establish, maintain, or destroy authority by relating it to a structure of norms, values, and data which are accepted as valid.[8]

Arieli points out that the limitations on political authority associated with constitutional regimes created a "new and intermediate plane between the individual and the state—society." Thus, the second ideological orientation to appear was social ideology which referred to "the totality of social existence and regarded all individual and social phenomena as expressions of one underlying principle of organization, or as fully determined factors of a closed system."[9] The latest social ideology to appear in the West is structural-functional requisite analysis.

The third ideological orientation to appear historically was national ideology which "considered the individual a citizen or member of the body politic because he was a part of the nation, a community bound by self-identification, which conceived of itself as absolute and self-determining."[10] In national ideology, the state expressed the unique personality of the national group. Arieli points out that unlike other Western nations, America has "claimed to possess a social system fundamentally opposed to and a real alternative to socialism and communism, with which it competed by claiming to represent the way to ultimate progress and true social happiness."[11] Thus, for Americans the myth of the state was never as strong as the myth of society. Following in the tradition of American ideology, Easton has based his political theory on a phantom collectivity—society. In Bentley's terminology, the society of which Easton speaks is a spook. It is a conception of the relevant collectivity to which the consequences of human actions should be referred. Therefore, society is a conception, not an object.

Requisite Function

Following from the judgment of society as a conception is the conclusion that societies do not have requisite functions. There can be no function of authoritatively allocating values for a conception. In *The Political System* Easton devotes an entire section to an attempted demonstration of the need for authoritative allocations in society. He begins by defining society once again as "the broadest grouping of human beings who live together and collectively undertake to satisfy all the minimum prerequisites of group life."[12] While every group has sets of tasks, the scope of which "embraces something less than all those conditions demanded for the survival of society as a whole," only "a society casts its net over all these tasks."[13] Among the tasks demanded for the survival of society as a whole is the authoritative allocation of values. There must be ways of "authoritatively resolving differences about the ends that are to be pursued, that is, for deciding who is to get what there is of the desirable things."[14] While there is no doubt that most people who live together have procedures for regulating the usages of cultural objects and the forms of social process, it is gratuitous to say that such procedures are demanded for the survival of society as a whole. Such procedures are demanded for the maintenance and/or extension of particular activities which may range from genocide to communion. To say that authoritative allocations of values are required for the persistence of a society is, analytically, to conceal one's ignorance with a word and, ontologically, to substitute an ideological phantom for the basic categories of human reality.

Easton's structural-functional requisite analysis can be criticized on the same grounds that Easton himself criticizes theories of the state. However, the criticism itself does not provide an adequate ground for empirical political theory. Essentially, Easton has been criticized here for mistaking an idea for a concrete entity. Society is merely one of the ideal collectivities to which human beings refer their actions. The new ground for empirical theory must be real rather than ideal. It must stem from an ontology of human existence adequate to account for all of the major philosophical, theoretical, and methodological contributions to twentieth-century political thought. Such an ontology is contained in the triadic description of the human act derived from the contributions of the master political philosophies of existentialism, pragmatism, and civilized humanism to clarifying the uncertain and threatening public situation of the twentieth century. Rather than adopting the mythical point of view of the social system, political theorists must adopt the point of view of the human being projecting himself into the future with respect to a civilization and the projects of others.

THE ONTOLOGY OF THE ACT

The basis of a political theory that will surpass current systems theories of political life is the complete human act. The complete human act is personal, social, and cultural. It has reference to values, morals, and history. Normatively, it involves the disciplines of axiology (value theory), ethics, and prescriptive political theory. Empirically, it involves the disciplines of psychology, sociology, and cultural anthropology. It is not a description that involves successive hierarchical layers or levels of analysis. Human activity is not viewed as a diffuse mass which is successively patterned by social stimuli and cultural patterns. Instead, human projections, social processes, and cultural objects are viewed as the coordinates of a single field.

Human beings project plans into the future that have reference to the usages of cultural objects and the plans of other human beings. Cultural objects are the content of a multitude of human projects that are interlaced in various ways. Through relating to one another, human beings fulfill or abort their planned usages of cultural objects. These three formulations are meant to show that the three phases of the complete human action are coordinate with one another. Each phase of the complete human act depends upon the two other phases for its appearance. However, each phase of the complete human act has an irreducible core. *Human projection, social process,* and *cultural object* are not three terms that ultimately refer to the same thing. They are phases of an act which is the basis of an empirical theory of the political system and a normative theory identified by the term *civilized and socially conscious existentialism.*

The Existential Component

The complete human act is a synthesis of the contributions of existentialism, civilized humanism, and pragmatism to clarifying the uncertain and threatening public situation of the twentieth century. From existentialism, the ontology of the complete human action derives the description of the human being as continuously projecting an image of the future. In every situation, the individual projects a set of possibilities and realizes one of them. If he believes that it is in some way absolutely necessary for a certain possibility to be realized, he acts in bad faith. Bad faith is, in fact, one of his possibilities. If he acts in full understanding that he is realizing only one of two or more possibilities, he acts in good faith. In either case there is no denial of the basic fact of projection. Human beings project plans into the future. They have projects, and these projects are more or less realized in their implementation. There is always a tension between projection and realization in human activity. The human being can never be fully defined by any empirical description of past or present behavior. Thus, transcendence of present behavior defines human existence.

Human existence cannot be defined in terms of an ultimately real personality. In line with Bentley's analysis, the personality is a spook, or an idea. The personality, or identity, can be termed *value consciousness* or *idealized self-image.* This does not mean that spooks are unimportant. Desired identity is a key element in human projects. Human actions are continuously referred to the creation or maintenance of identities. However, this personality is in no mysterious way real. There are several basic modes of value consciousness. The consequences of human actions for the creation and maintenance of identity can be referred to physical possessions acquired (identity through object—I am I because this land belongs to me), experiences enjoyed and suffered (identity through subject—I am I because I feel pain if I am injured), and the fulfillment of a plan (identity through action—I am I because I climbed this mountain). Further, value consciousness can be reflective and unreflective. In the former the identity surpasses given cultural models (I am Galileo because I say what I know), while in the latter the identity follows one or another received cultural model (I am Galileo's servant because I do as he tells me).

By themselves, projecting activity and value consciousness do not exhaust the description of human existence. The idea of projection does not include the description of the complete human action.

The Civilized Humanist Component

From civilized humanism, the ontology of the complete human action derives the description of the cultural object as the result of human projection and realization. In every situation, the most significant contents of human projects are cultural objects. *Cultural objects* can be defined as human productions which, if used in regularized ways, provoke uniform experiences. The regularized usages of cultural objects are their meanings. The meanings of any particular cultural object are variable. Thus, a plate can be used for serving food or as an ash tray. The word *free* can be used in an ideological pronouncement or in a philosophical monograph. Cultural objects are always part of a pattern or context. They are defined in terms of one another. In great part, human projects are planned usages of cultural objects expressed in terms of the symbolic cultural objects that make up language. Much of political activity is concerned with the maintenance and/or extension of access to or use of cultural objects. The accuracy of this statement can be grasped when one considers that food, clothing, and shelter are usually in the form of cultural objects.

The collectivities relevant for political theory are defined by the common usages of and references to cultural objects. Thus, for some problems the state, defined as a system of law, is important in political analysis. Those who make use of and refer their projects to the same law form a collectivity grounded in a set of cultural objects.

However, in the same way as personality, such terms as *society, nation,* and *mankind* refer to ideas. Just as human actions are referred to a self-concept, or identity, they are also referred to an idea of a relevant collectivity.

Parallel to value consciousness is historical consciousness, or the idea of a collectivity to which the consequences of one's actions are referred. One may choose to orient one's actions to the maintenance and/or extension of American society, the Free World, the West, the world revolution, or humanity, among many other possible collectivities. Perhaps the most important relevant collectivity in human affairs is the one that appears to be the most concrete—the family. People who lead primarily private, rather than public, lives generally refer the consequences of their actions to the fortunes of a domestic group. Historical consciousness arises from the realization that the consequences of human actions can extend far beyond the particular place and time of the individual chooser. This publicity of human action is based on the fact that the most important contents of human projects are cultural objects. Historical consciousness represents an attempt by human beings to control the extended effects of their activities by acting with reference to a particular collectivity. However, this attempt is usually vain in an age in which human actions are mediated through complex organizations and in which one's creations can be appropriated by others for uses that one never intended. Coupled with projecting activity and value consciousness, cultural objects and historical consciousness still do not exhaust the description of human existence. The ideas of projection and cultural object do not include the description of the complete human act.

The Pragmatic Component

From pragmatism, the ontology of the complete human action derives the description of social process as the mediation between various human projects directed at cultural objects. The foundation of social process is the fact that among the consequences of human activities are effects on the projects of other human beings. In the analysis of social process, these effects can be classified along a scale of awareness. First, there are consequences which are neither intended nor recognized by the perpetrator, and are neither intended nor recognized by the victim. This marks the limiting case of blind social processes. Second, there are consequences which are subject to the conscious regulation and determination by all parties to the relationship. This marks the limiting case of conscious social processes. Conscious social processes arise from the ability of human beings to anticipate one another's actions by making judgments about the character of one another's projects. Social processes are defined successively by the facts that people affect one another through their actions, that people can recognize that they affect one another through their actions, and that people can attempt to control the ways in which they affect one another through their actions.

Along with social processes go ideas of how people should control the ways in which they affect one another. Like personality and collectivity, morality is primarily an idea to which human actions are referred. Moral consciousness includes several components. First, it includes an idea of how various human projects should relate to one another. Among the different solutions to the problem of properly relating projects to one another are the rules that one should sacrifice the attainment of his own project to the attainment of another's project; one should arrive at a mutual compromise between the realization of his project and the other's project; one should strive to make his own project compatible with the projects of others; one should strive to realize his own project at all costs because his project is his very being; and one should only choose to pursue projects that realize certain approved values. Second, moral consciousness includes a judgment about the superiority, equality, or inferiority of one's own idea of how various human projects should relate to one another with reference to other norms prescribing the proper relationships among projects. Third, moral consciousness includes a decision as to whether one's idea of how various projects should relate to one another will govern one's action or whether it will be used as a rationalization to justify one's action. When an idea governs action, the person attempts to fulfill honestly a plan for the future. When an idea is used as a rationalization, the person acts on impulse and justifies his action after the fact.

Like historical consciousness, moral consciousness represents an effort by human beings to control the effects of their actions. One acts with the intent of relating the realization of his own project in a certain way to the projects of other human beings. As in the case of historical consciousness, this attempt at regulating the effects of one's actions is often in vain.

The Complete Human Action

The objective and subjective triads of the complete human action are respectively: projection, cultural object, and social process; and value consciousness, historical consciousness, and moral consciousness. Social processes are carried out with cultural objects. Violent conflicts are prosecuted with weapons. Communication is carried out through symbols. The primary contents of human projects are cultural objects. Symbols are the contents of projections. Tools and material are the contents of realizations. Human beings act with reference to one another. Projects are compatible or incompatible.

Human beings attempt to control the consequences of their actions for the realization of one another's projects or they leave these consequences unplanned. Objectively the complete human act requires a plurality of human beings, each projecting and attempting to realize a future with reference to a set of cultural objects and to the others. Subjectively the complete human act requires the reference of the consequences of an objective act to the realization of an ideal identity, an ideal collectivity, and an ideal pattern of relations among projecting human beings.

The description of the complete human act synthesizes the distinctive contributions of the three master political philosophies of the twentieth century. The existentialist insight that human beings are always projecting themselves ahead of their situations is given its due in the idea that one phase of the human act involves a plurality of human beings, each one projecting a future. The insight of civilized humanism that human beings exist in a cultural environment is preserved in the notion that one phase of the human act involves a reference to the creation or appreciation of cultural objects. The pragmatic insight that human beings affect one another in the efforts to realize projects is preserved in the idea that one phase of the human act involves the reference of the project of each human being to those of others.

Merit of this Description The description of the complete human action surpasses structural-functional requisite analysis in providing a ground for empirical political theory. Essentially, structural-functional requisite analysis makes one out of a number of possible forms of historical consciousness the basis for all political theory. Ultimately, it makes the idea of society the ground for a systems analysis of political life. Yet historical consciousness is only one moment of the subjective side of the complete human action. The objective description of the complete human action comprises an ontology of human existence or, in Justus Buchler's language, a metaphysics of the human process. It is such an ontology that provides a firm ground for empirical political theory because it is based on the irreducible and essential facts of human existence.

First, the ontology takes account of the fact that human beings are not encountered outside of social processes. Here the idea that the complete human act involves a plurality of human beings referring to each other is most important. There is no false abstraction of the isolated individual. Second, it takes account of the fact that human beings are continuously transcending themselves. Here the idea of projecting a future is most significant. There is no false apotheosis of a social process that submerges the individuals participating in it. Third, it takes account of the fact that human beings create, preserve, and destroy objects with regularized uses that provoke uniform experiences. Here the idea of a necessary reference to cultural objects in the complete human action is particularly important. There is no depreciation of the importance of past accomplishments in structuring human activity.

Characteristics of the Action The complete human action is individual, collective, and corporate simultaneously. It is individual in that it is the result of the projecting and realizing activities of a concrete human being. It is collective in that more than one person is always involved in the action. It is corporate in that a culture composed of objects with usages that can be learned comprises the primary content of projections and realizations. Based as it is on the essential facts of human existence clarified by the three master political philosophies of the twentieth century, the description of the complete human action is an ontology that underlies both the analytic categories of empirical political theory and the ideals of prescriptive political theory. Once the description of the complete human action presented here, or a similar ontology, has been made the basis for the further development of political theory, it is no longer possible to mistake the ideal for the real as the theorists of the political system have done. The description of the complete human action does not render political investigation antiempirical or unscientific. With the exception of social function, all of the formal categories of political analysis developed by the major empirical political theorists of the twentieth century are made meaningful by the ontology. In fact, the development of the ontology is a response to the periodic need to banish ideological elements and concepts without empirical referents from the mainstream of descriptive political theory.

THE ANALYTIC CATEGORIES
OF A HUMANIZED SYSTEMS THEORY

Cross Section of Activity

The fundamental categories of an empirical theory including the contributions of the major twentieth-century political theorists are expressed in the sentence: The political system is a set of cross sections of human activity that have reference to the maintenance and/or extension of other human activities, and which are organized and disbanded, dominant and subordinate. The notion of cross section of human activity, vital in the writings of such twentieth-century political theorists as Arthur F. Bentley, Max Weber, Gaetano Mosca, and David Easton, can now be fully interpreted. The cross section of human activity is merely a complete human action concerned with the manipulation and/or assimilation of a particular subset of cultural objects. There are as many cross sections of activity as there are usages of cultural objects. However, usages of cultural objects can be aggregated into more generalized groupings when they are related in some way to one another. For example, the complex activities involved in writing, publishing, and teaching in academic disciplines can be aggregated into a general cross section of activity defined as higher education. For the purposes of empirical theory the differences between general and particular cross sections of human activity are relatively unimportant. Any cross section of activity becomes politically relevant when it is made the object of another human activity that is concerned with its maintenance and/or extension. One may attempt to maintain, extend, or change the entire pattern of usages associated with higher education, or he may attempt to maintain, extend, or change only one or several of those usages of cultural objects.

As Bentley observed, making cross sections of activity the basic data of empirical political analysis involves the notion of *group.* The complete human act always includes a plurality of human beings acting with reference to a subset of cultural objects and each other. This does not mean that the group is a collectivity like Easton's society. Groups are defined by their relations to cultural objects, not by their self-sufficiency or by the functions that they perform. Members of a group may or may not be aware of their varied or common relations to a subset of cultural objects. When they become aware that their activities have consequences for the realization of one another's projects, conscious social processes may arise. Thus, through the notion of cross-sectional activity the complete human act is made the basic unit of analysis for empirical political theory.

The political act is the particular kind of activity concerned with the maintenance and/or extension of other human activities. Therefore, political acts exemplify certain usages of cultural objects. Human beings may use weapons of violence or threaten to use weapons of violence in order to maintain or extend particular activities. They may give or withhold cultural objects provoking desired experiences to attain the same ends. Finally, they may attempt to maintain or extend particular activities through the fraudulent use of symbols. These uses of cultural objects in political activities correspond to Lasswell's three ways of attaining socially available values. However, in place of Lasswell's consumer's point of view, there is an action frame of reference. As Bentley pointed out, political activity is representative activity in the sense that it attempts to secure the maintenance and/or extension of other human activities. Political activity is like all other human activities in that it involves multiple projections made with reference to cultural objects and to each other.

Organization

The second dimension of an empirical political theory based on the description of the complete human act is organization. The complete human actions that define a cross section of human activity are either organized or disbanded. Organization arises when the relations of human actors to cultural objects and to one another are regularized. Thus, organization has two primary components. First, certain usages of cultural objects are prescribed and proscribed. Second, certain social processes are prescribed and proscribed. For example, in military organization infantrymen are expected to fire their guns at the enemy and refrain from firing at their own side. Infantrymen are expected to cooperate with members of their own side and refrain from cooperating with the enemy. Organization at one extreme is an unconscious pattern of behavior and at the other pole a consciously determined set of relations intended to realize a particular set of results when they are instrumented. In the contemporary world many different forms of organization coexist. In the organization of work, the bureaucratic form of organization described by Max Weber and other twentieth-century organization theorists predominates. Here there is specialization of task coupled with hierarchical control. The relationships within a bureaucracy are supposedly ordered to result in the efficient realization of the goals set by those who stand at the top of the hierarchy. However, there are many other forms of organization in the contemporary world. Legislatures are not bureaucratic, although their committee systems exemplify a degree of specialization and their patterns of leadership display an element of hierarchical control. The relationships within a legislature are supposedly ordered to result in the making of laws that declare collective policies. Different from bureaucratic and legislative organization are the modes of organizing courts, families, and small businesses.

Organization of Organization Among the many ways of regulating the usages of cultural objects and social processes, some few become typical in each historical period. Perhaps the most significant recent historical development that relates to organization is the increasing importance of the organization of organization in the contemporary world. Theodore Lowi points out that the governmental regulation of economic activities is increasingly carried out by granting the officials of bureaucratically organized cross sections of activity rights and duties with respect to the usages of cultural objects and the forms of social processes. Earlier in the twentieth century, Elijah Jordan declared that the growth of administrative law, specifying the rights and duties of officials in public agencies, had ushered in a new historical period. Jordan holds that in the twentieth century law is no longer primarily concerned with regulating the activities of concrete individuals. Instead, the object of law is regulation of the usages of cultural objects by human beings in their corporate lives. According to Jordan, in the contemporary world property is owned primarily by bureaucratically organized cross sections of activity rather than by concrete individuals. Human beings realize their own projects only through participation in these bureaucratically organized cross sections of activity. Thus, the basic problems of human existence in the modern age are intimately connected with complex organization. Jordan holds that organized cross sections of activity in the modern age are principled to subjectivity in the sense that they are oriented to satisfy the desires of particular private individuals or interest groups. He urges that bureaucratically organized cross sections of activity be turned over to public ownership and harmonized with one another by the legislation of a parliament of professionals.

Whatever the defects of Jordan's defense of social planning by experts may be in the light of the fragmentation caused by specialization, his insight that individual human projects can only be fulfilled through participation in organized cross sections of activity is a vital contribution to contemporary political theory. When the cultural objects needed for the creation of a livelihood, the appreciation of peak experiences, and the creation of new cultural objects are owned and controlled by bureaucratically organized cross sections of activity, such organizations take on a decisive importance. The focus of the individual's existence as a responsible actor must be directed to organizational existence. This is why Jordan insists on maintaining that the full human action in the modern age is not an individual, but a corporate, action. He declares that institutions are the real actors in the contemporary world. In this respect, the argument of this study differs from Jordan's analysis. Here, the complete human action is defined as individual and social, as well as corporate. Jordan recognizes human projection in his idea that individual human beings continuously previse a future. However, he insists that while human beings can see, they cannot do. He holds that only organizations can realize purposes in the modern age. As opposed to Jordan's conclusions, this study concludes that only human beings acting mutually within organized cross sections of activity can realize purposes in the modern age. This revision, however, does not diminish the importance of Jordan's major insight.

Object and Project Orientation A second important distinction in the theory of organizations, not sufficiently recognized by Jordan, has been drawn and explicated by Friedrich Baerwald. For Baerwald, organized cross sections of activity are characterized by both object and project orientations. Object orientation refers to the cultural object that is created, destroyed, preserved, or experienced within the particular cross section of activity. Project orientation refers to the maintenance and extension of the organization of usages of objects and forms of social processes that characterize the cross section of activity. For example, in a university the object orientation is creating and transmitting knowledge, while project orientation includes maintaining the physical plant and financial solvency of the institution. Baerwald notes that every activity which involves efforts extending beyond a face-to-face group of human beings has both object and project orientations. Baerwald holds that project orientation makes human coexistence in extended spheres of space and time possible. However, he also notes that the justification for project orientation is object orientation.

Baerwald's distinction helps clarify why Jordan's parliament of professionals is a defective political formula. Jordan tends to divide organizational orientations into objective (public) and subjective (private). Public orientations have to do with perfecting and creating cultural objects and private orientations have to do with using cultural objects to satisfy desires. He believes that public ownership and professional control would allow the perfection, harmonization, and maximum appreciation of cultural objects. Behind this judgment is the principle that professionals have a predominantly public orientation while businessmen and politicians have predominantly private orientations. However, regardless of whether the orientation of professionals is public or private, Baerwald's analysis shows the defects in Jordan's proposal. The distinction between object orientation and project orientation cuts across the distinction between public orientation and private orientation. In the modern age, one's personal plans can only be realized within organized cross sections of human activity. Once one has patterned his plans to fit organizational requirements he develops a commitment to the project orientation of the organization. There are no free professionals in the contemporary world. There are professionals whose work is part of bureaucratically organized cross sections of activity. Through their membership in professional associations, specialists become committed to the project orientation of their organized profession. In many cases their career plans become dependent upon the fate of the organized profession. In this way, professionals in the modern world come to have interests as narrow and divisive as those of many businessmen and politicians, whether they have public orientations or private orientations. The unsolved problems of political change in the twentieth century are due in great part to the complications of private and project orientations that characterize contemporary human existence in organizations.

Public and Private Orientation A general theory of organized cross sections of activity must include both the distinction between object orientation and project orientation and the distinction between public orientation and private orientation. Analytically, public orientation and object orientation are the same. Both are concerned with the creation, perfection, destruction, and enjoyment of cultural objects. However, public orientation has two opposites, depending upon the type of project identified.

First, there is a private orientation, defined as the use of cultural objects to satisfy the desires of individuals within the cross section of activity. Second, there is project orientation, defined as the maintenance and extension of regularized usages of cultural objects that define the cross section of activity in its organizational phase. Intermediate between private orientation and project orientation is the use of cultural objects to procure the maintenance and extension of regularized usages of cultural objects that define cross sections of activity within broader cross sections of activity. This is the area of the interest group, and with respect to the entire culture every organization is an interest group divided between public function and private interest.

Further, private orientation can take the various forms of uses of cultural objects to procure personal values (value consciousness), values in social relationships (moral consciousness), and values for a collectivity (historical consciousness). The interrelationships between public orientation, project orientation, and the various private orientations identified by the terms *value consciousness, moral consciousness,* and *historical consciousness* define the outlines of a future theory of organized cross sections of activity. By virtue of its basis in cross-sectional activity, this theory will be ultimately grounded in the description of the complete human act.

Domination

Modes of Domination Cross sections of activity are not only organized and disbanded, they are also dominant and subordinate. In its widest sense, domination refers to the maintenance and/or extension of a particular cross section of activity at the expense of other cross sections of activity, whether or not there is any overt challenge to that maintenance or extension. Domination takes several forms that are closely related to aspects of the complete human action. *Suppression, oppression,* and *repression* are terms that express the three primary modes of human domination.

The suppressive act is one which uses cultural objects as means of controlling individual actions through the allocation of aids or hindrances to the realization of individual or group projects. The primary requirements of suppressive acts are control of cultural objects that can become important to the realization of the projects of others, and the ability to use these objects to effect control. Suppression includes the social processes of force, bribery, and fraud, as well as many others. Suppression is the most familiar way in which some cross sections of activity are maintained or extended at the expense of others. The range of suppressive acts corresponds to what is normally thought of as the range of power relationships. The application of suppression as a mode of human domination may be either conscious or unconscious. An example of unconscious suppression is the way in which people control the activities of others through unconscious variations of facial expressions and moods. Conscious applications of suppression, such as bribery, are too familiar to merit extended consideration.

Oppression is the mode of domination through which the maintenance and extension of particular cross sections of activity are obtained by systematic limitations of access to cultural objects. The enjoyment of particular cultural objects can be limited by their sheer location. One cannot enjoy the paintings in the Metropolitan Museum of Art unless one is in New York City. Patterns of income distribution, residence, educational attainment, and information all maintain and extend some cross sections of activity and deemphasize or eliminate others. While the denial of access to cultural objects through oppression may be backed up by acts of suppression, oppression is usually effected by the allocation of resources to cross sections of activity that are already dominant. All limitations of access to cultural objects are oppressive, but not all such limitations cause suffering or create the conditions for movements advancing claims to social justice. Certainly, the desires of most people do not include a visit to the Metropolitan Museum of Art. Therefore, the fact that many of them will never have the opportunity to walk through this museum is a source of neither suffering nor resentment. Quite different is the condition of many American blacks who deeply resent the denial of access to good food, clothing, shelter, education, and work.

The third primary mode of domination is repression. Repression is the mode of domination through which the maintenance and extension of particular cross sections of activity are obtained by the mere character of cultural objects. Repression is the restriction on human possibility implied by the existence of a particular set of cultural objects. For example, Benjamin Lee Whorf has pointed out that every human language emphasizes some experiences at the expense of others. For example, the Eskimo who have many words to describe different kinds of snow have a wider appreciation of snow than English-speaking peoples who have but one word. While every set of cultural objects is repressive in the sense that it excludes other cultural objects, the degree of repression can only be determined from the standpoint of another limited set of cultural objects. Repression is reduced by the creative activities of human beings who project new possibilities and attempt to realize them, and by encounters among people who use different sets of cultural objects. By restricting possibilities, repression maintains given usages of cultural objects and familiar patterns of social processes. The conscious attempts to restrict creative activity by totalitarian regimes and the efforts by these regimes to limit cultural contacts are demonstrations of the importance of repression as a means of maintaining and extending the domination of some cross sections of human activity over others.

Application of the Three Modes Suppression, oppression, and repression each have particular relevance to different phases of the complete human action. Suppression is most directly related to the phase of the human action expressed by the term *social process.* Suppression represents interference in the realization of one or more projects by activities oriented to the realization of other projects—for example, giving a person money so that he will vote for a particular candidate. Oppression is most directly related to the phase of the human action expressed by the term *cultural object.* Oppression represents a distribution of cultural objects that limits access for some and expands access for others—possibly, opening the polls in some neighborhoods only at inconvenient hours. Repression is most directly related to the phase of the human action expressed by the term *projection.* Repression represents a set of cultural objects that limits the scope and quality of human possibility—for example, denying to some the opportunity to learn to read and pass literacy tests. In human existence, patterns of suppression, oppression, and repression are closely interrelated, usually in such a way that they mutually reinforce the domination of a particular set of cross sections of human activity over others.

The notion of a dominant cross section of activity which is maintained or extended at the expense of other cross sections of activity can be clarified once the distinctions between suppression, oppression, and repression have been introduced. Cross sections of activity can be considered dominant in any of three ways. First, a cross section of activity can be maintained or extended at the expense of other existing cross sections of activity that are also bidding for maintenance and extension. This is the core process revealed in traditional theories of power and conflict. Contending parties use various means of suppression to further the realization of their projects. Second, a cross section of activity can be maintained or extended at the expense of an alternative pattern of activities that is projected by an observer. In this case, a particular pattern of access to cultural objects is contrasted with a different pattern of access to the same cultural objects. This is the core process revealed in modern systemic theories of power and conflict like Marxism where capitalists are expected to attempt to eliminate the potential power of the proletariat. Its perspective provides a necessary antidote to the limitations of liberal views of power and conflict like those of Robert Dahl and recent American interest group theorists. Third, a cross section of activity can be maintained or extended at the expense of an alternative pattern of activities, including new activities, that is projected by an observer. Here access is not restricted to existing cultural objects, but to cultural objects that might possibly exist if resources were devoted to their creation. This is the core process revealed in the twentieth-century political philosophies based on existentialism, pragmatism, and civilized humanism. It identifies repression as the most pervasive and general mode of human domination, and thereby places the other modes of human domination in their proper context.

Thus, a contemporary empirical political theory based on the description of the complete human action includes the analytic categories of cross-sectional activity, organization, and dominance. Cross sections of human activity can be organized or disbanded, dominant or subordinate. From the empirical theory of pluralism is derived the category of cross section of activity; from organization theory is derived the category of organization; and from the theory of political elites is derived the category of dominance. However, cross sections of activity—organized and disbanded, dominant and subordinate—can also be grouped into systems of human activity. The category of system is derived from current theories of the political system and represents the culmination of formalism in empirical political theory.

POLITICAL SYSTEMS

Traits of Political Systems

A political system is defined as the set of cross sections of activity—organized and disbanded, dominant and subordinate— which have reference to the maintenance and/or extension of other cross sections of activity oriented toward a specific set of cultural objects. There are as many political systems as there are sets of cultural objects, although depending upon one's perspective, some of these systems are interesting and others are trivial. Following Easton's terminology, a political system defined here is empirical, natural, open, constructively adaptive, and analytic. It is empirical in that it is defined by observable cross sections of human activity. It is natural in that the activities concerned with maintaining and/or extending other cross sections of human activity oriented toward a specific set of cultural objects are likely to influence one another if only in the elementary sense of having consequences for one another. A political system is open in that activities concerned with maintaining and/or extending other cross sections of activity are profoundly affected by changes in the quality and relations of the underlying activities. It is a constructively adaptive system in the sense that human actors are continuously summing up the system and projecting new possibilities for it. This does not mean that there is any strain toward maintaining the integrity of a system apart from exercises of suppression and patterns of oppression and repression. Logically, the political system is as subject to change as it is to efforts at pattern maintenance. In this study, constructive adaptation refers to the fact that the pattern of activities concerned with maintaining and/or extending other cross sections of activity is adaptable to the realization of a wide range of human projects.

Political activity is reflexive. It arises from the fact that human beings are capable of concern for the maintenance and extension of their primary activities. At its root, politics is project orientation. When the activities involved in project orientations of various cross sections of activity refer to the same cultural objects or the same human beings, political systems arise. This does not mean that the essence of politics is conflict. The interlacing of project orientations can also result in cooperation. The kinds of social processes typical of specific political systems cannot be specified in a formal political theory. Finally, a political system is an analytical system rather than a membership system. It is composed of cross sections of human activity rather than concrete human beings. Returning to the very ground of empirical political theory, a political system is composed of complete human actions. Thus, a political system is a broad cross section of human activity that has reference to a specific set of cultural objects. It is defined by representative activities which have relevance for the maintenance and/or extension of other human activities.

The Political System as a Cross Section of Activity

As a cross section of activity, a political system includes the three phases of the objective human action: individuals entertaining futures and attempting to realize them, individuals referring their projects to one another's plans, and individuals acting with respect to a set of available cultural objects. As a cross section of activity, a political system also includes the three phases of the subjective act: reference of the consequences of activity to the realization of personal values or a desired identity (value consciousness), reference of the consequences of activity to the realization of desired social processes or values in human relationships (moral consciousness), and reference of the consequences of activity to the realization of good for a collectivity (historical consciousness). As a set of organized and disbanded cross sections of activity, a political system is composed of activities characterized by public and private orientations, and object and project orientations. These activities are generally regularized with respect to usages of cultural objects and forms of social processes.

As a set of dominant and subordinate cross sections of activity, a political system is characterized by the modes of suppressive, oppressive, and repressive domination. Regularized usages of cultural objects and forms of social processes are maintained and/or extended by the allocation of aids and hindrances to the realization of human projects, by the distribution of access to cultural objects, and by the limited usages of the cultural objects themselves. Oppression and repression tend to maintain regularized usages of cultural objects and forms of social processes. Suppression can be used to maintain or disrupt regularized usages of cultural objects and forms of social processes. This is simply another way of stating the resistance to change observable in human existence.

As an empirical, natural, open, constructively adaptive, and analytical system, a political system is ultimately subordinate to human purposes. Composed of complete human actions, it does not transcend these actions as a superorganism. It can be changed through the projection of new possibilities. This is the creative activity which most effectively counteracts repression. It can be changed by the organization of people denied access to cultural objects. This is the militant activity which most effectively counteracts oppression. Finally, a political system can be changed through the mobilization of violence, wealth, and rhetoric. These are the means of suppression characteristic of day-to-day political conflicts. Ideally, political change would result from the projection of new and imaginative possibilities that would lure people to shed their narrow loyalties. However, the vision of a creative and cooperative politics is far from being realized in the contemporary world. Frequently, it is a vision that people cannot even take seriously. For the moment the dominant means to changing the political system are means of organized suppression. This fact has been important in determining the uncertain and threatening public situation of the twentieth century.

THE WAY TO POLITICAL VALUES

The ontology of the complete human action and the analytical categories of an empirical theory that can improve upon structural-functionalism do not exhaust the new directions of political thought in the last quarter of the twentieth century. From the ontology of the complete human action arise ideals for the political actor. In the discussion of the key methods of political inquiry in the contemporary world, several ideals for the political scientist are revealed. The proper uses of the historical, functional, and totalizing methods demand respectively a civilized, socially conscious, and freely creative human being. Political action in the twentieth century demands no less than the proper use of methods and, perhaps, more.

In encountering the uncertain and threatening public situation that characterizes present human existence the individual must become aware that the complete human act is not merely a conceptual tool, but a description of his very being-in-the-world. This awareness will save the individual from partial and distorted perspectives on his field of action. The individual will realize that in no situation is he merely an object. The complete human action describes the individual as capable of continually surpassing himself in projection and realization. One need never accept another's description of himself as binding. From this judgment follows the principle that the human being is a responsible actor. It is particularly important in the modern age to realize that even bureaucratic definitions of one's character can be surpassed.

Dilute and Full-Strength Existentialism

The existential commitment involved in accepting civilized and socially conscious existentialism is, in John Chapman's terms, both dilute and full-strength. Chapman distinguishes among dilute and full-strength existentialisms. Dilute existentialism involves adopting a set of attitudes and patterns of thought. With reference to the present study, one would adopt the broad historical perspective characteristic of civilized humanism, the awareness of social function characteristic of pragmatism, and the dedication to prevising new possibilities characteristic of the existentialist method of totalization. As a personal commitment, the individual can attempt to deepen and broaden his judgment with respect to the past, present, and future of human relations. This dilute existentialism is the minimum commitment advocated in the present study.

Full-strength existentialism involves adopting and working for a new vision of political organization: the transcendence of the nation state in the creation of an organized humanity. In the critique of contemporary theories of the political system an attempt was made to show that society as a self-sufficient unit of collective existence is ontologically unsound. In the contemporary world, only humanity meets the ontological tests for a collectivity. Full-strength existentialism has not been given an extended defense in the present study. However, it is implicit as the maximum commitment advocated here. Through gauging his particular relation to the public situation, each human being can decide upon his personal commitment with respect to that situation. Neither dilute nor full-strength existentialism is historically determined to become an important factor in the public situation. Both appear to be viable responses to the contemporary crisis.

Social Relations and Cultural Objects

In addition to transcending the view of himself as object, the individual will realize that he is always acting with reference to the projects of others. While existentialism liberates the individual from absorption into the life order, pragmatism provides the individual with social relations. As long as one remains conscious he is never fully detached from social processes. Even the stranded individual has his memories of social relationships. The individual who realizes that his actions have consequences for the projects of others and that the actions of others have consequences for his projects will attempt to exert some control over these effects. In the twentieth century he will be particularly concerned with controlling the secondary or indirect consequences of human activities. This social consequence carries over into purposive and cooperative social action. The political system is neither self-equilibrating nor self-improving. Through human efforts it can be made amenable to human purposes.

The last element in the political ideal is contributed by civilized humanism. Human projection and realization, and social processes can only be carried out through cultural objects. The ideal political actor in the twentieth century will be civilized in the sense that he learns to appreciate the worthwhile cultural objects that have been created in the major civilizations. His political activity will be concerned with expanding the range of human possibilities, maximizing access to worthwhile cultural objects, and minimizing the most debilitating exercises of suppression. The basic normative theory of the contemporary age is a socially conscious and civilized existentialism. Like the humanistic theory of the political system this normative theory is grounded in the description of the complete human action. Given a political theory grounded in an ontology of human action, fears that constructive political theory is dead are revealed as unwarranted, and new directions for creation are opened up for inquiry and action.

NOTES

1. David Easton, *A Framework for Political Analysis* (Englewood Cliffs, N.J.: Prentice-Hall, Inc., 1965), p. 38.

2. Ibid.

3. Ibid., p. 54.

4. David Easton, *The Political System* (New York: Alfred A. Knopf, Inc., 1953), p. 111.

5. Ibid., p. 113.

6. Benoy Kumar Sarkar, *The Science of History and the Hope of Mankind* (London: Longmans, Green & Co., Ltd., 1912), p. 23.

7. Yehoshua Arieli, *Individualism and Nationalism in American Ideology* (Baltimore: Penguin Books, Inc., 1966), p. 4.

8. Ibid.

9. Ibid., pp. 6–7.

10. Ibid., p. 7.

11. Ibid., p. 21.

12. Easton, *The Political System*, p. 135.

13. Ibid., p. 136.

14. Ibid., p. 137.

SUGGESTED READINGS

Baerwald, Friedrich. "Humanism and Social Ambivalence." *Thought*, 42 (Winter 1967): 543–560.

Buchler, Justus. *Nature and Judgment.* New York: Columbia University Press, 1955.

Ginsberg, Morris. *Essays in Sociology and Social Philosophy.* Baltimore: Penguin Books, Inc., 1968.

Hocking, William Ernest. *Man and the State.* New Haven: Yale University Press, 1926.

Jordan, Elijah. *The Good Life.* Chicago: University of Chicago Press, 1949.

Mukerjee, Radhakamal. *The Philosophy of Social Science.* London: Macmillan and Co. Ltd., 1960.

Santayana, George. *Dominations and Powers.* New York: Charles Scribner's Sons, 1951.

Sheldon, Wilmon H. *God and Polarity.* New Haven: Yale University Press, 1954.

Weinstein, Michael A. "Politics and Moral Consciousness." *Midwest Journal of Political Science,* 14 (May 1970): 183–215.

Znaniecki, Florian. *The Cultural Sciences.* Urbana, Ill.: University of Illinois Press, 1952.

INDEXES

INDEX OF TERMS

INDEX OF NAMES